Working from Within

Working from Within

Chicana and Chicano Activist Educators in Whitestream Schools

Luis Urrieta Jr.

The University of Arizona Press Tucson

The University of Arizona Press

www.uapress.arizona.edu

First paperback printing 2010
ISBN 978-0-8165-2917-9 (pbk. : alk. paper)

Library of Congress Cataloging-in-Publication Data
Urrieta, Luis.
Working from within : Chicana and Chicano activist educators in whitestream schools / Luis Urrieta, Jr.
p. cm.
Includes bibliographical references and index.
ISBN 978-0-8165-2611-6 (hardcover : alk. paper)
1. Mexican Americans—Education—United States—Case studies.
2. Mexican American teachers—United States—Political activity—Case studies.
3. Discrimination in education—United States—Case studies. I. Title.
LC2682.U77 2009
371.829'6872073—dc22

2008052139

Funding was provided by a University Co-operative Society Subvention grant awarded by The University of Texas at Austin.

Manufactured in the United States of America on acid-free, archival-quality paper and processed chlorine free.

15 14 13 12 11 10 7 6 5 4 3 2

Para José Luis Urrieta Martínez, Elodia Ramos Horta, y Rosa Angela Luquín Mondragón. Gracias por su lucha, su amor incondicional, y su apoyo infinito.

Contents

Acknowledgments

The completion of this book has been an ongoing journey. I would like to thank my mentors: Dorothy Holland, Kris Gutiérrez, and George Noblit. Thank you all for your input, insights, poignant concerns, and questions in the pursuit of this topic. Thank you for the incredible amounts of time and careful, yet always supportive, critiques of my work. You have all touched me in personal and academic ways. *¡Gracias!* I would also like to acknowledge Bernardo Gallegos, Carlos Tejeda, Sofia Villenas, Enrique Murillo, and Bryan Brayboy for all of their personal support and academic guidance.

The study this book is based on would not have been possible without the generous financial support of several organizations. First, the American Educational Research Association/Spencer Foundation Predissertation Award laid the foundation for this work. Special thanks to the Gates Millennium Scholars Program for their generosity and support. The Spencer Foundation continued their support of my work with a Dissertation Year Fellowship, 2002–2003. I would also like to thank Educational Testing Service for a summer research fellowship in Oakland, California, in summer 2001 that allowed me to engage in three months of data collection in the Bay Area. I would like to thank the American Association of Hispanics in Higher Education for their ongoing support and leadership mentoring in higher education issues. I would like to thank the University of Michigan's National Institute for the Study of Higher and Postsecondary Education for the Public Good. Through their Rising Scholar Award, I was able to continue my work on this topic. Finally, special thanks to a University Co-operative Society Subvention grant awarded by The University of Texas at Austin.

At the University of Colorado at Boulder, I would like to thank Lorrie Shepard, Margaret Eisenhart, Ruben Donato, Markie LeCompte, and Kathy and Manuel Escamilla for all of their support. I especially would like to thank the Chicana and Chicano Studies Program at the University of California at Davis, especially the students who inspired me and helped me to re-root. A shout goes out to Rick, Monique "La Puppet" Rocío, and Las Reds—Minerva y Noemi, Angie, Angeles, Rodolfo, Jisel, Celina, and Lisceth! I rest assured you will keep the world in check. I thank Adela de la Torre for her encouragement to write this book and for the valuable guidance. You knew it was possible even before I did! I would like to thank Beatriz Pesquera for her solidarity and guidance in Chicana studies and Inés Hernández-Avila for the *consejos* and blessings. Indeed, as I began to write this book, Inés gave a powerful *limpia*. I also thank my graduate assistant Lina Méndez Benavídez for all of her academic support.

At The University of Texas at Austin, I received financial support as a fellow in the Lee Hage Jamail Regents Chair in Education 2006–2008. I thank Larry Abraham for his support and kindness. I would like to acknowledge Jennifer Jefferson and Emmett Campos for helping me edit the manuscript. I thank Keith Sturges, Doug Foley, Octavio Pimentel, and Melissa Moreno for helpful feedback on the manuscript. Beth Hatt, Lan Quach, Ji-Yeon O Jo, Margarita Machado Casas, and Amy Anderson—thank you for being good to me all these years.

Most important, I thank my parents; this work is dedicated to them and to their struggles both in Mexico and in the United States. Gracias mamá y papá por darme amor, comprensión, y apoyo. Gracias por enseñarme a trabajar y a luchar por siempre lograr vivir una vida mejor. I thank my *compañera*, Rosa—this work would not be possible without you. Gracias por tu apoyo y amor, y más que nada por tenerme tanta paciencia durante este proceso tan largo y difícil. I also would like to pay my respects to the spirits and forces of nature that guide and protect me and to all my relatives in this world and the next. Projects like these are always the product of an entire community's efforts, and this project is no exception. I have been blessed in multiple ways. Any faults in this work are strictly my own.

Working from Within

1
Introduction

This book is about the lives of educators,[1] their schooling experiences, how they came to identify as Chicana and Chicano activist educators, and how they make sense of their multiple and often-contradictory roles as both activists and educators in whitestream[2] schools. The essential question addressed in this book is: Can Chicana and Chicano activist educators change whitestream schools by working within them? Chicana and Chicano activist educators are people who self-identify as Chicana and Chicano and who attend and/or work in the education field, but who see themselves, and are often seen by others, as activists, or agents of change.

To the extent that researcher identity and subjectivity never stray too far from the knowledge we produce (Delgado Bernal, 1998b; Davies, 2001), my goal is to be as transparent as possible about my lenses. With that in mind, I provide my autobiographical sketch to give the reader some insights about my background, motivations, and reasons for undertaking the study.

My father was the last campesino in a long line of farmers in the community of Nocutzepo, Michoacán, in Mexico, land of our ancestors the P'urhépecha. Michoacán is a land not only rich in resources but also in biculturalism and bilingualism, and of a complex racial ambiguity where the stepping stones of time created a magnificent, yet painful, mosaic of the Mexican nation. My father was the last campesino, but I am the first. I am the first to graduate from high school, the first to hold a BA, the only MA, and the only PhD. Relevant to this family past, I wrote a lot of personal reflections during my doctoral seminars while in graduate school at the University of North Carolina at Chapel Hill. I felt alienated and silenced, being the only Chicano/*indígena*[3] in my doctoral cohort after moving from Aztlán[4] to North Carolina. I tried endlessly to make my points about racial oppression and social justice heard, much less understood, by many of my privileged peers.

My educational background revolves around the strong influences of family members and my struggles growing up, and it is now incorporated into larger political and academic interests in identity and social change in whitestream schools. I was born in East El-Lay (L.A.), where I grew up in Mexican communities that richly influenced my life and set the foundation for who I am today. I became an avid reader at a young age. Realizing how much I enjoyed reading, my father, José Luis Oliverio Urrieta Martínez de la Salud (his full baptismal name), saved money and bought an encyclopedia on partial credit. Soon, I read almost every volume and excelled in school, forever changing my role within my family. I became the official translator, spokesperson, and advocate, translating documents ranging from mortgages to immigration papers. As a young boy, I spoke on behalf of my family and relatives with doctors, lawyers, bankers, and anyone who did not speak Spanish.

I did not completely understand as positive this experience of cultural mediation, or cultural brokerage. There was a contradictory feeling in me in always being sought out to go to city hall to translate. I harbored both feelings of being important and rewarded with a McDonald's "happy meal" and feelings of shame in speaking for people looked down upon and often not listened to, my own people. But it was not a shame anyone told me about; it was the hidden societal transcript of knowing, speaking, and translating in a "second-class" language for a "second-class" people. I began to look down passively on my relatives for not "trying hard enough" to learn and speak English: "Isn't this [the United States] the place where anything is possible?" In school, I was consistently reminded that one could be anything if he/she tried hard enough. I felt this way especially about my mother, María Elodia Jovita Ramos Orta de la Salud (her given baptismal name), because I began to see her as incapable of learning a second language, not just unwilling to.

School and the media actively contributed to these contradictory feelings of shame inside of me. My parents could not help me with my homework assignments because they didn't understand what I was doing, especially because it was in English. Both my mother and father only had a third-grade education, all that was available to them in the pueblos where they grew up. On television I always saw "American" (implying white) families helping their children do their homework or sending them to summer camp, things I thought "good" parents were supposed to do for their children. My parents rarely asked if I did my homework, and as a matter of fact, I was not always looked at as "normal" for reading so much. Rumor had it among my cousins that I would end up crazy if I continued to read so much. But the truth is that I was severely overweight and couldn't play like the rest of my cousins, I was always picked last for every team, and sometimes people fought over who would end up having me on their team. So, instead, I hid behind the pages of books. Surrounded by so many mixed messages of praise and shame, I began to see school as a defense mechanism for my differences and an opportunity to shine in the middle of the contradictions.

I excelled in middle school. I was recruited, unaware, into numerous programs directing me toward a college education, including tracking. Teachers continuously positioned me as a "smart" student and told me I was a "good" person, unlike most of the other kids around me. I passively accepted the position and began to believe I was different than the rest of my people. I learned to perform uncritically to my teachers' expectations and to in fact exceed them.

During that time, my father lost his job as a manager at a felt company, and I became an unlicensed public street vendor on weekends. We had just bought a nicer, bigger family home ten miles from East El-Lay in Pico Rivera that my dad was determined not to lose no matter how much work it took. This situation forced all members of the family, including children, to work in a variety of capacities. I disliked the stigma attached to my family and me as we tried to survive selling produce and eggs in the streets, but I also recall this time as the time when we became closer and resembled a Native woman's rug: we all cooperated like strings tightly woven together to form a beautiful design. It was a humbling experience that helped me identify with immigrant struggles, struggles that I had oversimplified before. This experience gave me strength, dignity, confidence, and the drive to be successful despite the contradictory conditions I was in.

The contradictions were well pronounced and hard to understand for a young adolescent. I knew our family's economic situation was not good because I stopped attending Catholic school, because I didn't have a lot of "nice" clothes,[5] and because there were times when there wasn't enough food. At the same time, I lived in a semi-private neighborhood, our house had a built-in swimming pool, and I was automatically placed in honors tracks when I transferred to public schools.

My teachers assumed that I must be better prepared than most of my peers because I came from a Catholic school. During school hours I became someone completely different from who I was on the weekends. At school, I was an honors student, I spoke only in English with my privileged peers, and I tried not to stand out. On weekends, I wore my old uniforms, I spoke mostly in Spanish, I knocked on people's doors, I solicited customers in parking lots, and I hid from the police in order to sell my share of eggs, oranges, and nopales (cactus).

Motivated by my cousin Cuco, my father later tried his luck at gardening as a business, which was a move that proved to be economically fruitful and labor intensive. I hated when my brother and I worked with my father after school on weekdays. This meant I had to stay up very late to finish the ridiculous amounts of homework I was assigned. No one seemed to understand my situation as a family member or as an honors student—not my father who needed my help, and not my teachers who assumed I had all the time in the world to do endless amounts of homework.

My father would often get angry at my brother and me for not working fast enough or hard enough. But, he would also become frantic whenever we told him we did not want to go to school anymore. He would make us work to exhaustion, only to ask if we were ready to go back to school. He hated when we scrapped the skin off of our hands, when we got blisters, or when we turned very dark from the sun. I began to make connections, perhaps the very same connections my father made in the very sensitive racial context of Michoacán where these were signs of racial, social, and economic inferiority. At the same time, he would make fun of us for not having "manly" hands and for not holding the axe hard enough, like a man, which resulted in blisters.

Several things became clear. To keep a "nice" house, you had to work hard. Families were groups of people and everyone had to unconditionally cooperate, like it or not. Implied was the message that *la sangre de indio* (indigenous blood) was strong, but *indio* features were not good; physical labor was dignified, good, and masculine, but also not of high social status. Schooling required a lot of tedious work for my ultimate goal, which was college at the time, and I realized that I would have to work harder than my other peers. The one thing I had sworn to myself was that I would not end up working as hard physically as my father and that I needed to give back to my family. I continued to make excellent grades and exhausted myself in high school trying to live the "American Dream." When I did encounter failure, I blamed myself—the myth of meritocracy was in place and I believed it.

In college I underwent a drastic identity shift when I learned about the War of the North American Invasion, the genocide of Native Americans, and the exploitation of Chinese railroad workers.[6] I embraced a strong and clear sense of ethnic pride, unlike any I had ever experienced before.

It was a euphoric experience that felt so good inside! I adopted a political stance, and I began to call myself a Chicano.

I also began to reflect on my life experiences and the many instances in which I had encountered racism. These encounters included subtle forms of discrimination and social and economic oppression, not only in the context of the United States but also in the rich family history my parents brought with them from Mexico. I realized that I had learned to ignore, to normalize, and to accept many of these forms of discrimination. I was upset and angry and felt a strong sense of urgency to change this hostile society. I also realized that I had not been "successful" in school because the system is fair and everyone has an equal chance, but because I was recruited into special treatment in honors classes and I was positioned as a smart person, unlike most of my Mexican American peers and my own family members. I was not as privileged as most of my peers within the honors program, yet I succeeded despite the many barriers set in my path within this tracking system. In some ways I succeeded because I became a passive survivor of schooling, the kind of child who follows rules, the kind who memorizes meaningless words without questioning, and the kind who jumps through the hoops.

When I came to my Chicano critical consciousness, I was convinced that schools were a good place to raise the consciousness of fellow younger Latina and Latino students. My identity shift as a Chicano helped me to change my views on Latina and Latino education in the United States; Latinas and Latinos were not failing in the educational system, the system was failing Latinas and Latinos. As a result of producing this identity consciousness, many Chicanas and Chicanos in my cohort at UCLA, including myself, entered community service–oriented professions, such as teaching, counseling, and social work upon graduation. We were determined to "change" the world. We wanted to go back to our communities and give back, even if only to give back the children their real names *en español*. In 1995, I became a bilingual social studies/language arts teacher in the El-Lay area. I made a conscious choice to work with bilingual eighth-graders, mostly of Mexican descent, in one of the poorest and most neglected schools in the school district.

I earned my master's degree while teaching full-time. In my master's program, I began to juxtapose critical theoretical frameworks with my daily experiences as a teacher. The lives of the mostly immigrant Latina and Latino students I worked with helped me analyze socially constructed paradigms and the role I played in maintaining them. Slowly, I began to look at issues of sorting through grading, tracking, testing, and labeling/naming as a long historical process of control and domination, and I suffered over how I was complicit in these institutional endeavors.

As a teacher, I also began to reflect critically on issues of identity and agency as I saw them manifest in the discourses of my students. I was fascinated to witness the many shifts that occurred as students negotiated identities in various situations. I realized that identities are shifting and plural, certainly not static as I had been taught. I had been taught that having more than one main identity was pathological and could even mean the onset of schizophrenia. This new understanding of identity as plural and dynamic freed me to be not only Chicano but also Mexicano, Latino, and of P'urhépecha descent. I was able to exist fully in my plurality. In my master's program and teaching experiences, I began to see how institutional and societal white supremacy is at the very foundation of the educational system. This link became much more apparent after whitestream voters passed Proposition 227, a measure that attempted to kill bilingual education programs throughout the state of California. After four years of teaching bilingual students, and with considerable encouragement from a Genízaro/Chicano professor, I decided to pursue a PhD in education in North Carolina.

In graduate school I questioned whether the academy was for me. Why did I feel so alienated? Was I too emotional? Was I being irrational? Questions like these fueled my interest in the production of Chicana and Chicano identities through educational experience. I questioned why I could see the inequalities that most of my privileged, mostly white, colleagues could not. Part of my identity as a Chicano compelled me to work for social justice and educational reform. After being a teacher in greater Los Angeles and witnessing the poor conditions of some schools and the poor treatment of some students versus others, at times, within the same school, it was clear to me why change was important because things were unjust. I asked myself, where had my peers been their whole lives?

I also realized that my Chicano/indígena identity is a produced identity that carries with it a deep sense of responsibility. This identity was one that I learned to produce during my undergraduate experience. But, the emotional, social, and theoretical aspects of sorting through my dilemmas as a Chicano, Mexicano, indígena, Californiano throughout my educational trajectory were not part of the whitestream academic discourse. During my time as a doctoral student, however, I was able to explore these issues using theoretical frameworks in disciplines such as anthropology, sociology, philosophy, and cultural studies. This course work, along with extensive fieldwork experience using a variety of research methods, provided me with a solid foundation in the practical and theoretical aspects of conducting various forms of ethnographic and qualitative research.

After making "peace" with the academy through my dissertation work as a Native researcher, I was able to steal the *patrón*'s[7] tools and commit myself to contributing to society by exploring issues of identity and agency in communities, like my own, that are severely underserved and exploited by traditional academic research. My perspective, life experiences, and training provided me with unique and innovative methodologies, decolonizing methodologies (Smith, 2001), and frameworks that incorporate the mentioned disciplines and approaches to research, writing, and teaching while also using Native paradigms.

My brown indigenous body and community ways of knowing are the very links allowing for praxis and the re/invigoration and challenge of traditional and conventional paradigms. My body and how it is read reminds me daily of who I am by the way I am stereotyped, judged, and treated in everyday life by people of other races and by other Latina and Latino people. The people whom I surround myself with outside of the academy remind me consistently of community ways of knowing and being.

But I still continue to question: Am I complicit in the colonial domination enterprise? How have my views changed for the better, or perhaps, for the worse? Where are the trenches of this battle for social change in education, in K–12 schools, in colleges and universities? Maybe the battle is in organizing student groups and through mentoring? Is there social justice value in publications and research? Are these all equally important ways to raise consciousness? Am I now approaching the highest state of colonization in the ivory tower, a handcuffed liberation, or even a real possibility for future emancipation?

Questions like these, with heavy emotional implications, drove my interests in Chicana and Chicano identities in this book. As a Chicano, I have always felt I should be doing something for my community. One of my obligations in the struggle for social justice was this urgent need to "give back" to my community and help others like me along the way. The emotional aspects of sorting through these issues in my everyday negotiations as a professor are not part of the academic discourse. As a former teacher, the contradictions were also present in my role as both an agent of the institution and an agent of social change. And so I look at the particularities of daily life and of moment-to-moment activism in the lives of Chicana and Chicano activist educators as a form of social justice work.

The general focus of this book is on Chicana and Chicano activist identity production and the shifts leading to a Chicana and Chicano consciousness. The study on which this book is based asked the larger question: How do Chicana and Chicano educators produce and negotiate identity, agency, and activism within whitestream schools?

My position and voice as a Chicano/indígena educator are a central component, not only in how my interests were shaped in the study but also in how I experience whitestream schools and negotiate my multiple selves within them for change and survival purposes. The study was designed as a "developmental"[8] study modeled on my own trajectory in whitestream schools from my identity shift as an undergraduate student to becoming a Chicano/indígena university professor.

The Study

I collected the bulk of the data in California between 2001 and 2003. The research method was participant observation (Davies, 2001). Four groups of self-identified Chicana and Chicano activist educators participated in the study: (1) undergraduates planning to enter the education field, (2) K–12 teachers, (3) graduate students in education programs, and (4) education professors. Drawing on my experience and the literature on the Chicana and Chicano Movement, I intended to focus on three general areas: (1) Chicana and Chicano activist identity production, (2) activist agency, and (3) negotiating change from within whitestream schools.

I used a snowball sampling method to identify participants (LeCompte and Schensul, 1999). A brief initial conversation (via telephone or e-mail) asking about identity issues and activist commitments was used to screen participants. To participate, participants had to primarily self-identify as Chicana and Chicano, fit into one of the four groups above, and have a strong self-described Chicana and Chicano activist orientation.

Each group consisted of six people (three men and three women); a total of twenty-four people participated (for further details see Urrieta, 2003a). Participant ages ranged from 19 to 57. Appendix 1 shows the general profile of the participants in this study. Pseudonyms are used in this book for all participants.

I analyzed interview narratives carefully before, during, and after transcription. Life history and ethnographic interview data are the primary sources of data analyzed; however, ethnographic observation data is used throughout the book. Interviews were, for the most part, conducted in English.[9] When words, phrases, or sentences were said in Spanish, I wrote them in *italics*. All of the interviews were conducted exclusively through dyadic interaction.

Initial interviews were life histories; later interviews focused on the daily practices of Chicana and Chicano activist educators in whitestream schools. I particularly paid attention to the negotiation of identity and commitment to the Chicana and Chicano worldview when looking at educators' self-reported practices as activists. I also observed participants in school settings while conducting ethnographic observations. Chicana and Chicano folk notions, like "playing the game," surfaced during interviews and were eventually incorporated into the research.

A constant comparative method was used to analyze and triangulate data (Creswell, 1998). A constant comparative method "combines inductive category-coding with a simultaneous comparison of social incidents observed and coded" (LeCompte and Preissle, 1993:256). This method allowed me to look carefully at the abundant data collected on Chicana and Chicano activist educators' experiences and approaches to change in whitestream schools. Interview transcripts, fieldnotes, classroom observation transcripts, artifacts, and documents were used to triangulate and further develop categories for coding. From interviews, emerging themes were identified and used to complement the data analysis. Larger domains of data were later grouped according to the themes identified from all of the compiled data. Themes included experiences in K–12 schooling, Chicana and Chicano identity production, practices of educational activism, and negotiating and strategizing change by playing the game.

A Reflection on the Unexpected

When I first set out to gather the data for the study, I was somewhat cynical. My romanticized and stereotypical notions of activism and activists, at that time, led me to believe that to be an activist and an educator in whitestream schools simultaneously was an oxymoron. I believed self-professed Chicana and Chicano activist educators were deceiving themselves if they thought they could bring about change in education from within schools. Chicana and Chicano activist educators were being co-opted by the system of white supremacy[10] into believing that they were working for change, while conforming to the rules and expectations that ultimately uphold whitestream models of schooling. In a nutshell, I wanted to debunk the idea that activists working from within could bring about change.

My early interviews, because of my cynical assertions, were more like interrogation sessions. My line of questioning ran something like this: Do you *really* think you are making change? What have *you* done that you think is important for social justice? My goal was to show that Chicana and Chicano activist educators' efforts to work change into the system were futile and deceptive. During the process, however, I began to not just see but also to feel the passion for social justice in the lives of the people whose experiences I share in this book.

How my participants made sense of their multiple roles in whitestream schools proved fascinating and hopeful. The metaphor of playing the game as a way to rationalize why and how these Chicanas and Chicanos were strategizing change into their practices as activist educators was repeatedly brought up. Statements such as "I've learned how to play the game" or "I've gotten good at playing the game" were often made during interviews. Intrigued with this sense-making metaphor of how to strategize change from within, I eventually incorporated this theme into my interview protocol and later into my analysis.

The metaphor of playing the game was clearly and commonly understood by the Chicanas and Chicanos in this book, but participants' different interpretations of the metaphor made for a complex issue. Some of the complexity lies in the fact that this is a gendered, power-laden way to make sense of activism. Games tend to be based around competitiveness, with the goal of winning, and games also tend to be male-oriented quests for power and prestige. Most participants viewed the system as a game and conceptualized themselves as players in that game. What some Chicana and Chicano activist educators considered necessary negotiations with institutional expectations in the game, others called costly compromises. What some considered strategic ways to survive with dignity in the system, or being good at playing the game, others called selling out, or the active denial of the ethnic self or community for personal, primarily economic, gain.

My analysis of the data led me to ask hard questions about playing the game versus selling out. Playing the game is a commonly used metaphor, not just in the Chicana and Chicano community, but also in other ethnic, class, race, gender, and activist communities. Selling out usually implies a betrayal, or abandoning the pursuit of an original goal or cause. Playing the game versus selling out can be problematic, however, because it is frequently framed as a rigid dichotomy.

In this book, I raise questions about where the agency lies in the tiny middle ground, in between the "cracks" of this dichotomy, as this tension is an extension of yet another dichotomy, reproduction versus resistance. And while surely there is something to gain and/or to lose by either playing the game or selling out, there is also the "in-between" that needs to be further explored. Using Mexican folk knowledge, I attempt to explore the in-between spaces by using the concept of *transas* in the final chapter of the book.

Transas literally means "transactions," which in Mexican folk knowledge are strategic and commonly known, but usually clandestine, practices used by people with less power to subvert, or get around, the system. There is generally a negative perception of transas in Mexican mainstream culture, but from the view of oppressed Mexicans, *el que no transa, no avanza* (s/he who doesn't conduct such transactions, doesn't advance). Transas are therefore calculated practices that do not follow mainstream prescriptions and are conducted to benefit the oppressed against the injustices of the system. Wealthy and powerful people also conduct transas, but because they are privileged by the system, their transas are perceived as fair and normal and have come to be the accepted way of conducting business. The same argument can be made about the normalized transas of privileged groups in any society, including in the United States, where white privilege is one big transa benefiting whites. Folk knowledge, like transas, was important to the Chicana and Chicano Movement and to Chicana and Chicano identity.

Identity, Worldview, and Activism

The Mexican American community has been involved in a struggle to improve the educational conditions of their children ever since the U.S. invasion and continued occupation of Mexican territory (Gallegos, 2000). This struggle includes the successful litigation of court cases against segregation a decade prior to *Brown v. Board of Education* in 1954 (Moreno, 1999). But, perhaps the most active events surrounding education occurred during the early Chicana and Chicano Movements.

The term "Chicana and Chicano," as an identity, was embraced by activist youth at the Chicano Youth Liberation Conference held in Denver in 1969 (Muñoz, 1989). A pursuit of social justice, not only a quest for identity, emerged from this event (Castro, 1974). To most Chicanas and Chicanos, but especially those of the 1960s and 1970s generation, to be Chicana and Chicano also meant to be an activist. Activism in this book is defined as the active participation, in various ways, of people who lobby around a particular set of issues (Urrieta, 2005b). Although stereotyped and attributed primarily to radical movements, activism is also practiced in different ways by conservative movements (Urrieta, 2005b).

Education is and always has been important to the Mexican American community. Inequities in schooling inspired mass protests by Chicana and Chicano students during the late 1960s throughout the Southwest. But inequities and the systematic denial of access to resources, especially to college preparation courses, were not the only issues inspiring student protest. Chicana and Chicano students in the 1960s demanded that schools hire Chicana and Chicano teachers who reflected their cultural experience and who could serve as role models, a demand yet to be fully met today. Another demand included that curricula center the Mexican American experience as part of the core curriculum in schools (K–12), which was a demand that district administrators never intended to meet. The 1960s student protests were partially successful, but the limited changes that occurred, especially at the K–12 level, were short-lived, or incomplete.

In terms of identification, people are not born Chicana and Chicano—they become Chicana and Chicano (Alarcón, 1990). Chicana and Chicano, like all identities, is embedded within a social, cultural, historical, gendered, and political context. Chicana and Chicano ideology professes that Chicanas and Chicanos embrace their people, *la raza*, and work toward self-determination. This call for solidarity in struggle does not only include the more educated, or the professional class, but all of la raza, especially those considered undesirables[11] by the whitestream.

Raza,[12] contrary to most whitestream analyses of the term, does not literally or simply mean race. Raza connotes a people with a similar social, cultural, and historical experience with oppression. Raza is a term of affirmation and empowerment (Castro, 1974). Chicana and Chicano identity today is like other culturally and politically constructed identities, functioning more like verbs than like nouns. Identities are often thought of as nouns, an extension of who people are in essence. Conceptualizing identities as verbs shows how identities are informed by who people are in practice and how that practice is lived in daily life.

This book is organized into three main parts. The first section examines the twenty-four participants' K–12 schooling experiences and the positioning of most as smart students by their teachers. This positioning, occurring mostly during the post–civil rights era, allowed these select students access to college-bound curriculum and eventually to higher education. Despite their positive positions, the participants were not represented well in the curriculum, especially in social studies. Because of portrayals ranging from invisible to hostile, participants felt disconnected from full American citizenship and from most of their ethnic/cultural peers.

The second section of this book focuses on identity production and identity shift. Participants' shifts in identification as Chicanas and Chicanos occurred as a result of being immersed and politicized in Chicana and Chicano social/academic circles, or what Holland and colleagues (1998) call figured worlds. Holland and colleagues (1998) define figured worlds as places where people come together to construct/form joint meanings and activities. In these Chicana and Chicano activist figured worlds, usually on college and university campuses, participants learned to refigure who they were, mostly through a re-vision of their past experiences and historical perspectives, and emerged as members of a Chicana and Chicano cultural world. This larger Chicana and Chicano cultural world engaged in an enduring struggle against the United States' physical and cultural invasion of what is known as Aztlán, the U.S. Southwest, or Mexican America.

Participation in these Chicana and Chicano activist figured worlds involved a reinterpretation of worldviews and often led participants to perform activism. Education was often seen as a major site for potential contention and struggle, a place to raise consciousness. The development of Chicana and Chicano consciousness by the participants was later negotiated in the context of whitestream schools that are alienating and castrating of social justice agendas and the pursuit of democracy for people of color. Chicana and Chicano activist educators, however, were creative and innovative in negotiating these agendas for social change.

The third section of the book examines how Chicana and Chicano activist educators negotiated their social justice agendas against the institutional boundaries and constraints of the whitestream schools that they worked in. There were undeniable barriers in schools that limited Chicana and Chicano activist educators' consciousness-raising agendas and their activist practices. These practices were negotiated by rethinking more traditional forms of activism, such as protests, marches, and demonstrations, to more strategic, day-to-day, moment-to-moment, innovative, and planned or spontaneous improvisations for social change. One of the intended outcomes of this book is the re/thinking of activism as a daily practice through the many creative and subversive ways Chicana and Chicano activist educators provided more democratic spaces in whitestream schools, especially for students of color.

I found my participants' activist practices to be enlightening and inspirational. From the study I also concluded that activism needs to be rethought by viewing daily "moments" of agency in practice as activism. Agency and activism, through this perspective, are tools embedded in the mundane details of daily interactions. The Chicana and Chicano Movement of today continues through local micro movements, *movimientos locales*, under the umbrella of a continuing macro Chicana and Chicano social movement. Most important, I found the lives of Chicana and Chicano activist educators to be fascinating, inspiring, and complex. This work is a testimony of their lives, and eight case studies will be presented throughout the book to highlight the multiplicity, creativity, and variety of their work, commitments, and dedication for change and social justice. The next chapter briefly provides an overview of the Chicano and Chicana Movements and my analytical lenses.

2
How the Story Goes . . .

> Play the game! I always tell them [the students]. I say, understand there's only one game in town. So play the game, but don't be controlled by it.
> —Rafael, Chicano Activist Teacher

Rafael, a Chicano middle school teacher in Southern California, tells his Latina and Latino students that there is only one game in town, implying that to do well in school, there's only one accepted route to success—the whitestream. Rafael, however, does not advocate that his students simply and uncritically assimilate to whitestream expectations. He tells his students to learn how to play by the whitestream rules that govern the system, but not to be controlled by them. Some could argue that Rafael is complicit with the goals of whitestream schooling by promoting a type of assimilation; others might argue he is being subversive in order to penetrate and infiltrate the system, and yet the issue is not so simple.

For Chicana and Chicano activists, to work or not to work within the system has been an ongoing dilemma since the late 1960s. Many Chicana and Chicano activists view institutions such as schools with distrust and contempt. For generations, Mexican American children have suffered from an unjust system that shortchanges their educational aspirations and minimizes their self-esteem (Valenzuela, 1999; E. García, 2001). Few people within the large category of Latina and Latino or Hispanic actively and consistently call themselves Chicana or Chicano. But, those who do self-identify in this way often feel strongly about their political convictions and visions for a better world, and some devote their entire lives toward furthering their vision of democracy. The Chicana and Chicano activist educators in this book are such people, and they come out of particular social, cultural, and historical contexts.

Historical Racialization of Mexicans in the Whitestream

Prior to the U.S. military invasion and subsequent occupation of Mexican territories, between 1836–1848 (Acuña, 2000), Mexican people had already been racialized as inferior (R. Gutiérrez, 2001). Manifest Destiny was justified by racial theories of Anglo-Saxon superiority (Menchaca and Valencia, 1990) that viewed Mexicans, in a pseudo-religious, racist mindset, as un-industrious, un-Christian, amoral, and genetically inferior half-breed "Indian/savage" people not worthy of occupying vast amounts of land (Horseman, 1981). Mexican men were especially dehumanized. R. Gutiérrez (2004: 262) documents: "Mexican men were typically portrayed as a breed of cruel and cowardly mongrels who were indolent, ignorant, and superstitious, given to cheating, thieving, gambling, drinking, cursing, and dancing." This dehumanizing process justified the invasion and military takeover of Mexican America during the War of the North American Invasion, today known in the whitestream as the Mexican American War and as the U.S. Southwest.

After the war, the Treaty of Guadalupe Hidalgo (1848) guaranteed Mexican citizens left on the U.S. side of the border equality and citizenship under the law. The United States, however, failed to uphold their promise (Menchaca, 1999). According to Donato, Menchaca, and Valencia (1991:33), from its inception, the California state government through "the California constitution (1949) prohibited 'Indian-looking Mexicans' from voting and only extended that privilege to 'White-looking Mexican' males." Regardless of physical features, by 1900 people of Mexican descent in the United States were racialized and dispossessed of most of their political influence and their economic wealth and were relegated into segregated quarters (barrios) throughout the Southwest (Pitt, 1966). Donato, Menchaca, and Valencia (1991:34) write: "In California the residential segregation of the Mexican began as early as 1850 and the process was completed by 1870." In San Francisco, San Jose, Santa Barbara, Los Angeles, San Diego, Santa Cruz, and Monterey, Anglo-American settlers restructured the old pueblos by constructing new subdivisions in the towns and prohibiting Mexicans from moving into Anglo neighborhoods. Throughout California the residential segregation of the Mexicans was enforced by use of racial harassment and violence, and in many cities by the use of housing covenant restrictions prohibiting Mexicans from residing in the white zones (Hendrick, 1977). By means of social segregation, policing, and denial of access to economic resources, the Mexican population in the "occupied territories," as Acuña (2000) has referred to the Southwest, came to occupy a racialized subaltern status to Anglos.

Mexican American Children in U.S. Schools

U.S. schooling enterprises were, at first, "tolerant" of Mexican children's linguistic and cultural differences; however, by the end of the nineteenth century, formal schooling institutions became increasingly intolerant (San Miguel, 1999). The focus of formal schooling shifted from one of basic academic training to that of socializing and Americanizing, which resulted in growing hostility toward the Spanish language and Mexican culture. Mexican children were denied access to white schools as early as 1892 (G. González, 1990). By the 1920s, school segregation was fully implemented throughout the Southwest in the form of either Mexican schools or Mexican rooms within schools (G. González, 1990; Donato, 1997).

Although *Plessy v. Ferguson* (1896) justified the legal segregation of blacks and whites, this legislation was used to justify the legal segregation of all non-whites. In California, legislators "sought to limit Mexicans' political and social rights on the rationale that Mexicans were Indians. They argued that because Indians by law were prohibited from voting, residing in white neighborhoods, and attending schools with white children, these laws also applied to Mexicans"(Donato, Menchaca, and Valencia, 1991:33). Mexican-descent children were segregated in deplorable conditions, with unequal funding and under low expectations, by unqualified, inexperienced, or inept, mostly white, teachers (G. González, 1990; Donato, 1997; San Miguel, 1999).

Psychometrics actively contributed to the rationale behind the segregation of Mexican American children (Valencia, 1997; R. Gutiérrez, 2001). This use of testing to justify segregation was tied to intelligence testing, Social Darwinism, and the eugenics movement at the turn of the twentieth century when people of color were "scientifically" categorized as inferior (Valencia and Aburto, 1991; Baker, 1998). During the 1920s, this led to the heavy implementation of tracking and vocational training programs for Mexican American students. The abuse of intelligence tests often led (and continues to lead) to the overrepresentation of Mexican-descent children in remedial tracks and special education (Rueda, 1991).

Another rationale for segregation was the issue of language. Since many Mexican American children were limited in speaking English, this was often used as the justification to keep them in separate classrooms. The issue of language became key to the litigation of successful court cases in favor of the Mexican American community in California in the 1930s and 1940s and in support of desegregation. Donato, Menchaca, and Valencia (1991:37) write: "In California, the Mexican parents of Lemon Grove were able to successfully overturn school segregation on March 13, 1931. *Alvarez v. the Board of Trustees of the Lemon Grove School District* represented one of the first successful desegregation court cases of Mexican students in the United States. The court ruled in favor of the Mexican community on the basis that separate facilities for Mexican students were not conducive towards their Americanization and retarded the English language competency of the Spanish-speaking children." Although the ruling intended to better Americanize Spanish-speaking students, it was a step toward desegregation that resulted in the *Méndez v. Westminster* (1947) court case that legally ended de jure segregation of Mexican children in California schools (Moreno, 1999).

Méndez v. Westminster (1947) is often cited by Chicano educational historians (G. González, 1990; San Miguel, 1996; San Miguel, 1999; Donato, 1997) as an important case toward the successful litigation of *Brown v. Board of Education* (1954). Both the *Alvarez* and *Méndez* cases, however, did not identify Mexican Americans as an "official" racial or ethnic minority group like African Americans and used language instead as a "proxy" for race. With regard to Mexican Americans and other Latino groups, language continues to be used as proxy for race (K. Gutiérrez and Jaramillo, 2006). It was not until *Cisneros v. Corpus Christi Independent School District* (1970) in Texas and *Keyes v. School District Number 1* (1975) in Colorado that Mexicans were legally recognized as an identifiable minority group (Donato, Menchaca, and Valencia, 1991). The early 1970s was also when the U.S. Census Bureau, influenced by legislators from New Mexico, also created the category Hispanic to identity this group in national census data (Muñoz, 1989; Oboler, 1995).

Early Mexican American Activism and Education

Mexican Americans were never passive victims. As early as the 1850s, Mexican Americans sought to maintain some forms of power and control over their children's education (San Miguel, 1996). High attendance rates in Catholic schools are often attributed to Mexican American parents' desire to keep their children in a less-hostile environment where their cultural and religious values were somewhat less under attack (San Miguel, 1996; Menchaca, 1999). Private secular schools were also started in an effort to maintain autonomy, cultural integrity, and the Spanish language; however, most were eventually closed (Salinas, 2000).

The League of United Latin American Citizens (LULAC) was formed in 1929. LULAC partially focused their efforts around issues of education and schooling for Mexican American children (Muñoz, 1989). Slowly, efforts for cultural recognition and educational attainment grew as the century progressed, mostly under assimilationist and Americanizing ideologies. Organizations such as the Mexican American Movement, Inc. (MAM) (1942–1950) sought to "combat the backwardness of the Mexican American community" through education (Muñoz, 1989:37). MAM, an organization made up of mostly Mexican American youth, emerged through the sponsorship of the Mexican Youth Conference (1934–1941) that was directly sponsored by the Young Men's Christian Association (YMCA) (Muñoz, 1989), a white Protestant organization with the aim of helping the "needy."

World War II was a time of violent attacks against Mexican American communities, especially youth. Muñoz (1989:37) writes about the Zoot Suit Riots in Los Angeles: "In 1943, World War II was at the height and thousands of soldiers of Mexican descent were dying on the battlefields. Tragically, their younger brothers were being attacked on the streets of Los Angeles by white sailors and marines on leave. Those confrontations, which became known as the 'Zoot Suit Riots,' were manifestations of a vulgar Mexican racism promoted by the Hearst newspapers, which publicly condoned and supported these racial attacks." Upon their return to a country that they had bravely fought for, Mexican American veterans were treated disrespectfully and unequally, although, through the American G.I. Bill of Rights (Gándara, 1995), limited educational opportunities did arise for some. The American G.I. Forum is an organization formed by Mexican American veterans after World War II to demand equal treatment in U.S. society (Muñoz, 1989).

The Association of Mexican-American Educators (AMAE), primarily a teacher organization formed in 1965, was the first to focus specifically on educational issues that addressed the concerns and needs of the Mexican American community. AMAE, however, was also initially heavily influenced by the conservative orientation of earlier Mexican American organizations. Its early founders were products of MAM and former participants in the Mexican Youth Conference (Muñoz, 1989). Several AMAE members were also veterans, now teachers, who had benefited from the G.I. Bill. Despite their conservative politics, all of these early organizations contributed to the creation of a small number of Mexican American professionals, including teachers. Because of their belief in the ideal of American meritocracy and their push for assimilation, they became known as the Mexican American generation.

While their tactics and strategies were very different than those of the civil rights era, their contributions are part of the larger historical trajectory that led to the activism of future generations, including that of the 1960s. During this pre-1960s Chicana and Chicano Movement period, a few prominent activist figures did emerge to challenge the negative and unjust treatment of Mexican Americans. Ernesto Galarza is often recognized as the first Mexican American student activist. In 1929 Galarza was a graduate student at Stanford University and was active in defending U.S.-born Mexican migrant workers. Américo Paredes also stands out as a leading folklorist of southwestern, specifically Tejano, culture. In the field of education, George I. Sánchez stands out as the only Mexican American academic addressing issues concerning Mexican American children (Murillo, 1996). Sánchez focused his career on debunking popular myths about the perceived deficiencies in Mexican American Spanish-speaking children. "On the basis of his own studies Sanchez argued that Mexican American children were no less intelligent than any other American group" (R. Gutiérrez, 2001:211).

Chicano Cultural Nationalism

El movimiento Chicano (I purposefully selected "Chicano" rather than "Chicana and Chicano") officially emerged in the late 1960s and was initially a social movement of Chicano men in part "fighting to regain their manhood," in response to decades of physical, social, cultural, religious, and economic subordination to Anglos (Pulido, 2006:204).[1] Although the larger Movimiento Chicano of the 1960s and 1970s was not ideologically monolithic, a general ideology that addressed white supremacy head-on, often referred to as Chicanismo, emerged. According to Acuña (2000), despite a lack of solid unification, generally an "anger and reaction to an unjust system, whether macro or micro, was being acted out" (357) through

Chicanismo. Chicanismo took on different meanings for different people, but broadly meant having "pride of identity, and self-determination" (358). Self-determination included a strong sense of "community commitment" (Delgado Bernal, 2001).

1960s and 1970s activism usually revolved around community-based organizations that sought self-determination in the barrios (neighborhoods). R. Gutiérrez (2001) refers to community as *raza* and to Chicanos' (males) brotherhood as *carnales*. "*Chicanismo* meant identifying with *la raza*, and collectively promoting the interests of carnales with whom they shared a common language, culture, and religion" (R. Gutiérrez, 2001:214). Chicanismo, in the gendered dictates of the Spanish language, as well as the focus on carnales, was male centered. Chicanos in the Movimiento were charged with the duty and responsibility to fight for the barrio/raza, to vindicate their manhood from subordinate status, and to regain power.

Chicanismo became a culturally nationalist ideology fueling the focus of the larger Chicano Movement. The Aztec warrior, especially Cuauhtémoc, became a Mexica-centric celebration of resistance, bravery, and manhood. More-militant stances were often thought of as more "activist" or "down" with *la causa* (the cause), while leadership was based on traditional leadership practices like holding office and formal public speaking (Delgado Bernal, 1998a). Early activists in the Chicano Movement, parallel to other movements at the time, failed to see how gender permeated early strategies and ideologies to the exclusion of Chicanas while the activist and leadership roles Chicanas performed were unacknowledged (Delgado Bernal, 1998a). This form of activism, reacting to an oppressive past of subordination through emasculation, emerged with Chicano Cultural Nationalism.

Aztlán was claimed as the nation, or *pátria* (fatherland), of Chicanas and Chicanos (Pulido, 2006). Nationalist projects rested on cultural images to re/produce nation. Chicano Cultural Nationalism's cultural images focused on *la familia* (the family) and familism (family loyalty) as core cultural production. Chicanas in Aztlán were charged with maintaining and literally reproducing the culture. Chicanas' wombs, like indigenous women's wombs in Mexico, became the epicenter for the nation's reproduction (Hernández Castillo, 2001). Chicanas' bodies and sexuality became the objects of Aztlán's (the pátria's) physical and cultural re/production.

Chicano Cultural Nationalism endowed Chicanos with hypermasculinity. This hypermasculinity emerged out of a historical context founded on malestream[2] competition, the competition of men against other men for power in patriarchal, capitalist systems. According to Pulido (2006), militant activist movements were quests for power, and the acquisition of power tends to be a male-oriented goal. The various civil rights movements, at least initially, Pulido (2006:181) argues, were efforts to "reestablish the status and privilege of subordinated men."

The Chicana Movement and Chicana Feminism

The political activism of Chicanas was often devalued in the early movement. *Mujeres'* issues were rendered invisible, there was a disproportional focus on men as leaders, and there was a gendered division of labor and participation (A. Hurtado, 1989; Nieto Gomez, 1997; Pesquera and Segura, 1997). The limits imposed on mujeres disturbed Chicanas, given that Mexicanas/Chicanas were always active in social struggles, not just exclusively involved in family-centered activities or other activities dictated by tradition (Ruiz, 1987). Chicana feminists were often accused of being *agabachadas* (white-washed) or lesbians.

Chicana feminists created spaces to address mujeres' concerns outside of both the wider white feminist movements[3] and traditional Chicano spaces (Segura and Pesquera, 1998). Chicanos in the broader Chicano Movement sometimes viewed Chicana feminists as Malinchistas (sellouts)[4], forcing Chicanas to create their own consciousness-raising efforts (Blackwell, 2003). Despite the attacks, Chicana feminists were reluctant to separate from Chicanos' struggles (Nieto Gomez, 1997).

Chicana feminists immediately began to form their own struggle within the larger Chicano Movement to address the simultaneity of their multiple oppressions (A. Hurtado, 1989). The Chicana Movement developed a distinct Chicana feminist discourse through ideologies like Chicanisma, and later Xicanisma (Castillo, 1994), that address race, class, gender, and sexuality issues. Chicanas embody gendered and racialized political identities (Blackwell, 2003) and theorize from a unique social/cultural and gendered location (Alarcón, 1990; Anzaldúa, 1990; Sandoval, 1991; Castillo, 1994).[5] The focus on tradition and cultural expectations around la familia and cultural tradition were not only pre-scripted in terms of mujeres' roles but also in terms of men's and mujeres' sexuality. To challenge these sexual norms and expectations, lesbian, gay, bisexual, and transgender (LGBT) perspectives were essential[6] (Trujillo, 1991). Issues of LGBT Latinidad also rose with the incidence of HIV/AIDS (Rodríguez, 2003).

Mestizaje

Although *mestizaje* embodies a historical location of racism and indigenous erasure in Mexican society (Urrieta, 2003b), the new mestiza enabled Chicana feminists to take resistance, culture, activism, and contradiction issues in new directions (Sandoval, 1998; Delgado Bernal, 2001).[7] Delgado Bernal (2001) elaborates on the concept of *la conciencia mestiza* (mestiza consciousness) by positing that "the mestiza identity is a dual identity that is located at the crossroads of racism, sexism, classism, homophobia, and patriarchy found in the dominant society and in Chicana and Chicano communities" (626). Mestizaje is a powerful counterhegemonic claim against modernist identities in which "a mestiza consciousness is born out of oppression and is in a conscious struggle against it" (Delgado Bernal, 2001:626). Mestiza consciousness embodies Chicanas' experience with the contradictions of multiplicity.

Emma Pérez (1999) discusses mestizaje and Chicana feminism as a "third space," a hybrid space created from a time lapse in the interstices between colonialism and (post)colonialism. From this third space, Pérez (1999) claims, Chicana feminists can learn to align their agency both with men's community struggles in terms of race and class and in relation to gender and sexuality. Pérez (1999) does not reject the idea of nationalism as a tool for organizing and refers to Chicana feminism as feminism-in-nationalism, where "one negotiates within the imaginary to a decolonizing otherness where all identities are at work in one way or another" (7). Third space, hybridity, and mestizaje, often used in complement, help Chicanas and Chicanos theorize the possibilities of these concepts for libratory purposes.[8]

Chicana and Chicano Activist Educators

Most people today know little about the 1960s Chicana and Chicano struggle for equality. Students in my college courses often ask me with genuine ignorance what the difference is between Hispanic, Latina and Latino, Chicana and Chicano, or Mexican American. Chicana and

Chicano as an identity is sometimes used synonymously with Mexican American and is at times used uncritically even by Chicana and Chicano academics. Some Latinas and Latinos go as far as declaring Chicana and Chicano issues as old-fashioned or outdated and prefer to use terms like post-Chicana and post-Chicano at this historical moment. The Chicana and Chicano struggle for equal education is far from dead, and both the Chicano and Chicana movements continue today. Chicana and Chicano identities continue to blossom in community organizations, as they do on the campuses of colleges and universities.

But, why study Chicana and Chicano activist educators? What is unique about Chicana and Chicano activist educators? Chicana and Chicano identity deserves to be studied in more complex ways in education because it is in formal and informal educational contexts that people enter the figured worlds of Chicana and Chicano activism and learn to become Chicanas and Chicanos. The focus on Chicana and Chicano activist educators in this book is an attempt to honor the complexity of this identity and its historical importance and is not meant to exclude other Latinas and Latinos who are also activists *and* educators. Chicana and Chicano identity, however, is a product of the social, cultural, and historical context already outlined that, in the Chicana and Chicano worldview, dates back to the invasion and subsequent continuous occupation of Mexican territory.[9] The participants in this book are the benefactors of the expansion of the multicultural perspectives that emerged during the civil rights era. These new social justice agendas are a determining force in current social movements, including Chicana and Chicano social movements.

The participants in this book generally defined activists as people with a critical literacy of the world who understood the issues affecting not only raza but also all oppressed people. Having this critical literacy, however, is only a step toward activism. To be an activist means actually doing something to challenge oppression. Doing something meant a variety of different things to different participants, ranging from formal protest on college campuses to teaching a unit on the genocide of Native Americans to fourth-grade students.

What was consistent in participants' narratives about activism, regardless of gender or age, was a sense of urgency to act upon the world in support of, and for the educational rights of, the communities they felt committed to. In that respect, the participants are similar to other people in the world who commit their lives to a struggle or cause. What is peculiar and inspiring about the participants in this book is their commitment to enter the very institutions that they are most critical of, endure the hardships of compromise with dignity, and yet remain hopeful and innovative as they try to make changes from within. The analyses presented in this book are based on several bodies of theory, especially on social movements, identity and agency, and Chicana and Chicano, Mexicana and Mexicano frameworks.[10]

Social Movements and Chicana and Chicano Identity

Social movements have changed since the 1960s as a result of the network economy because labor demands have changed from factory labor and the production of goods to labor focused on the production of services (Castells, 2006). Place and locality have become the sites for contestation/resistance to the privatization of public services like welfare, health care, and education, and to the encroachment of neoliberalism (Castells, 2006). Social movements, in this new global context, provide different means for studying identities, such as Chicana and Chicano identities, struggling for social change that are continuities, yet different identities than those of the 1960s.

The idea of coherence in social movements needs to be revisited in this new postmodern era (Morris, 2000). Melucci (1989) begins to reconceptualize social movements through an anti-essentialist approach by stressing that contextualization is crucial for studying today's social movements because today's movements tend to occur in relation to place and space in specific micro-localities as opposed to massive collectives. The continuing struggles of Chicana and Chicano activist educators, although they emerge from larger, specific enduring struggles, are particular to whitestream school contexts.

Because notions of the proletariat shifted with the economic shifts in capitalism, new social movement theorists emphasize culture, not class consciousness, as the site for struggle (Harvey, 1990). Social movements are now understood as transformations of adaptable and multiple discourses, especially of culture and identity, in new contexts (Melucci, 1989; Calhoun, 1994). Social movements revolve around particular communities embracing cultural and identity politics (Calhoun, 1994) in response to a dislocation of linear time and space (Castells, 2006). The Chicana and Chicano identity in the 1960s emerged from the postmodern context that enabled narratives to be questioned (Rust, 1991). The Chicana and Chicano Movimientos did not function as unified coherent class-based social movements, but as quests for power within a larger context of multiple forms of oppression under the banner of cultural/ethnic identity.

In the larger Chicana and Chicano Movement, activism and agency exist in multiple places with multiple loci and in daily, moment-to-moment "practice" (Bourdieu, 1977). Holland and colleagues (1998) view identity "as a sign of self in practice, not as a sign of self in essence" (31) and the focus on identity as a practice and not as an essence is important in this book. The *name* Chicana and Chicano is one that is "consciously and critically assumed" and serves as a "practice" to dismantle "historical conjunctures of crisis, confusion, political and ideological conflict and contradictions" (Alarcón, 1990).

Because improvisation can effect and affect permanent changes in future expected responses, critical *moments* during the interaction process are important for recognizing agency (Bourdieu, 1977). Agency is liberated, in a sense, from traditional stereotypes and Western expectations of what activism or agency in a typical social movement are usually limited to (e.g., class consciousness, mass demonstrations, armed revolution, etc.). In this notion of social movements, agents each have individual opportunities to act in the world, even when bound heavily by cultural and social norms (Holland et al., 1998).

Geographic location is also important when analyzing localized social movements. Globalization and technology have disrupted the traditional relationship between space and place (Harvey, 1990). Place is important for identity politics and collective action as it relates to physical and cultural location (Castells, 2006). The larger Chicana and Chicano Movement exemplifies different aspects of reactionary localized social movements—those movements that respond to neoliberal market expansion, economic dislocation, and globalization by advocating for place.

While a broad historical context of oppression linked the enduring struggles of the larger Chicana and Chicano Movement together through Anglo and U.S. military conquest, the local expressions of these historical processes were and are different with each locality. César Chávez' and Dolores Huerta's struggle in organizing farm workers against California agribusiness, Reies López Tijerina's fight to reclaim centuries-old Hispano land grants in provincial New Mexico and southern Colorado, Sal Castro's and Corky Gonzáles's quests for Chicano identity and demand for educational equality for urban youth in the barrios of Los Angeles and Denver, and José Angel Gutiérrez' effort to organize Tejano political power in south Texas were all expressions of local contentious practices embedded within an already durable, larger Mexican American struggle prior to the 1960s. There were also different points of contention within each local struggle, as with Chicana feminists' justified response to early Chicanismo. Focus on local issues is an important aspect of this book because each Chicana and Chicano activist educator engaged in both individual and collective struggles in local whitestream schools. Although some argue that the Chicana and Chicano Movement ended in the 1970s (Chávez, 2002), it is important to highlight the continuity of movement struggles (Pulido, 2006) through activist generational cohorts (Whittier, 1995). The Chicana and Chicano activist educators in this book are members of multiple generational cohorts in the larger Chicana and Chicano social movement.

Taylor (1998) contends that gender[11] is a fundamental part of social movements[12] even when gender issues are not targeted by the specific movements. Gender in a malestream society founded on patriarchy is like race in a whitestream system founded on white supremacy—enmeshed in all aspects of daily life. Einwohner, Hollander, and Olson (2000) concluded that social movements evaluated and perceived as feminine were often viewed as less threatening and were given legitimacy with more ease than those perceived to be more masculine, which were often viewed as aggressive or militant.

Feminine qualities in movements, such as non-violent demonstrations, are interpreted as peaceful. For example, César Chávez' and Dolores Huerta's farmworkers' struggle increasingly received considerable support, sympathy, and legitimacy for their cause over time because of their commitment to non-violence, prayer, and hunger strikes. On the other hand, more active attempts to make demands heard, like Reies López Tijerina's armed struggle to reclaim Spanish land grants in rural New Mexico and Colorado, were met with National Guard intervention, incarceration, delegitimization, and other forms of violent physical repression. Legitimacy for peaceful movements, however, usually comes with a double bind: "representations of femininity may help them [peaceful social movements] establish legitimacy, but limit their eventual [political] effectiveness" (Einwohner, Hollander, and Olson, 2000:693).

The general gender perception in social movements is that politics and political power are usually associated with masculinity and that feminine ideas are usually associated with service and volunteerism, which are usually dismissed. Thus, organizing for community building (generally viewed as the goal of organizing for women) is considered less threatening than community organizing as a means to power, especially political and economic power (generally viewed as the goal of organizing for men) (Taylor, 1999). Gender is a fundamental part of social movements and of social movement analyses (Taylor, 1998) and is therefore necessary in my analytical framework.

Identity and Agency

Identity is a concept not only constituted by the labels people place on themselves and others but also about how people come to understand themselves, how they come to "figure" who they are through the "worlds" that they participate in, and how they relate to others within and outside of these figured worlds. My framework for studying Chicana and Chicano activist educators' identity and agency is mainly drawn from Holland and colleagues' influential book *Identity and Agency in Cultural Worlds* (1998).

Holland and colleagues' theory draws from different (sometimes opposing) schools of thought, including culturalists, constructivists, and universalists, and from the work of Vygotsky (1978) and Bakhtin (1981). Holland and colleagues (1998) suggest that cultural production and heuristic development are important processes for identity analyses because they move us away, although not completely, from cultural determinism and situational totalitarianism to make way for the importance of improvisation and innovation (agency). In this sociocultural practice theory of identity and self, attention is focused on identities forming in process or activity in four contexts discussed throughout Holland and colleagues' book: figured worlds, negotiations of positionality, space of authoring, and world making. Of the four, figured worlds play most prominently in my analysis.

Figured Worlds

Figured worlds, Holland and colleagues suggest, are sites where identities are produced. People "figure" who they are through their activities, in relation to the social types who populate these figured worlds, and in social relationships with the people who perform in these worlds. People can develop and maintain new identities in figured worlds.

Holland and colleagues broadly define figured worlds as "socially produced, culturally constituted activities" (40–41) where people come to conceptually (cognitively) and materially/procedurally produce (perform) new self-understandings (identities). According to Holland and colleagues, figured worlds have four characteristics:

1. Figured worlds are cultural phenomenon to which people are recruited, or into which people enter, and that develop through the work of their participants.
2. Figured worlds function as contexts of meaning within which social encounters have significance and people's positions matter. Activities relevant to these worlds take meaning from them and are situated in particular times and places.
3. Figured worlds are socially organized and reproduced, which means that people are sorted and learn to relate to each other in different ways in them.
4. Figured worlds distribute people by relating them to landscapes of action; thus, activities related to the figured world are populated by familiar social types and play host to individual senses of self.

Figured worlds are therefore processes or traditions of apprehension that give people shape and form as their lives intersect with figured worlds. In figured worlds, people learn to recognize each other as a particular sort of actor, value certain outcomes over others, and recognize and attach significance to some acts and not to others. Whether people are passively drawn into or actively recruited into them, or enter particular figured worlds by some other means, depends on who they are and their personal social history (history-in-person). Holland and colleagues contend that we may never enter some figured worlds based on our social rank or position (or the lack thereof), while we may deny outsiders access to others. Some figured worlds we may learn fully, and others we may miss by contingency. And, I would add, we may yet enter other figured worlds only temporarily and peripherally, while in others we may come to assume positions of relative power and prestige.

Because figured worlds are socially organized and performed, they depend on interaction and people's intersubjectivity for perpetuation. In them, people "figure" how to relate to one another over time and across different time/place/space contexts. Holland and colleagues write that these ways of interacting become almost like "roles" (41), but not in the static sense of the older concept. The significance of figured worlds is that they are recreated by work, often contentious, with others; thus, activity takes on increased importance.

Culture, Possibility, Power

Although Holland and colleagues claim that figured worlds can be called "as if" realms, most are more substantial than fantasy. Holland and colleagues' sociocultural practice theory of self and identity focuses attention on figured worlds as sites of possibility, but also recognizes that figured worlds are social realities that live within dispositions mediated by relations of power. Because figured worlds are peopled by characters from collective imaginings—such as class, race, gender, and nationality—people's identity and agency is formed dialectically between and dialogically within them. Holland and colleagues' concept of figured worlds is therefore a useful concept to study identity and agency in education. Figured worlds are not set on previous static notions of culture. Figured worlds focus on activity and emphasize the importance of power.

Figured worlds are historical phenomenon, and each figured world is in turn organized by "cultural means" (53), or narratives, storylines, and other cultural genres, that help organize the figured world. These narratives provide a significant backdrop for interpretation and cultural resources that are durable and socially reproduced. These cultural means, Holland and colleagues claim, illustrate the influence of culturalists in their work.

Although narratives may be used by participants as though they were pre/scriptive, narratives are commonly horizons of meaning against which incidents, acts, and individuals are interpreted. From social constructivism and practice theory, Holland and colleagues add that figured worlds happen as social processes and in historical time. Figured worlds are encountered in day-to-day social activity and lived through practices. Identities are thus formed in the processes of participating in activities and practices organized by figured worlds.

From Marxian theory via Leont'ev's activity theory and Foucault's analyses of power, Holland and colleagues (1998) and Holland and Lave (2001) recognize that activities within figured worlds are meshed with trans-local systems of power and privilege. Relationships, practices, acts, courses of action, people, and cultural resources within figured worlds are tied to powerful, trans-local institutions. Different elements within the figured world take on variations of rank and status according to widespread relationships of hierarchy, and figured worlds themselves are organized around positions of status and influence. It is important to reiterate that regardless of the hopeful agency, creativity, and imagination available in figured worlds,

Holland and colleagues' (1998) theory remains situated in the dialectic between structure and agency because, although we shape our identities in practice, the languages available to us are the products of people, institutions, and ideologies embedded in unequal structural power relations.

Artifacts and Materiality

Holland and colleagues highlight the importance of artifacts as mediators of human identities and action. As "psychological tools" (60), artifacts provide the means to "evoke" figured worlds. Artifacts gain credence in connection to figured worlds and assume both conceptual and material aspects as practical instruments for daily use and as artifacts of collective memory; Holland and colleagues, citing Cole, claim that artifacts bring "developmental histories" (62) of past activities to the present. Each artifact, such as, for example, an apron, brings with it a unique history (and herstory) related to its origin and its use(s) in the past beyond its own existence and uses in the present.

In figured worlds, people learn to ascribe meaning to artifacts, such as objects, events, and discourses, and to people as understood in relation to particular figured worlds. Holland and colleagues also contend that artifacts help mediate the thoughts and feelings of individual participants, such as the thoughts and feelings a national flag evokes in people, both individually and collectively. Artifacts, such as a national flag, often provide for people the means to position themselves for themselves, and before others. Holland and colleagues do not stop at description when it comes to artifacts, but argue that artifacts can also offer possibilities for becoming, possibilities to expand the possibilities (so to speak).

Conceptual and Material Understandings

Holland and colleagues focus specific attention on two processes of self-making (identity): conceptual and material. Conceptually, figured worlds provide the contexts of meanings for concepts or domains of action, for artifacts, for action (behavior), and for people's understandings of themselves. People learn new perspectives of the world in figured worlds, and through them, participants learn to ascribe to artifacts and actions new meaning, passion, or emotion. Figured worlds also provide people with the capability to influence their own behavior in these worlds. As people's subjectivities become better organized around certain issues important to the figured world, their behavior manifests the ascription of new meaning, and they favor certain activities and practices over others. Materially, people enact everyday performances of these senses of self, and these performances in turn reify relative positions of influence and prestige in and across figured worlds.

Agency

Holland and colleagues (1998) highlight the importance of improvisations of cultural forms when used for agency purposes and propose two forms of improvised agency—spontaneous innovation and self-directed symbolization. Spontaneous innovation is the type of agency performed when people encounter difficult situations for which they have no formulated response. In such cases, people improvise in situ with a response. Self-directed symbolization is performed when people use symbols, such as artifacts, or activity, such as their own imagination, to mediate a type of response to particular situations. An example of this would be when people imagine their audience is naked to overcome the anxiety of speaking in public.

When such improvisations are interpreted as agency rather than as a disruption, a disorder, or a pathology of normalized behavior, these improvisations increase the potential for a temporary or permanent new way of doing things. Improvisations can become the basis for a reformed subjectivity and can incite collective action (Holland et al., 1998). Chicana and Chicano identity and activism in whitestream schools often seeks to improvise change into daily social interaction.

Inden (1990:23) defines human agency as: "The realized capacity of people to act upon their world and not only to know about or give personal or intersubjective significance to it. That capacity is the power of people to act purposively and reflectively, in more or less complex interrelationships with one another, to reiterate and remake the world in which they live, in circumstances where they may consider different courses of action possible and desirable, though not necessarily from the same point of view."

Inden suggests that to maximize the potential to exercise agency, agency must be reflected upon and understood. Individuals and collectives must *see* that they *can* act purposively and reflectively in the world either spontaneously or through intended self-direction. Purposeful and strategic interrelationships, or networks with like-minded others, are necessary to strategize for change at a larger and broader scale. To Holland and colleagues (1998), personal agency exists within the conundrum of a seeming contradiction between humans as social producers and humans as social products. In Chicana and Chicano activist educators' practices in this book, the participants developed the realized recognition of their ability to act critically upon the world with the understanding that there were inherent structural contradictions limiting their social practice.

This notion of agency incorporates cultural production.[13] Agency, especially activist agency, is a conscious and strategic form of active and strategic cultural production. Since it is lobbying for a particular set of issues, activist agency is produced within the confines of contradiction and is freed in part from traditional expectations. Chicana and Chicano activism in whitestream schools is under this conscious understanding of agency, being both culturally *produced* in whitestream schools and working within them to *produce* new and transformative cultural forms.

"Playing the game" for the Chicana and Chicano activist educators in this book is a strategic understanding of power and a critical exertion of activist agency, while also simultaneously a critical and conscious perpetuation of the system. As long as playing the game is not taken for granted, Chicana and Chicano activist educators remain aware of their agency to not follow (completely) the prescriptions of normalization (the whitestream game). When the belief in the possibility for change is taken out of the game, either through self-defeat, a loss of hope, or unconscious submission, then the game becomes normalized and is no longer being played; agency is subverted.

Participation in the process of whitestream schooling can and often does become normalized for some people (at which point selling out occurs). The surrender of activist agency is often justified with the phrase, "that's the way it (the whitestream system) is." When conformity to the whitestream game occurs, the willingness to conduct *transas* is surrendered. For the Chicana and Chicano activist educators in this book, part of the motivation for playing the game without selling out involved a redefinition of activism by working within whitestream schools with the aim of changing them from within. The participants held strongly to their cultural agency despite the challenges and constraints.

The next chapter focuses on how the twenty-four participants in the study experienced K–12 schools. Most were positioned as smart students by their teachers, and this positioning gave them access to rank, power, and prestige. However, positive positioning and academic success in whitestream schools did not free them from experiencing cultural alienation and feeling disconnected from full American citizenship.

3
Positioning Mexican American Students in Whitestream Schools

Mexican Americans have historically not been positioned as smart students in whitestream schools (G. González, 1990; Donato, 1997, 2007; San Miguel and Valencia, 1998).[1] My understanding of positioning is drawn from Holland and colleagues' (1998) second context for the production of personal and social identities: positionality. Postionality refers to the positions "offered" to people in different figured worlds (whether that be of a "loud student," "bad student," "successful student," or "smart student"). Holland and colleagues state that positionality is an analytically separable counterpart to figuration because when positioned, people are not as actively engaged in self-making, but rather are limited to varying degrees of accepting, rejecting, or negotiating the identities being offered to them. Similarly, in figured worlds, people encounter narratives born out of historical significance (both oppressive and liberating) as well as a distribution of power, rank, and prestige (or the lack thereof) that they either accept, reject, or negotiate to varying degrees.

Mexican American students have not often been positioned as smart in schools, despite the Mexican American community's rejection of this positioning. Chicana and Chicano education historians document the ways that Mexican American students have generally been labeled as intellectually and culturally inferior as seen by schools (G. González, 1990; Donato, 1997, 2007; San Miguel and Valencia, 1998). Donato (1997) documents high dropout rates, low expectations, segregation, the use of child field labor, vocational training, and the gross misuse of testing as sources of lack of achievement for Mexican American students throughout the Southwest during the past century. As an extreme, but not uncommon, case, Donato cites that Thomas Garth, a university professor in the 1920s, maintained that, based on his "scientific" findings, 80.5 percent of Mexican children tested were retarded (26). Such is the legacy of negative positioning that Mexican American children inherit in the figured worlds of whitestream schools. Interestingly, most of the participants in this book were not positioned in this way.

Positioning and Academic Success in Whitestream Schools

Almost all of the twenty-four participants were selected and positioned as "smart" students from an early age by teachers in the schools they attended, unlike the majority of their ethnic peers. Once positioned as smart, participants were separated into honors or gifted tracks, which made them aware of their positioning and gave them access to relative forms of power, rank, and prestige in the figured world of smart students. In private or rural school settings, participants acquired rank and prestige by being separated into ability groups. Participants positioned as smart were generally treated better in school and enjoyed attending school. Andrea stated: "I just knew that school was a place where I could do well. Ever since I was little, I was told I was smart." Similarly, María said: "I was a very successful student. I mean I always liked school, and so I did well in school." Most of the participants, like Andrea and María, reported that they were aware that they were expected to perform well academically, and they did.

Most participants could not recall how exactly they ended up being positioned as smart in schools.[2] Participants, for the most part, attended predominantly Latina and Latino schools, but were one of the few students positioned as smart. Participants reported feeling culturally isolated in honors and gifted classes and even teased by their own ethnic peers. As a result, some of the participants associated negative characteristics with students of their same ethnic group.

The few exceptions to such early positioning were three male participants who entered the school system as primarily Spanish speakers. A fourth exception was David, the oldest participant. David attributed his late positioning as a smart student to the low academic expectations of Hispano students in Colorado at the time of his youth (Donato, 2007). According to David, his athletic ability was the impetus for being recruited into the figured world of smart students.

The few participants not positioned as smart reported that they fought against the "bad student" stereotype. Their predominantly white teachers, they said, had negative perceptions of most Mexican American students. In Julián's experience, a narrative to be elaborated later, teachers became frustrated with him for not knowing whitestream culture. White-stream cultural artifacts, such as a bonnet or spinning wheel, although they seemed like "little things" to his teacher, were completely foreign in his cultural historical world. Despite his negative experiences, Julián became an avid reader and was later identified as "college material" in high school.

Jaime, who entered the public schools as a Spanish speaker in the 1980s, is another case of having to fight to be placed into a gifted and talented academic track. Jaime was placed in bilingual education programs in elementary school. He claimed several teachers tried to "test him out" to track him as "gifted," but his family moved often, and so his identification was delayed until the fifth grade.

> I was in bilingual education until the fifth grade because every time a teacher wanted to test me into the gifted program, we would end up moving. So in third grade a white teacher . . . took four of us out and gave us separate work to prepare us for this test. I took the test and got labeled as gifted and talented, but then we moved again, and I was again placed into a bilingual classroom. It wasn't 'til fifth grade that I won a math competition that they [the teachers] finally checked my record and saw I had been labeled GT two years before. Then I was moved to the GATE [Gifted and Talented Education] classes.

Every time Jaime changed schools, he was automatically placed into bilingual classes based on home language survey data and other narrow and deterministic criteria for language placement. Bilingual students are generally not positioned as gifted by whitestream teachers. Thousands more like Jaime are bilingual and gifted and will never be identified because whitestream notions position children in bilingual classes as remedial (González Baker, 1996) or "at-risk." In the figured worlds of schooling, bilingual education classes generally do not have high ranking or prestige in the distribution of power, with the exception of dual-language programs in white middle-class communities.

Juan was also an exception to being positioned as smart. He entered an almost entirely Latina and Latino Catholic school as a Spanish speaker in the 1970s. Johnny, as he prefers to be called, remembered being pulled out for "special" classes in reading, but was fully aware that "special" did not mean good. "I remember them [the teachers] sending me to special reading classes, but they were all in English with no Spanish support. So I learned how to read, but I didn't really understand what I was saying. I guess I knew I was slow and that made me feel bad." Johnny later transferred to public schools and was also automatically positioned as a bilingual student. Johnny admitted he felt "more comfortable" because "other kids would speak Spanish," but he did not feel that his classes were "challenging." Johnny recalled insisting he be placed in honors classes in high school because his older brother was in an honors track. "After several times, I would say after the seventh time, he [the counselor] got mad at me and told me, 'If you don't make it [in honors classes], don't say I didn't warn you and come back crying to me!' He finally authorized the permission for me to transfer to honors classes."

Until Proposition 227 passed, Johnny reported he received As and did exceptionally well in his honors courses and later attended the University of California. Johnny was a bilingual elementary school teacher in his home community.

Except for these cases, all of the participants were offered smart student positions early on and were aware that they were positioned in this way. Most were tracked in early elementary school, either in separate groups, gifted and talented classes, or magnet schools. When participants moved away from these positions, their early label as smart helped them to re-position themselves as smart once again. The exceptions mentioned fought to be positioned as smart students, and they gained this position later in their schooling experience.

Although Alicia was positioned as a smart student in elementary school, she was the only female who was not in high academic tracks throughout her schooling experience. Alicia became a single mother at age 15 and eventually attended continuation high school. Years later, when Alicia met her husband, a Chicano teacher, she reconnected with her early experience as a smart student. Alicia eventually completed her associate of arts degree at a local community college and her bachelor's degree and teaching credential at the University of California. Alicia now works as a history teacher at a predominantly Latina and Latino continuation high school.

Participants' separation into "smart spaces" generally created physical and social distance from other Latina and Latino students. Smart spaces are defined as the privileged physical and social spaces of high rank and prestige in the figured world of schooling, exclusively designated for students positioned as smart. Isadora, for example, thought of the "regular" students, those in the general track, as "dumb." At the time of the study, Isadora recognized these students as members of her own ethnic/cultural group by using the term *raza*. "There were raza at my school, but they were in regular [classes]. . . . Everyone always talked bad about the regular kids. . . . It's kind of bad, but I did feel like, oh, I'm not a regular kid. I felt extra special or something. . . . I don't think I ever outwardly made fun of them, but I know I would look at them and think, you're dumb!"

Other participants, like Isadora, also reported that they internalized negative conceptions of their own people. For Juanita, the distinction between herself as a Catholic school student and students in public schools, even if in the same predominantly Latina/o neighborhood, had a racialized class connotation.[3] Juanita remembered referring to public school students as *la chusma* (low class).

Some participants identified honors and gifted tracking as culturally isolating because physical separation from members of the same ethnic group led to cultural and social distancing. Therese, for example, recalled that: "it [school] was kind of isolating because my best friends didn't think they were smart. Like my little *Chicanita* friends, one of my friends I remember . . . she was in the slower class, and she was like, 'You know I'm not smart like you.' She would always say things like that. . . . K–6 a lot of my friends were white. . . . High school was a little different; all my friends were Asian. It just transformed because they were in the honors classes." Even though Therese lived in a predominantly Mexican community, she experienced cultural isolation in school. Therese's physical removal within community is an example of the segregation-within-schools effect of tracking (Oakes, 1995).

Smart Students in Whitestream Schools

Eight case narratives, four from *mujeres* and four from men, representing the four groups studied (undergraduates, K–12 teachers, graduate students, and education professors) will be presented. These narratives are condensed from long sets of life history and ethnographic interview data and are written in the first person. While all of the participant narratives were interesting and enlightening, the eight cases were chosen to reflect the diversity of Chicana and Chicano activist educators' experiences. While their personal social his/herstories led them to the figured world of Chicana and Chicano activism, each one had a very distinct and unique his/herstory-in-person. Each participant read their respective narrative and approved of it for the original study. Personal narratives highlight the centrality of experience to identity work.

While these narratives are not generalizable to all Chicana and Chicano activist educators, they are provided to better understand Chicana and Chicano experiences in K–12 schools. The eight narratives selected are diverse and representative of the most common themes found in the study, such as positioning in whitestream schools, recruitment and identification in Chicana and Chicano activist figured worlds, and playing the activist game from within whitestream schools. Narratives are never neutral, so I make no naïve claim to neutrality—these narratives have a purpose. A complete list of all of the participants is provided in appendix 1. A brief introduction to each participant whose narrative was selected is provided in appendix 2.

Undergraduates

Julián. I was born in Mexico in 1981, and I came to this country when I was five. My aunt got me across the border using false papers [documents], but my parents had to pass through *el cerro* (the hills). My dad had already been here for a while and was used to jumping back and forth between Mexico and the United States. We lived in a garage for about three years in a community I would say is about 88 percent Chicano/Latino, 5 percent African American, and the rest white. I hear it used to be a predominantly white community before the 1970s. The first three years we lived in fear of being deported and that the health inspectors would come because of where we lived. Later, we moved and I eventually became a legal resident in 1993.

In Mexico I had already attended *la primaria* [primary school, usually grades 1–6], but I began school in kindergarten here, and I was in ESL [English as a Second Language] programs from then until eighth grade. My first elementary school was about 90 percent Chicano/Latino, but I just went through the mechanics of going to school, not necessarily knowing what I was supposed to do. Then we moved from one side of the city to another. The school I was supposed to attend was overpopulated, so I was bussed one hour each way to a predominantly white and Asian school.

I was pulled out of class to attend ESL classes, and it was demoralizing because at times the teacher would say things like, "Don't you know what a bonnet is? You don't even know what little things are!"—things that didn't exist in my household. It was very demoralizing, but at the same time it built a lot of strength in me because I was really able to see just how bad the situation was. Like how people mistreat you just for being who you are.

There was an Asian teacher there, though, that really had an impact on my learning. She had this game going to see who could read the most, and she really enticed me to reading. I think she really wanted me to read a lot in English, and in the end, she took me to Disneyland. I returned to my community for junior high, and that's when I first heard the term Chicano, but I didn't pay much attention to it. It wasn't until high school that my school had a stronger presence of Chicana and Chicano teachers. I was amazed!

We actually had a MEChA [Movimiento Estudiantil Chicano de Aztlán] in my high school, but it was more the Chicana and Chicano teachers that made a difference. I had some teachers who were really involved in the Chicano Movement, and they'd show us movies and talk to us about what happened and so forth. So I really started understanding and reading a lot more. My first Chicano book was *Always Running, Mi Vida Loca* by Rodríguez. Then I started reading Gary Soto's books and slowly started understanding, but didn't necessarily identify as a Chicano. I would say the Chicana and Chicano teachers were the ones that really encouraged me to go to college because before high school I had never considered the idea of college. I didn't even think it was an option.

What was great about these teachers was that they allowed us to call them by their first names like María instead of Miss Gómez. I especially remember her because she was so simple, and yet she was so forceful in pushing us academically. I used to be very shy and she helped me open up. I don't know exactly what she did; she just spoke Spanish proudly and she really motivated me a lot.

High school was hard, though, because everyone was tracked. We had three tracks, A, B, and C. The B track, the track I was in, was seen as the track for stupid and ESL students, so not much attention was paid to us. When they realized I was college material though, they wanted me to change tracks, but I made it a point to stay in B track and still get into college. I got college applications and looked carefully at what they required. I got involved in all kinds of extracurricular activities. Some white teachers discouraged me because of the track I was in, but instead of making me feel bad, they made me angry against white people and, if anything, motivated me to prove them wrong. It wasn't just white teachers that were discouraging. We had a Latino principal that was just as bad. His name was Mark, and he would get so upset when we called him Marcos.

I remember a person from the Early Academic Outreach Program [EAOP] came to talk to me and explained the whole college application process. Now, looking back, the EAOP is a good program because it targets minorities, but I'm more critical of it because they only target certain students according to GPA and that doesn't necessarily provide equal access, at least to information. After this visit, I created a peer-counseling program at the college center to counsel B-track students. My goal was to counsel students that were seen as not going to college and just get 'em basic information. The college counselor, *una güera* (a white woman) was always telling me, "Well, you don't really need to be telling them, they're not going to go anyway." You know what helped too, in seventh grade we took a field trip to a university, and almost every year, I would always go on field trips to universities, and somehow that created and sustained the belief in my mind that I was going to go to college.

Isadora. My mom was born in Chicago and my dad was born in Mexico. I was born in the Midwest because my parents used to live out there. We lived in Chicago, Texas, and Mexico, before coming to California. We came out here with my mother's brother who is like my second dad. He was working out here as a bilingual teacher, and I basically grew up in Latina and Latino neighborhoods.

I was in a bilingual class in kindergarten and first grade at the local elementary school. Because my father enforced Spanish at home, I didn't really speak English until I went to school. My dad made most of the rules in the house, and he figured with TV, school, and everything else, English would come on its own. I really don't remember anything in first grade. I just remember learning the vowels in Spanish. There was a teacher there who thought I was smart and told my mom about magnet schools because she didn't think I would get very far if I stayed at that school. So I ended up bussed to this very rich magnet school outside of my neighborhood.

I was the only "out" Mexican at that school because I think there were other Mexican kids there, but they didn't say they were. I never really thought I was different until the fourth grade when my mom and I got this big basket with all kinds of toys, drinks, canned goods, and other stuff. No one at my school got it except me—it was called a charity basket. I guess no one else there needed this stuff, but that's when I realized I was poor. The kids there always had things to share, like this one kid whose mom worked on the set for *Beverly Hills 90210*, and he brought in all kinds of autographed things to share. I never had anything to share with anyone.

My mom was always supportive of education. She wanted me to focus on school and didn't allow anything to distract me from it. That's because I was always being compared to all my girl cousins who knew how to do chores, cook, clean, and all that stuff. My dad would like it when I did that stuff, but my mom would tell me I would have the rest of my life to do chores. So there were a lot of things growing up that I wouldn't say were expectations, but more like limitations because I was a girl. For example, the school I attended had many resources, including an orchestra. I wanted to play the trumpet, but my dad said the trumpet was a boy instrument, so I had to play the violin. I hated it.

The school I went to was a good school, and there were raza kids there, but they were in regular tracks. Everyone talked bad about the regular kids, and I know now that it's bad, but I did feel better than them, I felt extra special. I remember teachers would tell me I wasn't like the rest of them because I worked hard and that made me feel good. I know there were kids in ESL classes there too, and I thought they were kind of dumb because they couldn't speak English. In terms of learning anything about my culture or my identity, I don't remember learning anything, except one time when a math teacher showed us the movie *Stand and Deliver*, but we had to get consent forms to watch it. So it felt like it was something bad. I mean I knew I was Mexican because my dad was really strict and my family was so close and protective, but I identified more as Hispanic. I remember my mom, my sister, and I used to make fun of my dad during the Olympics because he was born in Mexico and we were born here.

My uncle would always try to get me on the right track though. He would question me on stuff about being Mexican American. He would also take me places like bookstores, museums, and cultural fairs. He'd always have a book with him, and so we'd go eat, and he would just sit there and read while he ate, so I had to do the same thing. He exposed me to a lot of books, and so I read since I was a little girl. During the summer, instead of letting me run around, I would be his teaching assistant because he taught art classes at a local community center. I did that from first to eighth grade.

I heard the term Chicano for the first time in eighth grade from a white student teacher, and I would get upset because I didn't understand why he just didn't use the term Hispanic. By then I had more Latino students in my classes, but we all agreed we didn't like the word Chicano. More than anything we didn't like those words because they didn't sound like English. Soon after, my mom started taking Chicano studies classes at the local community college, and she told me all about being Chicana. So I began to call myself Chicana, but didn't understand what it meant. Around that time there was a march against Proposition 187, and my dad took us to the protest, and it made sense to me. It's weird because I wasn't anti-immigrant, yet I would make fun of them. It was so popular to use the word *chúntaro*,[4] or call Huntington Park Chuntyville, or Chuntana for Santa Ana, you know.

I kept getting contradicting messages, and my identity wasn't ever really strengthened or celebrated in school 'til the end of my first year in college. Because of the track and school I attended, college was an expectation. It seemed overwhelming at times because since ninth grade it was college, college, college! They had already planned out my next four years, AP this, AP that, community service here, there. They just kept throwing out all this information at us. I got encouragement, but it was not benign because teachers would tell me, "You're gonna succeed, you're gonna make it. You are not like so and so, you're not gonna be like *those* people." My own people! "You're not gonna be like those *cholos* (gang members)," they said. They would tell me I was better than them, and so I felt I was better than them.

I did have a couple of Chicano teachers in high school. My AP government teacher was the first. She started a club called La Raza Student Union, and she was more critical of mainstream things. She was really down-to-earth and seemed like your aunt or something when she talked to you. I still see her sometimes when she brings students to campus on field trips. There was another Chicano teacher who said he thought of me as his daughter, and that was very touching. During high school I had major surgery, and a couple of the Chicano teachers came to visit me at my house! An English teacher bought me Gary Soto books, and I had never read a book written by raza so that was like, wow! I got so much encouragement I applied to top schools because I was so confident, and I got accepted to all of them.

Teachers

Henry. I am a third-generation Chicano. My parents were also born here, and they are bilingual. I grew up in mostly middle-class neighborhoods, and I have two brothers. I am the middle child. I don't speak Spanish because when my older brother was growing up the pediatrician told my parents he wasn't talking because he was getting confused with two languages, so my parents decided on English over Spanish. We all realize now that was a bad decision because English we would have learned anyway.

My neighborhood was pretty racially mixed, but I really didn't associate with other Chicanos/Latinos at school. I used to be really, really critical of my own people. I used derogatory terms like wetbacks toward them. I was bad. I was so caught up in the "if you work hard you can achieve anything" mentality. I'd tell my parents I wanted to be a police officer, buy a Porsche, a nice house, and make all this money. I was caught up in the American Dream essentially.

My parents were always very supportive of education, but neither of my brothers did well in school. School for me was good; I got good grades from kindergarten on, but I never learned anything about myself, my culture. I mean I got the typical stuff, like the Mexican War. It's just typical of this system to make you blind to the reality, so they focused on the Alamo and made it seem like the Americans were so valiant and the Mexicans got what they deserved. My parents weren't down on other Mexicans, but they also didn't try to make us learn more about ourselves. I was just good at picking up things at school though, and my parents encouraged me. This provided me even more of a push to get a good education.

By seventh grade I knew I was going to college because I was recruited by a minority college outreach program. And that's the ironic thing: I was recruited because I was Latino, but I didn't see that. I was so caught up in being American I thought it was just because of my grades. To me being American overshadowed any kind of thoughts about being Mexican. My college admission essay focused on being proud to be an American and how college was yet another step in me living the American Dream.

Juanita. My mother and father are from Mexico, but I was born in the United States. I grew up in this city my whole life, but I didn't attend the public schools because my parents wanted me to have a "good" [represented quotations with her fingers] education. You see, to them a good education wasn't really about what you learn in books, but about being respectful, having morals, and being religious, so they sent my sisters and me to Catholic schools. I am the oldest, the first one to graduate from college, and the first to like school.

I had a very positive experience in school, even though now I realize we had to take a test to get in. So they didn't just take anyone, and we had to pay tuition. I liked school a lot because the teachers always told me I was smart, and we always thought the public school people were like the *chusma* (low class). And you know I think I did get a good academic foundation because I would compare notes with my best friend who went to public school, *una gringa* (a white girl) who was a year older than me, and I could do her homework. So, that made me feel good.

I didn't learn anything about my identity in school because I wasn't very Chicana or Mexicana at all. I knew I was Mexican because we ate tortillas at home, and I'd go to Mexico with my parents and speak Spanish and all, but you go through that phase where you just want to be like the mainstream culture. In this society it's white culture, and we just kind of wanted to dress like them, talk like them, and live like we saw them on TV. I remember one thing I would always say was that I would never, never, never marry a Mexican! I wanted to marry an American [white man]. And it's funny I ended up marrying an undocumented, Spanish-speaking, Mexican guy straight from the rancho.

I didn't want to watch TV in Spanish. I believed I didn't understand what they were saying because they were talking too fast. My parents wanted us to go to Mass in Spanish, and there was a Mass in English for the students, so I would get upset because I wanted to go with my peers. I also thought it was Mexican, or TJ [Tijuanero/a; used as a put-down]; we used to call it "TJ" to go shopping at the swap meet [flea market]. I wanted to get my clothes at Robinsons-May [department store]. I didn't want to watch *novelas* (soap operas in Spanish) and didn't even want to listen to Mexican music. When my dad would play a song loudly while he was driving, I used to get so mad at him because I was embarrassed, so I would scold him and tell him to turn off his *tan tan* music.

My parents were always very supportive of education, especially my dad. At the high school I attended, it was almost like an expectation we were all going to go to college. They had a reputation for having a 90 percent college attendance rate, even if it was to community colleges. My parents actually took me to see the local college campuses because they didn't allow me to go too far away, not even two hours away driving distance. So I applied to local, mostly public, schools and got into all of them, and my parents actually made the decision for the one with the best reputation. It's not funny, but tuition at my university was cheaper than my tuition when I was in high school. I think that's why they chose that school. They chose it for me, I didn't. I actually wanted to get away from them.

Graduate Students

Miguel. I was born in Mexico in 1967, but I was brought to this country when I was two years old. My father was an ironworker and laborer his whole life; my mother was a homemaker. They are both retired now and have since moved back to Mexico. My dad had a fifth-grade education and my mother a third-grade education. There are six children in our family, and I'm the second to the youngest, and all of us went to college, from two-year community colleges to professional degrees. My parents were always very supportive of education.

I grew up in a pretty racially mixed, suburban, working-class neighborhood in Southern California. Growing up, I always had conflicting ideas regarding my identity. I think because of the racism towards Mexicans in the community and my parents' own push for our educational success and assimilation, we were always implicitly trying to escape our identity. But at the same time, my parents were proud of their culture, and that was clearly transmitted to us and was also part of the motivation for our educational success. Growing up, especially in school, we experienced certain things in terms of racism, but it wasn't until later as an adult I realized what I experienced, but I never noticed because from early on I always did well academically, as did all of my brothers and sisters.

To begin with, I don't ever remember my identity being reflected in the curriculum, not to mention most of our textbooks were two decades old on average. The only time I remember I identified myself with the curriculum was in fifth or sixth grade when we studied the California missions. That was one of those few times K–12 I actually remember talking about anything remotely Latino or about Mexicans. I always remember that. But socially a lot of distinctions were made, even amongst Latino students themselves. It seemed like to survive you almost had to shed layers of your identity, especially any association with new immigrants, the kids white and some Latino kids called "wetbacks." In my experience, for example, school was the only place where I was kind of embarrassed about my parents not speaking English and me having to translate all the time because everywhere else in and around my community a lot of people spoke Spanish. So I grew up very conflicted in the reality of my community.

Academically I graduated in the top ten students of my graduating class, even though in retrospect the high school counselors really underserved us the most because of their stereotypes and preconceived notions of Mexican kids. So it was mostly because of minority recruitment programs, which we, the students, invited to our school, and the mentorship of my older brothers and sisters that I attended the University of California. By the time I was a junior in high school, four of my six siblings were already attending colleges or universities. My parents were always supportive of education, *siempre apoyándonos* (always supportive), but they were only peripherally involved in our schooling because of language barriers and because of work demands.

Therese. I was born in California and am a fourth-generation Chicana. All of my siblings did well in school. My sister is currently a teacher and is going back to school to get a master's in education. My brother is completing his PhD, and my little brother is about to finish his BS. My dad has worked for the same grocery store food chain for over twenty-eight years, and my mom works as a payroll clerk. They're hardworking people.

I think I've always identified as a Chicana, but with different levels of awareness, because my father was a Teamster and was very involved with unions and the labor movement, and because when I was born we still had the Chicano Movement. I remember being real young and having this T-shirt that had a person wrapped half in the Mexican flag and half in the American flag. On it we had our family name written in Old English type above it, and below the image it said 100 percent Chicano. So my dad's familiarity with the Chicano Movement once he got back from the service really shaped my identity at an early age. I'd say I was around eight when I realized who I was.

Grapes were like a sin in our house because of César Chávez. I knew all the famous Chicano icons growing up, they were like my heroes: Dolores Huerta, César Chávez, and people we saw on TV like Edward James Olmos. But my dad inspired us because he is a fighter. He is a firm believer in the public schools, and if anything didn't seem right to him, he would challenge principals and teachers, and we were proud of that because we knew our parents were gonna fight for us. So early on I knew I would survive anything because I was part of a fighter lineage.

We knew what it was like to be without, but we also learned about giving back to each other as a family and to the community. See, my dad was a striker, and sometimes he'd go without work for a long time, so we learned to be modest. He'd take us to a local hospital to see people with disabilities whenever we'd complain about not having things, and he'd say: "See how lucky you are. Yeah, you don't have that Barbie, but you're very lucky." That also taught us about giving to the less fortunate, and charity and goodwill were really engrained in us. My dad comes from a very large family; he has twelve siblings, and all of them were very involved with unionizing workers. So when any one of them was on strike, the family was very good about putting their money together and buying groceries and stuff to support one another during those hard times. So giving back wasn't just talked about: it really happened.

I remember I was ten years old when the whole family campaigned to get our first Mexican American mayor elected. We made signs and were really into getting a Mexican in office. So we did a lot of this giving back together as a family, and I learned giving back happened in a lot of different forms. It was like an empowerment type of thing, and I felt lucky. I had a roof over my head, I had good parents, they loved each other and weren't in a miserable marriage. They were actually happy and in love. I knew early on I had something not everyone had and it was a good thing. We were also very spiritually Catholic, but not fanatical. I remember going to church as a family, pretty much every week.

My K–6 schooling experience was pretty white because the majority of kids in my classes were white, and so I felt very isolated. The curriculum was also the typical Benjamin Franklin–type of stuff. I felt pretty isolated all the way through school because I remained in honors courses through high school, and most of the kids in those courses were not Chicano. Earlier in my educational experience, they were white and then Asian, although my community demographically was about 80 percent Mexican. I remember having Chicanita friends, one in particular, but she never thought she was smart enough to get into those classes. And my dad kind of set me up to think I could do anything and I was the "smart one," his little *princesa* (princess). The whole family did well academically too, but my sister was the all-star athlete, and my brother did both. In terms of leadership, though, my dad really encouraged me, and so I ran for office all through school. Our family was kind of known as the smart family.

But, yeah, early on I knew my family was different than my white friends' families and the Mexicanos too. Like whites didn't understand why mom would call my dad to make sure it was okay for me to go to the library with them. I couldn't spend the night anywhere; I couldn't do a lot of things. I mean, they just didn't understand like the cultural respect a woman has for a man and his word. I think they just thought we were weird. That was hard, it was, I mean it wasn't gonna kill me, but it was just different. And of course foods were different: we ate tortillas, they ate bread. In terms of Mexicanos I knew I was a *pocha*.[5] I really suck at speaking Spanish, and you just knew when you were called a pocha and you were it.

At home I would get some negative stuff about Mexicans, especially from my dad that I later tried to call him out on. I think now he really sees the big picture too because I mean he used to be so into unionizing and the companies would use Mexicano labor when they were on strike. So he'd say things like, "Mexicanos are breaking the strike!" and he got kind of bitter toward that community of immigrants just trying to survive. So later when I was in college and we had the anti-immigrant law on the ballot, Proposition 187, I told my dad some racist white people don't know the difference between me and someone who just crossed the border. He'd say: "No, you're different! Don't even say that! You're different!" I would tell him that wasn't true and call him out on all that stuff. So I think now he understands it's the people who have the power, not these poor people who fight for crumbs, that are to blame.

There were some things that really made a difference in terms of my education, and they didn't come from school necessarily. The first was when I was about nine, and my dad went to a community college to get his AA under the G.I. Bill. He was taking these English classes, and he chose me to study with. So I would quiz him on his vocabulary words, and my own vocabulary just grew tremendously. I started winning spelling bees, and I even won an encyclopedia set when I was in junior high. The other was we always ate dinner together and had very involved and complex discussions on issues. Except during those finals sports seasons, we'd talk about things like the labor movements, César Chávez, abortion, the women's liberation movement, faith, and politics. It really got us thinking, and I think that's what made a difference. The whole asking questions of children and making them think for themselves. Forming opinions really helped us early on, and it was around the dinner table. My parents aren't college educated; they're just educated.

Professors

Phillip. My mother is from Mexico and my dad was born here, but his parents are from Mexico. So I guess I'm second-generation Chicano on one side and third on the other. I have two siblings and I'm literally the middle child. I was born and raised in Southern California in a working-class neighborhood that used to be a steel town. When I was growing up, the population was primarily white, like 60 percent, Latino maybe 20 percent, and African American like 20 percent. Now the population has become predominantly Latino.

I was raised Catholic. We all did all of our sacraments and are still pretty active in the church. I grew up speaking mostly English, especially around my nuclear family, but I did speak a combination of both around my extended family, especially my *primos* and *primas* (cousins) and my *abuelitos* (grandparents). We used more Spanish around my dad's side of the family than my mom's. So I felt like I functioned in a lot of different worlds at the same time.

Growing up, my family and I moved from a more working-class community to a more upper-working-class to lower-middle-class community. So I attended an elementary school a lot more diverse than the junior high and high school I attended. I didn't notice many differences being made in terms of race in elementary school as I did later when we moved. Of course, some of the differences were in food: like we ate burritos for lunch and they ate ham sandwiches. I was very active in sports, and I played in a lot of Mexican soccer leagues, but at my new schools, the white kids had never even played soccer. They played the traditional baseball, basketball, and football.

Racism was subtle, like teachers making comments about Mexicanos, and it wasn't so much what they said, but the tone they said it in, which conveyed the message they didn't think too highly of Mexican kids. Most of the teachers were white, and I guess they didn't have high expectations. I remember the campus security guards being the most racist individuals. Once I locked myself out of my brother's car and was trying to get it open with a clothes hanger, and the campus security came at me like I was a criminal, no questions asked. I was like, this is a bunch of bullshit!

I always did well in school, ever since I can remember. I remember my mom trying to recognize and incorporate our Chicano/Mexicano ancestry into school projects, so I never felt ashamed of who I was. She once helped me do a project on the Aztec Empire, and we built all these little pyramids, and I don't recall the teacher being opposed to it. Mom worked as a bilingual teacher's assistant at another school, and she was always doing things to incorporate Mexican culture into schools. She did an assembly for Cinco de Mayo, got a *balet folklórico* (folkloric dance) going, and made the costumes for us and everything. If she wouldn't have done that, they probably wouldn't have done anything to recognize Cinco de Mayo. Other than that, there was nothing in the official curriculum that had anything to do with people of color, nothing at all.

Something that was instrumental in my success was my mom's knowledge of schools. I'm sure that probably affected the way teachers reacted to me, thinking I had an involved mom, that my mom was in the profession, and they should pay attention to me. She also did a good job of exposing me to the less-privileged kids she worked with. So I knew there were differences amongst Mexicans, but we were all Mexicanos. The thing I got from my dad was the love of sports, and I really did love playing sports. I wanted to be the best at anything I did, so I wanted to be the best in school, the best at soccer, the best at football, the best at everything. So college to me came as part of that motivation to be the best.

I always had parental support and was excited because I was going to be the first one in my family to go to college. I mean, my mom had attended community college for a while, but I was actually the first to go away to college. But, during my high school years my parents divorced, and that created a lot of turbulence for us emotionally, socially, and economically. We had to move out of our house and lived with my mom's parents for a while and later moved into a one-bedroom apartment. When I made my decision to go to college, I chose a college out of state to get away.

Anabel. I come from a small mining town in the Southwest that was pretty racially mixed, but also from a line of multiple generations of Mexican Americans. So I was always aware of my identity in a positive way. I remember my great-grandmother, for example, didn't really like to speak English, even though she knew the language, so I used to translate for her. Because the community was well established, I had many Chicano role models, but they were mostly men. My mother's brothers, for example, went to college, but my mother wasn't allowed to because women weren't allowed to go to college. So she really encouraged me to go to college from day one. With my father, it was more of a struggle because there were some real gender differences in my family, but both of them were always very supportive of education. They always took us to the library; they read to us, bought us little desks, books, and encyclopedias.

I remember school as a very happy place because I always did really well. I realize now I was tracked and even then I knew I was always in the high group versus the low groups. The academic program at our school was very good because it was designed for the kids of the elite, the chemists and so forth that also worked the mine. It also made a difference that our teachers and school administrators lived in the community, but there was a lot of racism, especially towards Native Americans because the reservation was close by. But, because I was competitive academically, I was allowed to cross some boundaries, like me and this other guy were allowed to go swimming in the country club pool when Mexicans weren't allowed in. The curriculum was just white, there was no mention of people of color, and you didn't even get to be negative.

My mom was instrumental in me going to college because I think she wanted to live vicariously through me. She was like a working-class snob and had very middle-class values. There were several things that helped me get to college: one was her encouragement; two, I was tracked; and three, school wasn't foreign because a lot of the Chicanos in my community did quite well. I mean there were a lot of teachers that came out of the local area, so early on I decided I wanted to be a teacher. I always had this inclination for service and helping others, and I guess that's partly due to my extraordinarily Catholic upbringing.

Educational Mobility

The participants' K–12 schooling experiences were consistent with Gándara's (1995) study of low-income Chicanos' educational mobility. Gándara's study documented Chicana and Chicano educational mobility when opportunities were opening up for minorities, specifically for war veterans through the G.I. Bill. Gándara's findings suggest the following to be important characteristics for low-income Chicanas' and Chicanos' access to higher education: (1) access to integrated schooling environments, (2) parental support, (3) a hard work ethic and the view of hard work as a mobility strategy, (4) family myths or folklore that created a culture of possibility where mobility was possible, and (5) an intense personal drive and persistence. These characteristics, especially access to the college-bound curriculum and to information and resources through integrated schooling, were important in accessing higher education. My study found similar results.

All participants had parental support for education, although men had more support overall than women. When both parents did not equally support educational attainment, at least one parent, often the mother, was very supportive. Findings specific to women will be discussed later.

All participants had a hard work ethic and often worked alongside their parents. The work they performed included doing farmwork, landscaping, fixing automobiles, and cleaning homes and offices. This work ethic carried through to working while in college. Participants like Therese worked at least three jobs throughout college and continued working part-time and running her own business while finishing her doctorate.

Several participants reported having a family folklore of wealth. Anabel, for example, described her mother as "a working-class snob." David's collective family memory was of being landowners in New Mexico and losing that land in the 1800s after the U.S. invasion. This family history motivated his educational mobility and also his identification with Chicano identity, Reies López Tijerina, and the Chicano land grant movement in New Mexico and southern Colorado in the 1960s and 1970s.

All participants expressed a strong personal drive. Phillip, for example, reported always striving to be "the best." Participants described themselves as persistent and goal oriented. They knew that educational mobility was a real possibility. Once positioned as smart students, educational mobility became an expectation reinforced through unconditional parental support for education.

With the few exceptions reported, participants were positioned as smart early on and were tracked in groups, classes, programs, or schools that got them into college-bound tracks. Positive positioning in school, high expectations for academic achievement, and participants' drive and persistence contributed to a very positive, but often judgmental, academic identity that viewed students in lower tracks as "dumb" or "lazy." High-ability tracking and all of the resources, rank, and prestige that come with it, peers from more privileged backgrounds, educationally mobile older siblings and romantic partners, and minority recruitment programs provided means to resources and information about college and financial aid to the participants.

My study differed with Gándara's (1995) work in that Chicana and Chicano teachers and Chicana and Chicano student recruitment efforts and organizations had a greater impact on K–12 student life for my younger participants. Chicana and Chicano teachers were reported to impact younger participants' lives by advocating for them and their parents in whitestream schools. For students like Julián, Isadora, Mariana, Jaime, and Rodrigo, Chicana and Chicano teachers provided opportunities for ethnic self-recognition and motivation to attend a university.

Jaime, for instance, was personally recruited to the University of California by Mechistas (members of MEChA). Through outreach, Mechistas encouraged him to change his original plan, which was to attend a highly commercialized technical institute. For Mexican American high school students, the impact of Chicana and Chicano student recruitment efforts through university conferences was as a means to access information. Rodrigo recalled attending a workshop on financial aid at a high school student conference hosted by MEChA de UCLA that influenced his decision to attend the University of California. Prior to the workshop, Rodrigo had no idea he could financially afford a university education.

Chicana/Mexicana Mothers' Pedagogies[6]

Mothers were instrumental in their daughters' successful navigation of patriarchy and in their daughters' quest for higher education. Although some fathers were not supportive of their daughters' educational aspirations, mothers were the most helpful to their daughters. Villenas (2001, 2005) highlights Latina mothers' pedagogies centered on moral education and *convivencia* (communalism) as the "resistance that occurs in direct and subtle ways in the intimacy of the home" (2001:22). The Chicanas in this book pointed to their mothers as key figures who helped them navigate the patriarchal structures of both the family and the larger society.

In her family's experience, Elena credited her mother with disrupting gender roles, at least among siblings. Elena recalled: "I think my mom was a little more equal than other moms I've seen, especially Mexican moms. Like my brother cooks and washes his clothing and stuff like that. She didn't have any, 'Oh, you do this and you can't do that' type of thing." Disrupting gender role expectations, or limitations as Isadora referred to them, was a step Elena's mother implemented in her household. This example reflects what Villenas (2001) refers to as resistance in the home. Mothers' resistance to the patriarchal order was conveyed in more subtle ways in other Chicanas' experiences.

Isadora's mother, for example, did not support her husband's push for household-gendered roles because she wanted her daughter to focus exclusively on her schoolwork. Isadora commented:

> My dad would compare me a lot to my other girl cousins. And my dad would be like, "Oh, you're lazy," 'cause I wouldn't do chores. He would say like, "Oh, look at . . . she already knows how to cook, and she already knows how to clean and . . . Oh, that's really good she does that." My family thought that was good except for my mom. My mom just wanted me to focus on school. She just said, "I'll do the chores and you just do your school stuff," 'cause she didn't want anything, anything to distract me from school. . . . I think she thought that . . . if I got married or something, like, "Oh, she'll have the rest of her life to do chores." So she never told me to do anything.

Isadora's father, although not necessarily against her pursuing higher education, imposed gender limitations on her time, which acted as a limit on her studies. Isadora's mother liberated her from these gendered limitations (expectations) by fulfilling those roles herself on Isadora's behalf.

Anabel commented that her mother was subservient and submissive to her father's rule, but that she wanted to live "vicariously" through Anabel's experiences. Like Isadora's mother, Anabel's mother supported her daughter's educational aspirations when her husband did not always agree.

> My mother absolutely from day one said you're going to college. My dad didn't. When I was ready to graduate and applying for schools, my dad would not fill out the financial aid forms 'cause he was too embarrassed for everybody to see how much he made. So he said, "You're not going to college, you're going to beauty school." I said, "Beauty school?!" I mean, I saw myself as a real scholar, you know? And my mother said, "No, I don't care what, she's going to college." And my dad said, "No, we can't afford it!" And I said, "I don't need your money; I just need to have you sign these forms." It was a real struggle with him. I never could talk back to my dad, we weren't allowed to, but that time I told him, "Well, if you didn't want me to go to college, you did everything wrong!" And he asked why. And I said, "Because you were at every parent/teacher conference and you helped me with my homework."

Anabel and her mother joined together to argue against her father's decision that Anabel should attend cosmetology school instead of college. Anabel claimed that her father, who internalized the oppression of patriarchy, was embarrassed about his income because he could not pay for his daughter's schooling. Regardless, Anabel's mother proved to be her strongest ally by verbally joining forces with her daughter and going against her husband's wishes.

Andrea's mother also supported her daughters in a vicarious way: "My mom says she always wanted us to go to college because she never got the opportunity to go. She wanted to pursue something after high school and she never did. And so as early as, I guess, elementary school, I remember my mom talking about, 'I want you all to go to college.' And because I was seen as a smart kid [in school] I always thought it was within my reach."

Andrea's position as a smart student corroborated well with her mother's support and encouragement for higher education. Overall, mothers' support of their daughters' education was a significant finding. Mothers found ways, creatively or directly, to either free their daughters from gender limitations or act as their greatest advocates for higher education.

Memories of Whitestream Schooling

Nearly all participants revealed that the rigidity of the whitestream curriculum that they experienced did not nurture or even discuss Mexican or Chicana and Chicano culture. Participants had either no memories or nearly no memory of learning positive information about Chicano/Latino culture or it being incorporated into the curriculum, except in uncritical ways. Participants remembered social studies and U.S. history curricula as the most hostile or culturally isolating.

Invisibility

While the age differences of the participants were significant, little had changed in their K–12 experiences with regard to whitestream social studies curricula and pedagogy.[7] Participants reported that people of Mexican descent, especially Chicanas and Chicanos, were almost invisible in the curriculum. According to Therese, "the curriculum was very white" and "all Benjamin Franklin–type of stuff." There was only minimal mention of other cultural groups. Elena said, "The curriculum was very traditional and standard. I don't remember ever, not even once, learning about Mexicanos in school [K–12], or blacks, or anything from different cultural aspects."

During one of her interviews, Anabel responded similarly: "Hmm. [Nods a 'no' response] No, 'cause probably to tell you the truth we were invisible. I mean there was no discussion of . . . I mean you didn't even get to be negative. There was no discussion of, except the stereotypical Alamo and stuff like that. It was as white a curriculum as you could get."

María said the community provided the students information about their culture, not the school curriculum. "We knew who we were from the community, more than from school. At school they didn't . . . I mean like Chicano history was like a non-invention at that point in the realities we were experiencing. It just didn't exist in high school. Latino issues, things like that weren't . . . You know, the whole meritocracy is what they were pushing down everybody's throats."

With a more emotional tone and making larger societal connections, Alicia responded:

> No! No, and I say that with an emphatic *No!* Everybody was white, the teachers were all white, the students were all Mexican. The teachers, I can't tell you in elementary school, but starting in junior high is when I started to see . . . high school I could fully see that . . . how . . . There was like no relationship, there was . . . okay, how do I say this? There was nothing culturally relevant whatsoever between our education and the area in which we lived and the fact that we were all Latino. Nothing whatsoever!

> In fact I grew up with, until the time I met my husband . . . I was 21 when I met José. And up to that time, I had it in my head . . . which sounds absolutely ridiculous, but that Mexicans weren't smart enough to be able to do anything. We were stupid. We couldn't get anything in life, and it was almost gonna be like our lot to be the downtrodden. And it, it's not because I wasn't proud, because that's one thing I had, because it was all predominantly Latino, we were brown and proud! I mean we were totally down for la raza. So it's not like I was looking down on our people, it's just you didn't see anything [different], and so then you start to think that's just the way it is. You know it's just the way it is. One of the things that attracted me to José was that I had finally met a Mexican person who actually had a degree. And I was like *what*?! I had never seen that before. And I was 21?! I mean that sounds so ridiculous like I'm lying, but it's the sad truth.

Invisibility had broader consequences for identity production for Alicia because she associated being Mexican with being the downtrodden. White teachers' positioning in the whitestream as being imbued with authority and power implied to Alicia that Mexicans "weren't smart enough" to be in these positions.

Through invisibility, Mexicans, like other people of color, are constructed as a stigmatized people (Payne, 2003). The glorification of whites, the lack of positive portrayals of Mexican-descent people in the popular media, and the extant conditions in Alicia's environment created an internalized negative self-image. Not being "worthy" of mention in the whitestream curriculum had a negative effect for Alicia: "Mexicans weren't smart enough to be able to do anything." Gutman (2004) argues that the absence of people of color in curricula implies that they made no contributions and creates an unequal impression of civic worth and of social entitlements.

Jaime responded in a similar way: "I don't remember anything being mentioned [in school] about Chicano. Maybe, not even, not even like . . . any issues about movements. I don't remember any of that. Mexican? *Nada* (Nothing), nothing man. Nothing I could identify with, like you know, 'Oh, you know, he's like me' or anything like that. Maybe the only thing was like the war of, what was it? . . . the war with Mexico. That was like the only thing. And I was like, what side am I supposed to be on?" Jaime expressed disconnection with either U.S. or Mexican citizenship. Learning about the War of the North American Invasion created conflict in either nationality and forced him to question his citizenship status, both as a Mexican and as an American.

Uncritical Portrayals

For some participants, uncritical portrayals of Mexican culture were the norm, and any kind of historical or critical understanding was nonexistent and, at times, discouraged. Uncritical portrayals refer to the stereotypical, essentialized, and festive approach to learning about people of color in U.S. schools (Banks, 2003). According to Banks (2003:15), this approach is the "contributions approach" focusing generally only on heroes, holidays, and other discrete cultural elements of multiculturalism.

Raquel remembered her experience in a Catholic girls' high school during the 1980s:

> LUIS: So, what did you learn about being Latina, Mexicana, Chicana, prior to going to college?
> RAQUEL: I remember some fucked-up shit Luis. I wish I had different things to tell you. [laughs] I mean I remember like in high school, for example, we were talking about Mexico. . . . It was global studies, my freshman class. And so like the teacher said, you know she's an older nun, she said, "Ok, everybody, you know, put what you know about Mexico on the board." . . . So then we had to pass to the board and write something on there. Y yo escribí del PRI y del PAN [I wrote about the PRI and the PAN—the two major political parties in Mexico]. Yo no más escribí PRI/PAN, no? (I just wrote PRI/PAN, no?) Porque cuando iba a México se veía (Because when I would go to Mexico you could see), you know, *muchas* (a lot) . . . it's like major [written] on the walls and everything. *Este* (And), and she's like ¿qué es eso? (what is that?) And I'm like, well . . . it's like, I just know they're like the two [political] parties you know and that's it. And then she's [the nun/teacher] like, "No! No! No! No!" and she erased it. And everybody just had like *pan dulce* (sweet bread) and tortillas and things like that. I mean it stayed very much at that level. It [Mexican culture] was just like *como un pinche* (like a fucking) ornament, you know? It was . . . uhm . . . strange things and that's it. It wasn't about another way of knowing the world, you know?

Whitestream schools' uncritical portrayal of Mexico focused on the strange and exotic, as well as on the foreign—Mexicans and Mexico are in another country—the subject was rarely approached as a connected U.S.

issue. According to Raquel, to take the conversation in a more meaningful direction such as politics, even in a foreign context, was cause for her being ignored and "corrected."

In predominantly African American and Latina and Latino areas, the essentialized images of Dr. Martin Luther King Jr., César Chávez, and Cinco de Mayo became part of the whitestream curriculum. Essentialization and uncritical incorporation of "Others" (especially pacifists) in the form of token and festive multiculturalism is problematic if left at that level. These uncritical portrayals often played themselves out as conflicts among minority groups in schools. Pitted against each other in competition for minimal representation in the curriculum, minority-minority conflict leaves the foundational basis (white supremacy) of whitestream curricula uncontested. Cary (2001) correctly asserts discourses that are assumed to be transformative, such as multiculturalism, can reinscribe normalizing practices that maintain the status quo.

Jaime, who attended high school in south central Los Angeles where teaching about Black History Month was unknowingly pitted against Cinco de Mayo festivities by the predominantly white teaching staff, mentioned that racial tensions eventually lead to "brawls" between students.

> Just all-out brawls! All-out brawls! People would come out bleeding. A dude was wearing his huaraches (Mexican sandals), and his nail fell off, and his toe was bleeding. The cops came of course. That was going on in a lot of schools [in that area] 'cause I remember my cousin like they had all these race wars and fights as well. They had Edward James Olmos go and talk to them. So, I think it was all over [the area schools]. And it still happens. . . . They're having the same racially motivated wars, like you know, Mexicans versus blacks.

According to Jaime, critical awareness of Black History Month and Cinco de Mayo was not being taught. Both Mexican and black identity were highlighted without a social consciousness of mutual respect, and especially without a critique of white supremacy. Identity, sustained through an "us versus them" "war" mentality between the Latina and Latino and African American students, created physical and psycho-emotional community harm—divide and conquer—while leaving white supremacy intact. The white teachers, according to Jaime, drove away every afternoon to their own neighborhoods on the other side of the city, but were partly responsible for the unrest they left behind. "They [white teachers] kinda played it off as if it didn't happen. It wasn't happening.

They never mentioned it in class, like it was going on . . . A couple of times they didn't let us go out. The cops locked all the gates. So we had to wait forever. It was like a prison, they locked us in, and we couldn't get out, but the teachers still got to go home."

White teachers' general silence and appeals to neutrality[8] failed to enable a larger critique of the social, cultural, historical, and economic context of their students and their community. By ignoring the root causes of historical inequality, these events became a black and brown issue, instead of an issue of white supremacy. Whitestream schooling does not promote the healthy and critical development or awareness of racial and social justice consciousness outside of the whitestream. Students were superficially taught about their ethnic/racial identities, and this discouraged multi-racial and multi-ethnic coalition building, promoted an uncritical understanding of larger power inequalities, and effectively undermined the struggle to end white supremacy.

Negative and Hostile Portrayals

Participants also reported "negative and hostile portrayals" of people of Mexican descent in whitestream schools. Henry said, "I learned typical U.S. stuff, the U.S.-Mexican War, that's always . . . I mean, you hear about that even in grammar school. I remember that. You know, you talk about things like the Alamo, and it's puttin' such a different life on the reality. Like the United States was so valiant and the Mexicans got what was coming to them. It was just . . . I don't remember any real positive stuff, to be honest."

Henry expressed anger at a system of schooling that kept him "blind" to inequality and injustice. "In terms of making me blind to the reality, that's just typical of this educational system as a whole. I mean, most people of color in this country, unless you have like parents that are really informed about the real issues, or you're lucky enough to have a teacher that's gonna wake you up to the reality of the United States, you could just go through the whole K–12 blind! That was me! A lot of that is definitely the educational system." Henry's memories of "typical U.S. stuff" were linked directly to whitestream social studies curricula and pedagogy. Marciano (1997) highlights what Henry called "typical U.S. stuff" as civic illiteracy when students are taught a one-sided perspective focusing on a heroic and teleological U.S. history of wars. Henry claimed such portrayals keep all students, and especially white students, blind to the reality and complexity of social and historical issues (Payne, 2003). History is never one-dimensional or exclusively one-sided (Loewen, 1995). Failure to explore the multiple sides of history and herstory in U.S. schools leads to institutionally sanctioned civic illiteracy.

The underlying message Johnny recalled receiving in whitestream schools was that being Mexican was a bad thing.

> JOHNNY: I would say it [being Mexican] is, or would say it was. Maybe not to other people, I don't know. I guess it just . . . it just was.
> LUIS: And what do you think causes it? You said you went to a school that was 98 percent Mexican heritage.
> JOHNNY: It starts off since elementary [school] . . . where teachers are not allowed to speak Spanish to the kids, and they [teachers] try to tell them [students) not to [speak Spanish], not necessarily to their faces, even though some teachers do. They're [Teachers are] always talking about White America and how beautiful it is and never mention a child's culture. They don't let them speak Spanish, and I guess people [students] begin to feel that's the right thing. With the majority [of teachers] talking about white people . . . the media, they impose on us that being Latino is bad.
> LUIS: So did you learn anything in school that was positive about being Mexican, or being Latino?
> JOHNNY: No! [laughs] In high school . . . no, I don't think so.
> LUIS: What did you learn about being Mexican?
> JOHNNY: Nothing! [laughs] I just learned that Mexican was bad.

Johnny learned that "being Mexican was bad" both in school and society through invisibility. As Johnny recalled, teachers "never mentioned a child's culture," with "the majority talking about white people." His mention of "White America" indicates, in his reality, the existence of a central white "American" context, or what Rosaldo (2003) calls national citizenship, that disconnected Johnny and others in marginal cultural positions from full membership. His sarcastic reference to "how beautiful it is," he later mentioned, related to his memories of "America the Beautiful," a patriotic song used by his teachers to teach him and his classmates English.

Andrea, a *Tejana*, was also told directly by her eighth-grade teacher that being Chicana and Chicano was bad. Her teacher equated the word Chicana and Chicano to gang members and to trickery. Andrea said:

> I remember when I first learned the word Chicano or Chicana; it was in eighth grade when I asked a white teacher what the word meant. She told me it was like thugs, they were like *cholos* or *cholas* (gang members). That was the first time I remember someone even talking about that. Then I remember another white teacher saying something negative about Chicanos. Saying it had to do, or it had its origin in the word *chicanery*. . . . It means trickery, which is what people thought of Mexicanos, that they're like sly or not truthful.

By associating Chicanas and Chicanos with "trickery," Andrea's teacher created a negative and hostile portrayal. Negative portrayals of Mexican people historically justified U.S. troops' invasion of Mexico and the subsequent and continuous dehumanization of Mexican labor in the United States.

Chicanas and Chicanos also formed an important part of the civil rights movements (Rosales, 1997). The civil rights movements in general are often disremembered (Payne, 2003) by whitestream history and social studies curricula, but Chicanas and Chicanos', Asians', and Native Americans' contributions, in particular, are often not mentioned. Chicanas and Chicanos' struggle for bilingual and social justice education, along with promoting a unique identity of self-determination, are important, often forgotten, contributions.

Samuel, who is darker skinned and more indigenous looking, highlighted the exclusion of positive images of Mexican indigenous-descent people. Samuel internalized messages of Mexicans as "the bad dudes" by personal (physical) dislike of his body and his culture.

> SAMUEL: I don't remember ever learning anything about ancient indigenous civilizations of what we now call the Americas. . . . I don't remember anything about that. And when you were represented, we were misrepresented.
>
> LUIS: How?
>
> SAMUEL: The El Paso experience, when I used to live in El Paso, Texas, that's really where I guess I have the most vivid memories of that. *Porque* (because) . . . *ahí en* (there in) Texas you know *está cabrón* (it's hard) and shit. Fuckin' . . . the history they teach you, man, it's fucked up, you know. It's the whole Texas pantheon of heroes, Moses Austin, Davy Crockett. . . . The kind of shit you go through every year. So, every time you see or talk about Mexicans it would be like the bad dudes, you know?

Samuel mentioned how social studies (history) curricula in Texas, through heroification, glorify a colonialist/nationalist set of white men as heroes (Loewen, 1995), reifying the stigma that Mexicans were/are "the bad dudes." To Samuel, negative portrayals were not exclusive to "Mexicans," but also to indigenous people.

LUIS: How did you feel when lessons like that were presented?

SAMUEL: I guess to some point you internalize it, or else you wouldn't hate the way you look, or the kind of food your family eats, and the way your relatives speak English. The fact they speak Spanish. But, there's always something . . . there's always a contradictory feeling as well. Your body tells you something even though you're not able to put it into words or counter the argument. Your body tells you when they're saying those things about you that it's not true because you get a feeling in the pit of your stomach that someone's lying to you.

LUIS: What are some of those feelings you say you internalized that you didn't like about yourself, about your culture?

SAMUEL: You begin to believe you're ugly, which is like being in the worst kind of prison because there's no way out. You're trapped by your body. There's no way out of it. You come home, and you're ashamed of the things your family does, your traditions, your culture, your language. There was a point there, probably during those El Paso middle school years, where I didn't want my parents going to school for those reasons. You know, because they didn't look white, and they didn't act white. And to my white teachers they would appear less-than, so I didn't want them to. 'Cause I guess to some point too you want to be accepted by those white teachers. You want them to praise you, and you want their acceptance.

LUIS: What did you do to compensate for that?

SAMUEL: I cried a lot, that's about it. . . . You know a lot of looking in the mirror and hoping I could peel my skin off and something new would emerge. Those kinds of things. That's what I really internalized the most and a big part of the struggle in my life. You know, you've got self-hate.

Fanon (1967) wrote that colonization worked best when the colonized internalized an inferior status. Colonized people who internalized an inferior status through internalized oppression would most likely cooperate with the oppressor whom they had accepted as superior to them. Samuel described his internalized oppression, even with his underlying doubt that the whitestream curricula and pedagogy were lying to him; he still came to rationalize (internalize) his self-hate. Samuel's internalized oppression not only projected a dislike for his physical attributes but also his family's and community's cultural attributes. Distance between Samuel and his family illustrates the disconnection between U.S. whitestream national citizenship and Samuel's family's Mexican cultural citizenship.

> Luis: How did it [self-hate] become more internalized [in middle school]?
>
> Samuel: I believed I was ugly. People think that doesn't affect a young male. It's not really acceptable for a male to come out and say that affects me. The fact I think I'm ugly hurts my feelings, and it does other things too. It tears me apart inside, but it does, but it does.

Samuel's case shows how sometimes full membership can be inaccessible, and negative curricular portrayals of Mexican people can become painful physical and cultural self-perceptions. The disconnections that result are between students like Samuel and their families, as well as between students of color and full American-connected citizenship. The implications of such disconnections in students are detrimental to both national and cultural citizenship.

Disconnections with American Citizenship

Schooling practices and curricula focused on whitestream culture as the standard for all students implicitly conveyed the message that Mexican Americans were less or not important (Gutman, 2004). For most participants, this compulsory indoctrination into whitestream society translated into mixed and contradictory feelings about their Mexican homes and their family's cultural citizenship. Whitestream curricula, pedagogy, and society conveyed the message that "being Mexican was bad" and full American citizenship was reserved as a white male privilege (Cary, 2001).

Lack of a critical recognition of Mexican American people in whitestream curricula created dissonance with American citizenship (Urrieta, 2004b). As Samuel aptly suggested, "Your body tells you when they're saying those things about you [even in the effort to convince you that you are somewhat American] that it's not true because you get a feeling in the pit of your stomach that someone's lying to you." The repeated memory of learning about the stereotypical Alamo and the Texas pantheon of heroes in schools pits people of Mexican descent against themselves. For people of Mexican descent, and other people of color, to fully accept "American" as an identity implies a denial and rejection (to varying degrees) of a racial/ethnic identity (Ladson-Billings, 2004).

People of color are portrayed as less valuable in society than white people by making them invisible, by portraying them in uncritical ways, or even by going as far as portraying them in negative and hostile ways (in equating Chicana and Chicano with chicanery, for example). Continuous attempts to uncritically and passively assimilate people by erasing them from history and displacing them from their social context are illustrative of Skutnabb-Kangas's (2000) argument that assimilation follows a logic of glorification, stigmatization, and rationalization.[9] Glorification was the active promotion of the colonizer's culture as superior. Subaltern culture was stigmatized as backward, language as gibberish, religion as evil, and institutions and traditions as unproductive. Assimilation and acculturation have traditionally been justified as the "greater good" of both immigrants and U.S. society (Houser and Kuzmic, 2001); therefore, assimilation has been part of U.S. educational policy with the excuse of creating a responsible citizenry.

Whitestream curricula and pedagogy function to sustain white supremacy through self-aggrandizement. Alicia's statement that she internalized the ideas that Mexicans were "not smart enough," "stupid," and had the "lot of being the downtrodden" comes to mind. White culture and history were normalized in participants' experiences, even when uncritical attempts were made by some white teachers to minimally include Mexican cultures, as was Raquel's experience in her high school global studies class. White culture and history as the norm in whitestream schools effectively denied full "American" citizenship to the participants (Cary, 2001), especially by constant references to Mexicans as enemies and foreigners, as was the case with several participants.

By erasing, or re-telling the colonialist history of Manifest Destiny as something just and teleological, U.S. society rationalizes its past and present dehumanizing attitudes toward people of Mexican descent, thus stigmatizing "being Mexican as bad." Samuel tells of the worst kind of stigmatization in internalizing and rationalizing cultural and physical self-hate. His eloquent words recall his metaphorical comparison to a prison, and not just any prison but the worst kind of prison: his body, a body constructed as ugly that he could not escape from, and skin he could not peel off.

Implications of Positioning

Mexican American students positioned as smart students by whitestream teachers are a small and elite group. This is alarming, given that the total Hispanic population in the state of California was 36.17 percent in 2007, with Mexican residents and U.S. citizens of Mexican descent accounting for over 25 percent.[10] In 2005–2006, Latina and Latino student enrollments (K–12) in California schools accounted for 47.6 percent, with non-Hispanic whites at 30.3 percent (California Department of Education 2006). Latinas and Latinos, however, accounted for over 50 percent of the K–12 dropouts in 2000–2001 and only 32.48 percent of the high school graduates.[11] The participants in this book, enrolled in honors, gifted and talented, and advanced placement courses in K–12 schooling, unquestionably form part of an elite and select group.

A significant implication raised in the study is that being positioned as smart students and being allowed into smart spaces did not guarantee full, connected citizenship for the participants. Assimilation was, by some, internalized in oppressive and painful ways. The participants agreed, in hindsight, that they were positioned as smart students at the expense, to varying degrees, of their ethnic/cultural identity. When family and community provided ethnic/cultural nourishment (K. González, 2002), whitestream schooling clashed with Mexican American culture, and contradictions over whether Mexican cultural identity was a positive or negative identity emerged. Native elite in colonial contexts, like the participants in this study, also experienced the denial of full membership rights and internalized oppression, but often benefited economically, through rank and prestige, from such positioning (Fanon, 1967).[12]

I do not argue that Mexican American students should not be recruited into smart space and be positioned as smart students like the participants in this book. There should be population parity in such separation to avoid cultural and ethnic peer isolation, and there is a need for a critical, anti-racist revision of whitestream curricula and pedagogy, especially in social studies.

The first implication, population parity, moves beyond the expectation that all students be positioned as smart in schools, although all should be. Population parity argues that all designated categories of students in school reflect a parallel percentage with the population. If 10 percent of the students in a given school will be positioned as gifted and talented, and the school population has a 50 percent Latina and Latino student population, then 50 percent of those coveted spaces should be reserved for Latina and Latino students. Unfortunately, not all parents have the same power, rank, and prestige in the figured world of schooling, and not all students are viewed in the same way, and these gifted and talented slots are usually taken by the people with the most access to power, rank, and prestige. For people with privilege, equality generally sounds great, until they are asked to give something up to make things equitable, like their child's slot for AP Calculus. Demanding population parity in all school programs, although not perfect, is a step toward equality and greater access to underprivileged students.

The second implication asks that critical anti-racist curricula be implemented K–12 and be taken seriously by administrators, teachers, and parents. I am not referring to festive and superficial inclusion such as "taco day" on Cinco de Mayo, but to meaningful and hopeful inclusion that examines the United States' troubling historical experience with race and other "isms" and our current unsolved problems with them. Historical minorities should be included in such curricula. I am referring specifically to African Americans, Native Americans, Asian Americans, and Latinas and Latinos, especially Mexicans and Puerto Ricans.

We are not foreigners or newcomers to Mexican America. For Mexican American students in the Southwest, meaningful engagement would include a multi-perspective analysis of their group's historical contributions, such as cheap labor, to U.S. society. Meaningful engagement would also not shy away from the problematic annexation of Mexican land into U.S. territory, as well as current critical issues faced by the community such as the high dropout (pushout) rate, immigration, language, and identity issues.

The following chapter addresses conceptual and procedural identity production, especially participants' experiences in *becoming* Chicana and Chicano activist educators. All participants in the study eventually enrolled in colleges and universities. There, participants encountered cultural spaces, Chicana and Chicano figured worlds, where their identities shifted.

4
How Some Mexican Americans Become Chicana and Chicano Activist Educators

> The name Chicana is not a name that women (or men) are born to or with, as is often the case with "Mexican," but rather it is consciously and critically assumed and serves as point of redeparture for dismantling historical conjunctures of crisis, confusion, political and ideological conflict and contradictions.
> —Alarcón, 1990:250

Alarcón points out that Chicana and Chicano are not identities that people are born with, but ones that they come to consciously assume.[1] Assuming the Chicana and Chicano identity implies taking on a strong political orientation and a commitment to struggle against white supremacy, to work toward individual and collective self-determination. Service to the community (Delgado Bernal, 2001) is valued above personal and economic gain. To become individualistic and work for self-gain is generally thought of as selling out (Urrieta, 2005a). Not all Latinas and Latinos are willing to undertake Chicana and Chicano community-oriented responsibilities. Becoming Chicana and Chicano involves an identity shift important to understand, especially as it relates to the reasons why many Chicana and Chicano activists decide to become urban educators. Chicana and Chicano activist conceptual and procedural identity production is the figuration by which people's identities shift over time. In this study, Mexican Americans shifted to Chicana and Chicano activists with a desire to raise consciousness (teach for social justice).

The twenty-four participants in the study came to produce Chicana and Chicano activist identities and later decided to become educators to raise consciousness and "give back to the [their] community." Participants' complex process of identity production and the shift to Chicana and Chicano activist identity through participation in local micro Chicana and Chicano activist figured worlds will be highlighted.

Identity

Identity is defined from a cultural production perspective as people's ever-changing perception of who they are as opposed to a psychological or strictly racial perspective on identity development.[2] Identity is a dynamic co-constructed cultural phenomenon. Holland and colleagues (1998) broadly define identity as "self-understandings, especially those with strong emotional resonance" (4). Whether as individuals or as collectives, people make sense of who they are personally and politically, and they convey these meanings to others (Calhoun, 1994). Even when more durable identities are formed, how durable identities are understood and how their meanings change over time become lifelong processes.

Identity is therefore relational. Sarup (1996:47) states: "Identity is always related to what one is not—the Other. . . . Identity is only conceivable in and through difference. . . . That one is not what the Other is, is critical in defining who one is." Similarly, Holland and colleagues (1998) incorporate Bakhtin's concept of "dialogism," or the capacity for people to have internal, often contradictory, dialogues that allow for self-making. Self-making is part of the internal dialogue by which people make sense of who they are. "People tell others who they are, but even more important, they tell themselves and then they try to act as though they are who they say they are" (Holland et al., 1998:3).

By engaging in self-making, individuals construct conceptually a sense of who they are as individuals and in collectivity. The understanding of identity used in this book is one of becoming, not of being. To avoid essentialisms, Holland and colleagues (1998) state identity is in constant flux. As such, identity is always a site for self-making, embedded in a collective past and produced in practice through life experiences. Importantly, identity production is also mediated by cultural artifacts and discourses that are also capable of improvisation, embodying internal tensions and contradictions. Like the U.S.-Mexico border in borderlands theories, all identities are both real and artificial, both socially constructed and internalized into a physical and material "reality" (Anzaldúa, 1987; Alvarez, 1995; Elenes, 1997).

People produce identities through participation in cultural activities that allow them to engage conceptual and procedural identity production (Holland et al., 1998). The conceptual process is the cognitive understanding, or mental self-making process, of identity production. This process involves individuals' dialogic mental sense-making of who they are and who/how they want to be. The procedural process is the physical engagement or practice of a new identity, the physical "performance" of a new self (Alexander, Anderson, and Gallegos, 2005). Figured worlds, by focusing on activity and improvisation while expanding the fluidity of culture, are a good conduit for exploring Chicana and Chicano activist identity production.

Figured Worlds and Identity

Figured worlds highlight the importance of activity and improvisation, rather than essentialize culture by looking for behavioral patterns (Rosaldo, 1989). While cultural organization and reproduction remain important, figured worlds highlight cultural production and heuristic development as key to identity analysis. In figured worlds, the attention is on the "figures," on people and how they *participate* in these worlds on a daily basis, rather than on the material culture, and patterns of behavior and cognitive sense-making of people across time and space in bound systems. In figured worlds, people (sometimes) better organize their subjectivities around particular issues and emerge with shifts in identity production.

Figured worlds are formed through social interaction, and in them, people "figure out" who they are in relation to those around them. The significance of figured worlds is in how they are recreated by people's social engagement with each other in localized and temporal spaces that give voice to particular landscapes and experiences. Through participation in figured worlds, people can reconceptualize who they are, or shift who they understand themselves to be, as individuals or as members of collectives. Through this figuring, individuals also come to understand their ability to craft their future participation, or agency, in and across figured worlds.

Identity is an important concept to consider in understanding how figured worlds function in relation to the various ways people are positioned in society, such as by gender, class, race, or as a smart student. Chicana and Chicano identity is viewed as a process of *becoming*, not as a fixed state of being, because it encompasses different gender, class, race, sexual orientation, age, and linguistic positions. Identity, mediated by cultural artifacts and discourses, is thus a site for self-making. From this perspective, improvisation, where a person strategically uses the cultural resources at hand to devise a new action or response to a specific situation, is an important part of identity production processes. Improvisation can lead to the creation of an altered sense of self (Holland et al., 1998), or to a new way of "figuring" who one is.

In figured worlds, people are ordered and ranked, and power is distributed. For example, all of the members of the honors track at a local high school are positioned as smart. But, not everyone within this figured world has an equal claim at being considered smart, because some members consider themselves, and are considered by teachers, parents, and peers, to be smarter than others.

The process of sense-making in figured worlds is always embedded in a collective past, or *history-in-system*, because figured worlds are historical phenomenon. But sense-making is also created in practice through life experiences, what Holland and Lave (2001) describe as *history-in-person*. History-in-system, or history for short, refers to the actual and structural sequence of events that occurred, whether that history is the official history, a revisionist perspective of history, or the collective memory of events. History-in-person (H-I-P) refers to each person's individual subjective experience, or personal social history (Holland and Lave, 2001). H-I-P accounts are narratives told by people about their lives and past experiences. Each one of us has a H-I-P. This chapter explains how the twenty-four Mexican American participants in this study *became* Chicana and Chicano activists by participating in the figured worlds of Chicana and Chicano activism. Eventually, their Mexican American identities shifted as they re/made themselves as Chicana and Chicano activists and later as Chicana and Chicano activist educators.

Macro and Micro Figured Worlds

I propose thinking of figured worlds in different magnitudes, macro and micro figured worlds. Macro figured worlds are those larger conceptions spanning across time and space, often functioning more like abstract constructions than specific local practices. According to Holland and colleagues (1998), figured worlds are dependent on social interaction and activity.

Macro figured worlds remain dependent on social interaction across imagined community space (Anderson, 1983). An example of a macro figured world is the imagined community of the middle class, which is more of an abstract construction of people going beyond a certain location in time and space. People tend to attribute characteristics to the middle class that may or may not manifest in the same way in local practice, but people nevertheless generalize to this imagined community (Anderson, 1983).

Micro figured worlds are local, temporal, and specific manifestations of the larger macro figured world. For example, in a gated middle-income neighborhood outside of Denver, Colorado, specific middle-class cultural practices may be taught to young children in relation to where they live and the people who live around them. Such a hypothetical neighborhood may be a site for micro middle-class culture and identity—a local middle-class micro figured world. Access to micro, local figured worlds allows for entry into larger macro figured worlds through the acquisition of social, cultural, and economic capital necessary for successful functioning in those worlds. For people not born into the middle-class macro figured world, for example, recruitment into the micro figured world of "smart students" can eventually lead to access to the larger middle-class macro figured world (Urrieta, 2007b).

The Macro Figured World of Chicana and Chicano Activism

Through collective identities, social actors recognize themselves and are recognized by others as part of broader social groupings (Della Porta and Diani, 2006). All identities have sets of ideas attached, explicitly or implicitly stated, constituting what that identity is about. These coordinated and collective bodies of ideas or concepts function as each identity's ideological view about the world, especially when identities are reactionary and formed in response to perceived historical aggressions (Castells, 2006). Chicana and Chicano identity shares some of these qualities.

There is a general lore about being Chicana and Chicano that forms the basis for the Chicana and Chicano macro figured world. Broadly, the Chicana and Chicano figured world is premised on a revisionist perspective of history, an asset of heroes, artifacts, and decolonization and social justice discourse. The Chicana and Chicano identity is said to be one of self-determination, or decolonization, and of a struggle in unity with a community and against Anglo-U.S. racism for social justice (Muñoz, 1989; Chávez, 2002).

Discourses become identity artifacts at a macro level and manifest locally as the "language" of these identities' micro figured worlds. The local languages of Chicana and Chicano figured worlds are derived from the larger macro discourse of the Chicana and Chicano Movement that "officially" embraced the Chicana and Chicano identity in the 1960s (Chávez, 2002; Oropeza, 2005). Although these discourses have changed since the 1960s, varying by space and time (context), and in some cases becoming more pre/scripted (restrictive) and in others more open to dialogue and transition, the decolonial (Pérez, 1999) macro-perspective of the discourse remains consistent. *La lucha*, or the struggle for equality in U.S. society, fuses the resistance behind the labels Chicana and Chicano, a continuity in resistance, which is sometimes traced back to past indigenous peoples' struggles (Forbes, 1973), with a highly political, some would argue even militant, ethos that dissuades many from ever becoming Chicana and Chicano activists (I. García, 1998). In California, where the study was conducted, this identity has been more salient and durable than in other contexts in the Southwest where terms like *Manita* and *Manito*, *Hispana* and *Hispano*, *Spanish* (New Mexico/Colorado), Mexican American, or *Tejana* and Tejano (Texas) are more prevalent.

The main principles of Chicana and Chicano activism identified by the participants referred to joining *la causa* (the cause) in an attempt to empower themselves and their communities. Empowerment often meant the recognition and appreciation of Mexican and Chicana and Chicano culture and its strong indigenous roots. This empowerment arises through self-validation and epistemological self-recognition; it also rises in a struggle by means of activism on behalf of *raza* (Oropeza, 2005).[3] In an abstract sense, these principles comprise the Chicana and Chicano activist macro figured world. Cultural artifacts important to Chicana and Chicano activism include the Mexican flag, the Virgin of Guadalupe, the United Farm Workers flag, and the colors red and black, as well as other cultural symbols of Mexican/Southwestern origin, while Emiliano Zapata, Che Guevara, and César Chávez have become the most prominent heroes of this larger cultural context (Rosales, 1997).

The Micro Figured Worlds of Chicana and Chicano Activism

Most of the participants in the study were formally exposed to local Chicana and Chicano activist figured worlds in colleges and universities. Local micro figured worlds were historical phenomena that participants reported entering or being recruited into and depended on social organization and participation for continuity, but were part of specific local contexts. In these figured worlds, participants' thoughts, feelings, wills, and motivation (Holland et al., 1998) were formed as individuals produced Chicana and Chicano activist identities.

Participants reported shifting to a new sense of self through activity in local micro Chicana and Chicano activist figured worlds. Local figured worlds were the sites of Chicana and Chicano activist identity production. These worlds provided participants with identifiable cultural, political, social, and historical landscapes, access to a more enduring identity, and other persons similar to them whom they could relate to in the midst of the alienating whitestream university environments they found themselves in. Participants "figured" out who they were as actors in relation to landscapes of people and action in Chicana and Chicano activist local figured worlds. Participants produced, or began to produce, identities as Chicana and Chicano activists by participating in the activities organized in Chicana and Chicano activist micro figured worlds.

Participants reported that their involvement in ethnic student organizations, courses taken, work-related training in ethnic or multicultural organizations, peer groups, and orientation programs for low-income and minority students in college and university local environments made an impact in their Chicana and Chicano activist identity production. The ethnic student organization overwhelmingly reported as influential in participants' Chicana and Chicano activist self-making was MEChA (Movimiento Estudiantil Chicano de Aztlán), which traces its creation to the Chicana and Chicano Cultural Nationalism of the 1960s (Muñoz, 1989). Other influential student organizations included Chicana and Chicano Teatro (theater), Danza (Aztec dance), and Balet Folklórico (folkloric dance).

Participants reported that specific courses were important for Chicana and Chicano activist identity production and included offerings in ethnic or Chicana and Chicano studies, history, sociology, anthropology, and Spanish. Classes important for Chicana and Chicano activist self-making usually exposed students to epistemological diversity.[4] Critical perspectives and analysis, multiculturalism, revisionist perspectives in history, and Spanish for Spanish speakers were reported as life-changing experiences. Topics that made an impact on participants in these courses dealt with the historical presence of Chicanas and Chicanos, Latinas and Latinos in the United States, and the history of Latin America, as well as current issues in the Chicana and Chicano, Latina and Latino community. Participants remembered studying Malcolm X, Paulo Freire, and Gloria Anzaldúa in these courses. Other scholars mentioned included Beatriz Pesquera, Denise Segura, Antonia Darder, Luis Valdez, Luis Rodríguez, Guillermo Gómez-Peña, Gary Soto, Carlos Muñoz, and Mario Barrera.

Work-related training in ethnic and multicultural organizations on campus was also mentioned as important for Chicana and Chicano activist self-making in local contexts. Work-related training included learning about diversity issues such as race, class (issues), gender, and sexual orientation, or working with diverse populations. Participants reported that work-related training usually involved learning how to conduct research on topics related to the Latina and Latino community. The development of organizational and cooperative leadership skills for peer-counseling positions and the directorship of a mentorship program was also mentioned as important for self-making. In these positions, participants moved from a more passive type of Latina and Latino self-making to a more active role of Chicana and Chicano activist identity production because of the greater visibility they enjoyed on campus and the programs that they represented. As more prominent positions were assumed, participants became more active in constructing their identities for themselves and for others.

Fellow Chicana and Chicano students' peer groups were also reported as important for self-making. Older undergraduates, and to a lesser degree graduate students, assumed the role of mentors to younger undergraduates because they had a more complex understanding of the worldview and practices of Chicana and Chicano activism. Having this more sophisticated understanding, they often engaged younger students in important conversations about being Chicana and Chicano activists. More advanced students functioned as *significant narrators* (Sfard and Prusak, 2005) of the local Chicana and Chicano figured worlds they participated in.[5]

Peers were also significant in sharing their life experiences, especially *testimonios* (Beverly, 2000), about their past experiences with racism and discrimination. By listening to peers' testimonies about how they experienced racism, several participants reanalyzed their past experiences through a racialized lens and also learned to tell their own personal testimonies about experiences with racism. As in Cain's work with members of Alcoholics Anonymous (Holland et al., 1998), this narrative was significant since people who might not have thought about themselves as members of an oppressed racialized group used these narratives to reanalyze their H-I-P through a racialized lens.

Peer groups also helped socialize some participants to the politics of the Chicana and Chicano worldview. Because some of the participants had been socialized in conservative K–12 whitestream schooling and family environments, exposure to classes, student organizations, and professors with more progressive (radical) views of history and current issues challenged participants' prior understandings of the world. This new exposure to ideas and revisionist history often left some participants shaken up, angry at the injustices they now could see, or confused with the struggle to self-make in the midst of new perspectives and narratives. Isadora, for example, recalled: "I was angry because I was made to believe [from the dominant perspective] I was better than all my people [for doing well in school]. I realize I had kind of been taught to make fun of my own self by making fun of my own people [putting down Mexicans and other Latinas and Latinos]. Now, I also understand Chicana and Chicano is not exclusive to Mexican Americans; it's more than that. It's about constantly struggling to be more aware [about issues], a process of self-education and learning from other people, other raza."

Isadora experienced, like most of the participants, a conceptual re/figuring of who she thought herself to be, while also exploring a new understanding of her relationship to others in this figured world.[6] Isadora understood herself to be "Chicana," not necessarily as a noun to describe herself, but as a *verb*. Chicana to Isadora meant a "constant struggle," a "process," and "learning." Often, more advanced peers, already more comfortable with this new knowledge, helped novice participants deal with the challenge of re/figuring or authoring themselves in these new paradigms.

Other significant local micro figured worlds for Chicana and Chicano activist identity production were student orientation programs for low-income and minority students. Especially significant were those programs experienced during the summer prior to entering the university as first-year students. In these programs, new students usually lived in the dormitories, had peer counselors, attended special topics forums, and took courses on topics that exposed them to more progressive perspectives. Due to this intensive (usually about three- to six-week) exposure, many participants reported this experience as the beginning of their Chicana and Chicano activist identity production.

Identity Production

Identities are produced in the process of participating in the activities organized in figured worlds (Holland et al., 1998). In Chicana and Chicano activist micro figured worlds, participants' subjectivities became better organized around certain issues and causes, which allowed them the opportunity to figure out a new sense of self. In this process of identity production in figured worlds, subjectivities became better organized when

participants had the opportunity to corroborate their own H-I-P with a new perspective of history or herstory within the social life and activities of the local micro figured worlds that they were participants in. Identity production is composed of two processes: conceptual identity production and procedural identity production (Holland et al., 1998).

Holland and colleagues (1998) offer that shifts in identity are conceptually a new figuration of the world that involves a change in how people view and act in the world. Usually, people reinterpret their own pasts when identity shifts occur and develop new understandings of themselves and their lives with a stronger emotional investment in their new world. As new external objects, symbols, and ideas become internalized, people begin to express these internalizations as identities conceptually and in practice (Voloshinov, 1929; Leont'ev, 1978).

Procedurally, people increase their participation in the activities that validate the cultural forms particular to their new view of the world. Through individual and group activities, people in identity production accept and use the forms of the figured world as devices for mediating not only their conception of themselves but also their new view of the world. For example, many participants reported embracing Mexican/Chicana and Chicano cultural artifacts to demonstrate to themselves and to mediate to others their new identity production. Such artifacts included displaying the Mexican flag in their offices, classrooms, cars, or homes.[7] Changing their clothing style was important for others, such as using articles of indigenous clothing like colorful embroidered blouses, rebozos (shawls), huaraches (sandals), or intricate, long earrings. Other cultural artifacts included using the language of the barrio (neighborhood—urban), pronouncing and insisting that others pronounce their names *en español*, and playing (loudly) Mexican folk and popular urban music.

History-in-Person and Conceptual Identity Production

People conceptually organize or reorganize their subjectivities around certain ideas or issues in the process of producing identities in figured worlds (Holland et al., 1998). Shifts in identity affect how people conceptually view and act in the world because of a reorganization in subjectivity. Conceptual shift, in part, relates to how people develop new understandings of themselves and their lives, including how they reinterpret their own pasts. People develop significant emotional investments in this new world and their new landscapes of perception. Shifts in conceptual

identity production, however, are not uniform because people enter identity production experiences with different life (histories/herstories) or history-in-person and conceptual understandings. Therefore, people were drawn into local Chicana and Chicano activist figured worlds for different reasons that resonated with who they were (at that time) and their past experiences.

H-I-P is important in Chicana and Chicano activist conceptual identity production because people with certain life experiences tend to be drawn into, or are easier to recruit into, the figured worlds of Chicana and Chicano activism. The use of life history interviews revealed that H-I-P was significant in participants entering the micro figured worlds of Chicana and Chicano activism. The following four participant-reported life history experiences were noteworthy for all participants in Chicana and Chicano activist identity production: (1) the influence of religion, (2) the importance of family relations, (3) the importance of time and space (context), and most important, (4) past experiences with oppression.

The majority of the participants in the study talked about having a strong religious upbringing prior to attending the university. From these religious experiences, participants conceptually learned to have a strong commitment to serve others. Volunteerism and charity were emphasized in their family lives, as well as a strong sense of empathy for the less fortunate. In some religious institutions, participants also learned, at least in rhetoric, to demand justice for those wronged. Most participants were raised Roman Catholic, but two participants raised as Pentacostal Christians also expressed similar religious orientations for service. Approximately half of the participants shared that they remained, at least peripherally, involved in religious organizations, but even those who did not, highlighted religion as a significant part of their early-life conceptual formations that led to their activist orientation.

Family relations were also highlighted as important life experiences for participants' activist orientations. Participants often expressed growing up with strong family commitments and responsibilities, like chores, babysitting, cooking, translating for parents and other family members, and contributing to the family's income either with labor or with money from an early age. Some of the labor included doing farmwork, cleaning other people's homes or offices, fixing cars, landscaping, or other types of work they performed alongside their parents. Several of the Chicana participants also reported having to provide childcare for their mothers and relatives as well as doing household work in their mother's absence.

Experiences with strong family commitments helped create a sense of commitment and obligation to others' needs. This sense of commitment that participants reported helped them to be open to Chicana and Chicano community commitment issues and the concept of *la raza* as a way to demonstrate obligation and camaraderie to similar people in need.

Time and space (context) was also a significant factor in how and why participants entered the figured worlds of Chicana and Chicano activism. The older participants, like Rafael, Anabel, Ruth, and David, lived through the movements of the 1960s and 1970s and were drawn into their causes because they were surrounded by them. For the younger participants, the organizations that resulted from the movements, both on college campuses and in the community, were important for Chicana and Chicano activist identity production. On college campuses, MEChA, as well as Chicana and Chicano studies departments and progressive professors in various departments, became sites for their critical engagement. Most of the study participants of the post–civil rights generation benefited from an expansion of a multicultural perspective deriving from the social movements of the 1960s, especially the Chicana and Chicano Movements and the people and organizations that resulted from these.

Space was also significant for participants like Phillip, Raquel, and María, who found themselves in university environments where the presence of other Latina and Latino students was not sizeable. Participants in more extreme cultural isolation either had to create sites for critical engagement, as Phillip did when he helped start a Chicana and Chicano student organization on his campus, or came to develop a critical Chicana and Chicano self-making process later in their careers as educators in urban schools. María and Raquel, for example, who worked with urban children in barrio schools, were amazed by the conditions of these schools, the low expectations, and the mistreatment of Latina and Latino students, and they were drawn to become Chicana advocates for social justice in these schools. Most participants were eventually drawn to members of their same ethnic/cultural group due to varying degrees of social and cultural isolation.

The documented alienation of Mexican American students in whitestream university environments (Gurin et al., 2002; Fry, 2004; Haro, 2004) also facilitated participants' recruitment into the figured worlds of Chicana and Chicano activism. Many of the participants expressed that during their initial experience with the university they sought out peers of their own ethnic group for company, especially through ethnic student organizations on campus.[8] Juanita, a bilingual elementary school teacher, for example, said that in the university, "even if you don't want to, you're kinda drawn to your own group."[9]

Seeking out peers of the same cultural group, seeking out classes on Latina and Latino or Latin American topics, or doing community volunteer work led to recruitment into Chicana and Chicano activist figured worlds. Being in those Chicana and Chicano spaces allowed participants access to the languages of Chicana and Chicano discourse communities. Concepts and terms to reinterpret social and cultural relations were important for conceptual identity production and included terms such as raza, *la causa*, *communidad*, *compañera/o*, and the diminutive "*ito*" or "*ita*" such as in the *cariño* (endearment) terms *Chicanitas* and *Chicanitos*, grounded in familial, organic cultural knowledge and authentic caring relationships (Valenzuela, 1999). These terms often carried over into professional educational spaces by Chicana and Chicano activist teachers' references to "my kids," rather than "those kids" or professors' references to themselves as *padrinos* or *madrinas*, godparents (mentors) of Chicana and Chicano graduate students, rather than formal terms like "advisor" or "chair." In all cases, these alternative meanings and epistemologies provided conceptual access to the cultural capital of the broader Chicana and Chicano activist figured world.

Participants also expressed that momentous experiences with oppression made them receptive to the social justice discourse of the Chicana and Chicano activist macro figured world. Experiences with oppression ranged, but generally were about racial, class, gender, body image, and sexual orientation discrimination. Depending on participants' specific experiences with oppression, some of these forms of oppression were highlighted more than others, but the oppressions were not mutually exclusive.

Participants with darker skin and indigenous features, like Samuel, Pedro, Rita, and Andrea, recalled oppression based on skin color. Often, fellow family members were the perpetrators of skin color discrimination since a form of internalized oppression in the Latina and Latino community is privileging lighter skin (Urrieta, 2003b). My analyses showed experiences with oppression allowed participants to be more open to alternative perspectives in regard to the historical discrimination of Mexican Americans, Mexicans, and other people of color, as well as to be empathetic to others. Participants reported that their experiences with oppression helped them better understand Chicana and Chicano activist perspectives, especially the acknowledgement and celebration of indigenous heritage.

Chicanas' Added Lenses of Oppression

Mujeres were particularly aware of gender discrimination from early on. Ruth, a university professor, former school administrator, and bilingual K–12 teacher, remembered being oppressed by her family's and church's gender and patriarchal expectations for women because of her early non-conformity to gender roles and lesbian sexual orientation. The gender expectations Ruth experienced as oppressive in her early life included that women not teach men and that women wear long skirts, veils, and long hair. Ruth's early career choice to become a minister was not a possibility in her church.

Aida Hurtado (1989) contends that there is no private sphere for people of color because the public sphere invades their lives, especially women of color. Chicanas were aware of their multiple oppressions from early on, especially gender oppression. Chicanas knew that men, according to Andrea, held mujeres back. "When my dad died, my mom took a turn around. She was like men are shit [laughs], and she was like I can do anything without a man, and I can do it even better. And she put this in our mind, especially me and my sister, us as women, we didn't need a man. And as a matter of fact, men would hold us back." Andrea noted that her mother had been in a seriously abusive relationship with her deceased father. Andrea's mother prepared her daughters to face men in society by making them strong women. Andrea's mother did this by disrupting male privilege among her own children. Andrea said: "He [my brother] always felt that we were unfair with him because he didn't have the privileges I guess that most men have, especially in Mexican families, you know, that create that patriarchal system. Well, mom, although she has a very patriarchal father, she did the opposite of it in my family, and as a matter of fact, it felt like we as women had more rights than, than any men that I knew." The disruption of patriarchal male privilege in everyday life, in Andrea's family, empowered Andrea and her sister to feel that they had rights, even more rights than any of the men around them.

Therese, who reported having a good relationship with her father despite his "mach[o]" ways, was aware of men's abuse over women because one of her school friends was being sexually molested by her own father. Therese stated: "One of my *Chicanita* friends, she was molested by her dad. . . . She would tell me not to say anything, so I ran home and told my mom." Although Therese's father made his daughters exempt from his sexist views on women, Therese was aware at a young age that some men sexually abuse women, including their own daughters. Knowledge of men's abuse of women and girls later made Therese appreciate her parents', especially her father's, overprotectiveness of her growing up, which ironically is also in line with patriarchal expectations.

Isadora also reported that the gender limitations (expectations) her father had for her were evident to her from an early age. "It wasn't so much expectations, but more like limitations because I was a girl and there was a lot of things I couldn't do. Even little, really simple things, like sleep over at people's houses or . . . Like we had orchestra and I really liked to play the trumpet, and my dad said the trumpet was a boy instrument, and I would be better off playing the violin. Whatever my dad said went, so I had to play the violin. I hated it." Gender limitations for Isadora included doing gendered chores, for which she was called "lazy" when she didn't perform to her father's wishes. Isadora's father also constantly compared her with her "girl" cousins who cooked and cleaned for their fathers.

Chicanas revealed that they were warned early on that men often "use" women for their own personal gain. Andrea and Juanita were specifically warned (in a prejudiced and gendered way) that undocumented men sometimes use U.S.-born Chicanas to obtain legal residency. Andrea stated: "Like, oh, if you're a Mexican American and you marry a Mexican immigrant then they're using you to get their citizenship. I remember family members saying that."

Andrea's family members cautioned her about future romantic involvement with Mexican immigrant men. Although the argument can be made that this is a prejudice against undocumented immigrants, in terms of gender, it conveyed the message that men often use women romantically for their own personal gain. Similarly, Juanita recalled hiding the fact that her boyfriend (now husband) was undocumented from her parents for fear that they might think that he was only using her to get legal residency.

Alicia also knew that men use mujeres for sex. When mujeres became pregnant, men, according to Alicia, "had little remorse" about deserting them and their children. Alicia gave birth to her first child at age fifteen. "Our kids' dads were a bunch of losers. They had no responsibility about . . . no guilt toward the children they had. They could care less. So I got a new little family going with my friends [women]. And we were all in the same boat. That's when I really became conscious. The disparities between the haves and the have-nots, how race played into it, how it was us poor Mexican women."

Alicia knew first-hand how often childraising responsibilities are placed exclusively on mujeres and how men use mujeres for sexual activity and then leave without "guilt." Later, Alicia added:

> I'll tell you right now. For a long time I wished to God I had been born a man. I even went through a period when I was a teenager, wishing that if I could be a man I could be the one to leave my responsibilities. . . . The way gender, the women's struggle, comes in is obviously guys don't gotta do this because they're not the ones who stay with the kids. Even if you didn't wanna stay with your kids, it didn't matter. You were gonna stay with them. All of us ladies wanted our kids because those are our kids. We might not have been the absolute greatest moms, but we weren't bad mothers either. None of the kids' dads paid child support. It was up to the woman to pay the rent, be it through welfare or working, pay all the utilities and have money for food, and for clothes, for gas. I mean, how the hell? And this only happened to women, it was only women. We were constantly struggling, "What are we gonna do? What are we gonna do? What are we gonna do?"

Alicia understood oppression from a unique gendered, racialized, classed, and sexualized perspective. Because she was living it, Alicia could see how women were affected unequally by having children and how society treated teenage women condemningly for engaging in sexual activity that produced children.

Alicia knew that poor single mothers of color generally lived in impoverished conditions that men could walk away from. Importantly, women create support networks to face oppression, *convivencia*, which highlighted these women's resourcefulness, *sobrevivencia*. Trinidad Galván (2005) defines sobrevivencia as a type of survival and resiliency that goes beyond mere economic survival and that includes cherished everyday interactions and measures (11). Alicia's reference to her "new little family" of support that were all in the "same boat," and constant reference to a collective *we* (women), reflect these support networks and women's ways of being and knowing in convivencia and in sobrevivencia.

Years later, when Alicia enrolled at the University of California and took classes on race, class, and gender oppression, she was often taken aback and was at times angry at her classmates' willingness to theorize her own experience. During an interview, Alicia commented: "When I was at

UC, we had whole classes . . . Every class that I took was the intersection of race, class, and gender. And they're all theorizing, THEORIZING what it feels like to live in a ghetto, or a low-income area, or barrio. Theorizing! I'm like, what the hell! I've been there! I know!"

What was being covered in Alicia's university classes was all too familiar to her. The fact that academics theorized about the experiences of people like her amazed Alicia and is also telling of her ability to understand theory because she did not have to imagine herself in the conditions they were theorizing about—she had actually lived in such conditions. Women's awareness of their multiple oppressions, although unfair and grossly unequal, gave Chicanas added lenses and creative resourcefulness from which to struggle collectively against the limitations placed upon them. The figured worlds of Chicana and Chicano activism provided mujeres and all participants with spaces of authoring—Holland and colleagues' second context for identity production.

Space of Authoring

Holland and colleagues credit their context, "space of authoring," to the influence of Bakhtin's concept of dialogism. Dialogism is the ability of people to self-/sense-make through multiple internal dialogues (Henríquez et al., 1984). When people are being socially identified by others, they are offered positions that they must accept, reject, or negotiate, and they must make choices and respond (according to Derrida [1996], a non-response is also a type of response). Holland and colleagues state, following Bakhtin, that the world must be answered—authorship is not a choice, but the form of the answer is not predetermined.

The participants in my study authored themselves as Chicanas and Chicanos in the spaces of authoring that local micro Chicana and Chicano activist figured worlds provided. Participation in local Chicana and Chicano activist micro figured worlds was a source of empowerment for many participants who previously had not recognized the value of their community or home cultures. The process of Chicana and Chicano conceptual identity production and self-authorship, however, involved "learning," but not necessarily performing, the practices of being or becoming a Chicana and Chicano activist. The process of Chicana and Chicano conceptual identity production and self-authorship was an individual cognitive internal dialogic process of continual formation. But, the empowering part of this self-authoring process was that it involved participants in the Chicana and Chicano practice of decolonizing the mind, or of conceptual self-determination.[10]

To self-author conceptually as Chicana and Chicano activists, participants had to mentally corroborate the new revisionist perspectives of history that they had learned with their own H-I-P and reinterpret their own past experiences. For example, in his conceptual process, Henry realized that he had been "kept blind" about himself and his people's history by the whitestream educational system. About his experience training for a peer-counseling program, Henry recalled: "During those two weeks we talked about issues of gender, race, homosexuality, and that made my eyes go, wow! It's almost like you're living in the dark and then somebody shines a flashlight, boom! All of a sudden like you wake up and realize that everything you believed and thought isn't true." His new conceptual understanding led to his subsequent "conversion" into "seeing the light," to his new self-authorship, or to what he referred to as "being born-again as a Chicano."

A reinterpretation of the personal and collective past was important in the process of conceptual Chicana and Chicano activist identity production. Especially important was reanalyzing personal past experiences through a racialized lens and learning to testify about past experiences with racism. Part of coming to self-author as a Chicana and Chicano activist also includes conceptually coming to understand the capacity to have multiple identities that are related and negotiated at once (Villenas and Moreno, 2001). For several participants, understanding this "multiplicity" was a new concept that, prior to this awareness, was not considered "normal."[11]

After coming to understand the Chicana and Chicano worldview, many of the participants recalled wanting to take more classes on Chicana and Chicano topics. Other participants also expressed early feelings of anger toward white supremacy and wished to be exclusively in the company of other Chicanas and Chicanos. Most participants drew more from their past personal experiences, community knowledge, community lore, and the value of their community and cultural informal education to not only re-author themselves as Chicanas and Chicanos but also to re-make sense of the world. When participants came to conceptually view themselves as Chicana and Chicano activists, their subjectivities became better organized around this new identification and its causes.

Procedural Identity Production

Holland and colleagues (1998) contend that shifts in procedural identity production are dictated by activity in figured worlds. This process of identity production is premised on people's participation in group activities and the practice and enactment of cultural forms particular to that figured world. In some cases, people take up the new forms of the figured world as devices for mediating their new conceptions of themselves and of their world.

Participants reported that participation in "Chicana and Chicano activities" allowed for a shift in procedural identity production that often complemented the conceptual shift in how they viewed the world. The reported and observed practices that favored Chicana and Chicano procedural identity production were organized around four themes: (1) intellectual engagement, (2) activist rites of passage, (3) leadership, and (4) raising consciousness. Raising consciousness, defined as teaching for social justice, is important because this practice is what motivated participants to enter careers in education, especially in urban areas.

Practices of intellectual engagement involved participants in several types of group activities outside of academic courses. These practices centered on the use of peer study groups to learn new perspectives on history and herstory and on understanding oppression. Many participants reported they developed an incredible desire to learn "their own history" that had been denied to them during their K–12 experiences. As practices of intellectual engagement, participants reported reading, studying, and engaging in critical discussions with peers about their newly encountered knowledge. Some of the predominantly English-speaking participants, for example, reported actively trying to learn, or relearn Spanish, while participants who identified more with their indigenous heritage tried to learn indigenous languages, especially Náhautl. In Chicana and Chicano procedural identity production, participants came to use Chicana and Chicano and Mexicana and Mexicano cultural symbols such as art, music, language, and clothing that they previously did not listen to or use. The majority of participants also found a new appreciation for their parents and ancestors, and their struggles and knowledge. This new appreciation manifested in spending more time with, and talking more often with, parents and family members. At this point, people like Samuel and Daniel reported that they reestablished estranged relationships with their fathers. Many participants reported that listening to "elders" became an important learning activity, especially because many had previously dismissed the wisdom of older family members. In terms of material culture, Mexican music, especially *corridos* (Mexican folk ballads), became important cultural tools for participants (as well as other cultural symbols) for mediating identity.

Other Chicana and Chicano group activities that participants reported as significant for procedural identity production were activist "rites of passage." These rites of passage included more traditional radical movement activities used in local contentious practice (Holland and Lave, 2001; Urrieta, 2006), such as organizing and participating in boycotts, marches, and protests, and getting arrested for civil disobedience. Participants reported having engaged in at least one of the listed rites of passage through their involvement in ethnic student or community organizations. These local contentious practices, especially being arrested, marching, and protesting, helped strengthen a sense of empowerment and self-authorship (to themselves and to the world) as agents of change. These rites of passage metaphorically and procedurally gave birth to their activist agency. Through these activities, participants reported that they came to *see* and *understand* their capacity to be agents of change in the world, as Inden (1990) suggests. Some participants reported that engaging in organizing activities especially provided them with important procedural skills they later used and further developed when they undertook leadership roles in ethnic student and community organizations.

The majority of participants also reported organizational and cooperative leadership roles in student and community organizations as significant activities for their Chicana and Chicano activist procedural identity production. Leadership positions such as being committee coordinators, program directors, and peer counselors were remembered as important. Although the goals and aims of the organizations the participants represented did not always have activist orientations, the positions they held in them, according to the participants, allowed them opportunities to mediate their conception of themselves and of the world as Chicana and Chicano activists. In these positions, participants remembered mentoring other, more novice Chicanas and Chicanos, and they thus became significant narrators themselves, like others before them, of Chicana and Chicano activist identity production. Importantly, Chicana and Chicano activist educators reported that they began to develop "an incredible desire to raise consciousness" during the Chicana and Chicano activist procedural identity production process.

Chicanas Discovering Options

Chicanas reported that they discovered that more options than they knew were available to them as mujeres through Chicana activist figured worlds. Chicana self-discovery, identity production, and self-authorship involved learning/hearing about prominent figures like Sor Juana Inés de la Cruz, Frida Kahlo, Las Adelitas, Angela Davis, Dolores Huerta, Emma Tenayuca, Patricia Tijerina, Geraldine Gonzalez, and others in ethnic or women's student organizations and through college courses in local Chicana activist micro figured worlds. Faculty role models, especially Chicana/Latina faculty mentors, became important for Chicanas' identity production, as were Chicana student organizations.

For older participants like Ruth, being in college was a time of self-discovery. Ruth recalled being inspired: "Angela Davis was also influential [to me] because she was so unconventional about how she approached politics and the fact she came out in the 60s as a Communist Party candidate for president. For me like . . . how could somebody be that brave and bold to come out and risk her whole career?"

Prominent strong women enabled Ruth to acquire a stronger Chicana feminist perspective that allowed her to reinterpret her herstory-in-person (H-I-P). Like the other Chicana participants, Ruth reinterpreted her past experiences through a racialized and gendered Chicana feminist lens. Chicanas also learned to tell stories about their past experiences with sexism and the intersections of both racialization and sexism with other forms of oppression.

Chicana/Latina faculty members either directly or indirectly became mentors, *madrinas* (godmothers), to younger Chicanas (Urrieta and Méndez Benavídez, 2007). Mentoring often occurred indirectly through taking courses with these mujeres. Mariana recalled the impact of women role models in her identity production process: "In college I started diverting from the traditional mindset I had of being a woman. I saw these women professors and they were doing something. Most of them were very active in the community, so I think that's what interested me in that field [gender, ethnicity, and multicultural studies]. They're not the traditional housewife and they're happy. At first I thought having a family was what made a woman happy, and now I see women can do more to be happy. There's more options for happiness."

Mariana's exposure to mujer faculty allowed her to question the traditional gender limitations placed on Chicanas and Latinas (such as being a housewife) and also to see there were other options in women's lives. Mariana directly questioned the gendered constructions of what constitutes happiness in women's lives and concluded that there were "more options for happiness."

Chicana student organizations provided Chicanas with important spaces for self-authoring. Andrea learned to appreciate the value of women's spaces through participation in a woman-centered student organization: "I learned [through this women's organization] that we need to connect ourselves with other women so we learn to nurture that part of us. Because when we don't focus on that part of our lives, it's easy to ignore the needs of being a woman, or the struggles of a woman. I think it's an ongoing process of discovery, of knowing what it really means to be a woman, knowing what it means to participate in society and everyday interactions as a woman."

In mujer-focused spaces, Andrea explored how learning to be a woman is an ongoing process because the malestream and patriarchy do not nurture women's ways of being outside of pre/scribed norms. To explore what it means to be mujeres, Chicanas shared the belief that there is a need for Chicanas to connect and nurture Chicana ways of being and women's ways of knowing.

Not all women focused their energy on women-centered organizations, however. Therese, although she appreciated these organizations' efforts, set her personal limits as to what she considered to be her "moral" boundaries, especially regarding sexuality. Therese explained why she became active in MEChA instead of a Chicana woman's organization: "There was a woman's group I was involved in at UC. But they weren't conservative with their bodies. So I decided not to be one [laughs]. . . . This group was a bit too risqué for me. So I ended up quitting. . . . They were really strong women; it's just morally I didn't agree with them. But it helped me to be around those women who really thought for themselves and were really strong. But . . . when their strength conflicted with my morals I quit."

Therese's example is important because even though Chicanas were open to exploring their discoveries of themselves as mujeres, they were also bound by past experiences with religion and other traditions. H-I-P indeed influenced what Chicanas and Chicanos were willing to explore and be open to. Participants like Therese, for example, were not completely open or easily influenced by their new surroundings. Even when Therese appreciated the strength and intelligence of the mujeres in this Chicana women's group, she decided not to remain in this organization or to push the limits of her sexual experience due to her strong Catholic influence. Therese's example corroborates with Pulido's (2006) findings on Chicana activist members of the Third World Left Movement. Pulido (2006) concluded that Chicana sexuality and the influence of Catholicism suggest that Chicanas are more hesitant to embrace new sexual practices and are more sexually conservative. Regardless of the self-discoveries that Chicanas made, all emerged with shifts in their identity production. Self-authoring as Chicana activists implied that they were committed not just to Chicana and Chicano racialized issues but also to gender issues.

Activist Identity and Activist Agency

Participants' agency as activists was a product of their identity shift and participation in Chicana and Chicano figured worlds. According to Holland and colleagues (1998:60), "Figured worlds in their conceptual dimensions supply the contexts of meaning for actions, cultural productions, performances, disputes, for the understandings that people come to make of themselves, and for the capabilities that people develop to direct their own behavior in these worlds." For the participants, coming to realize that they could act upon the world as activists was due primarily to their immersion in Chicana and Chicano activist figured worlds. Holland and colleagues (1998:40–41) state: "Figured World then provides a means to conceptualize *historical* subjectivities, consciousness and agency, persons (and collective agents) forming in practice." Chicana and Chicano activist macro and local micro figured worlds provided participants with a notion of Mexican Americans' subaltern historical membership and the agency embedded within cultural resources by valuing Chicana and Chicano culture. The practices and activities of the Chicana and Chicano figured world in dealing with societal and institutional racism and discrimination enabled activist agency.

Self-authoring as Chicana and Chicano activists gave participants hope that, as Bourdieu (1977:19) argues, "the imposition and inculcation of the structures is never so perfect that all explicitness can be dispensed with." Raquel understood this and stated it well: "I think what we're trying to do [as activist educators] is find those cracks in the system, *no*? . . . because like hegemony, their control isn't perfect. It's not perfect. It's not total . . . even when we get to a place where we feel it is." To understand activist agency as a daily practice is to know that there are institutional/structural constraints but also that activist agency is drawn from community and personal cultural resources, social networks, and leadership roles to "find those cracks in the system."

Using Chicana and Chicano activist educator identity production as a model, studying activist identities and activist agency can be more accessible with the following understandings:

1. *All* people have agency or the ability to act upon their environment(s).
2. Activist agency is embedded within daily *conscious* practices in critical moments eliciting responses or the lack thereof.
3. Activist identity is embedded within multiple cultural or figured worlds.
4. Activist identities are an important basis for activist agency.

Activist identity produces activist agency, and activist agency is more likely to seek out more opportunities for change.

Chicana and Chicano activist agency, as a daily moment-to-moment practice, is informed by a critical, always developing, and continuous state of consciousness. *Being* Chicana and Chicano in moment-to-moment practice is a way of life. Because Chicana and Chicano agency is contested by the whitestream, it is constantly renegotiated in daily practice. To make identity a *verb* and more than a descriptive label, Chicanas and Chicanos continuously engage in moment-to-moment self-authorship and strive toward further developing a critical state of consciousness.

Chicana and Chicano consciousness in practice is not only active awareness of agency in moment-to-moment interactions but also taking the responsibility to seize moments to act purposively and subjectively in the world (Urrieta and Méndez Benavídez, 2007). That critical state of consciousness is an endless but necessary process of life-long analysis of historical social injustice, the unlearning of white supremacy, and healing from the pain of internalized oppression, but it is not limited to this. The process is about awareness of the multiple oppressions of other groups of people in the United States (including women, LGBT [lesbian, gay, bisexual, and transgender] issues, class, immigration, etc.) and throughout the world.

Understanding activist agency, activism, and their redefinitions is an important part of Chicana and Chicano figured worlds but is even more so outside of those "safety zones," where identifying as Chicana and Chicano comes with certain stereotypical assumptions. Activism of a highly militant ethos involving violence and direct physical action is a misguided male-centered expectation of Chicanos (I. García, 1998) by our society. Broader, less-romanticized conceptions of activism helped the participants in my study decide strategically what physical acts they considered valuable and durable for social change versus others. For the participants, strategy and negotiation were focused on individual decisions about what daily actions and practice were important for change, without also underestimating the power of collective action. Both conceptual and procedural shifts in identity production highlight activist identity production as the basis for activist agency, a form of agency much more likely to seek out opportunities for change.

"My Whole Life Just Changed"

The eight narratives introduced in chapter 3 continue in this section. The narratives focus on participants' experiences in Chicana and Chicano activist identity production. By participating in the macro and local micro figured worlds of Chicana and Chicano activism, Chicana and Chicano activist conceptual and procedural identity production occurred.

Undergraduates

Julián. I graduated ranked fourth out of a class of eight hundred, but I was told I could have been valedictorian had I changed tracks. I was admitted to the University of California. Our school was given ten scholarships for the top ten students, all of which came from A track, except for me. Thinking back, that was not right because there were a lot of other good students who were much, much more motivated than those who got the praise and "good" classes and were never given the opportunity. There's an article by Marcelo Suárez-Orozco at Harvard, I think, that talks about how immigrant students are amongst the most motivated. Now I realize it's true. Some B-track students worked so hard to learn and get a chance, but they were lied to because this system never intended to give them the same opportunity.

I attended a summer orientation program for students of color sponsored by the affirmative action program prior to my first quarter at the university. In several ways it was good because we were taught things I have yet to encounter here in a regular quarter, other than in maybe an ethnic studies course: themes in comparative literature, for example, like on power, ideology, economy, political science, community, and race. Topics I had never really heard of. It was also great in terms of getting credit for starting a quarter early and socially in making friends and meeting people from various communities. My critical awareness was heightened. But, one thing that was bad was that we were discouraged from getting involved in ethnic student organizations because they said they were radical and we would be restricting ourselves to our own ethnicity. So at first I hated MEChA.

Coming from a school of 98 percent raza (by raza I mean Chicano/ Latino), I was shocked when the regular quarter started and I was the only Chicano student on my dorm room floor. I tried to maintain the friendships I made in the summer program, but after about six months, I decided to give MEChA a chance. There, I quickly began to understand what people took as radicalism is really a type of progressivism. I got involved pretty quickly. By the first month I was already secretary for the youth conference; the next year I was the youth conference co-chair. This year I'm the youth conference co-chair and the vice-chair of MEChA. Being Chicano is something I learned because it's a self-realization. It's a process. The process of what Freire calls *conscientización*. It's not something that occurs from one moment to another: "Yeah, I'm Chicano!" It's a construction, an understanding, a lifelong process.

When I use the word Chicano, it doesn't necessarily mean Mexican, or of Mexican descent, it's more of an identity of cultural formation that represents the struggles binding different communities. It's an identity of self-formation, self-determination. This process is not really defined, but more of an individual process of your own endeavor and how comfortable you are with who you are. You know, people are afraid of who they are! I think the work of Franz Fanon is so important because I read *The Wretched of the Earth*, and he talks about how the colonized person wants to be like the colonizer and it's true. Divide and conquer, divide us amongst ourselves and divide us amongst each other as minorities. So being Chicano is more about being progressive in your understanding of self culturally and also where you're at in your journey and seeing how you can help out your community. You have a responsibility to the community, and you draw from it because it has an abundance of assets that are not valued. This process of Chicana and Chicano conscientización is nonstop: it always continues.

The activism that comes with this self-determination is in not being afraid of saying what you feel and what needs to get done to raise consciousness. So I'm a student activist. Activism to me is going to meetings, coalition building with other student organizations and community organizations, and getting involved in university committees. As an activist, you have goals and objectives of why you are doing what you're doing because it's not just about showing up at a march and that's it. I mean marches, protests, rallies are all important, but it's about doing the everyday work, about creating programs and not just screaming at the top of your lungs. To create programs and coalitions, it takes talking to people, going to meetings, creating resolutions, talking to people from professors to community members and getting input from everyone. It's really time consuming and has taken a toll on my studies and especially my social life, but it's really something that needs to get done. A lot of people don't take the time to do it.

Isadora. I started attending the University of California in the summer through an orientation program for minorities and poor whites, and it was a really good experience. The teachers started breaking down all these big words like capitalism, institutionalized racism, worker exploitation, and it was like learning a new vocabulary to talk about things that I knew existed but had never considered. I was amazed because I never thought people could actually organize classes around these topics. In one class, I remember we read the autobiography of Malcolm X, and people had told me who he was, but they had never really told me who he was! For an assignment we had to go talk to our families and find out alternative stories to what we got in school, and my mom and I had a very emotional conversation about my grandfather and his involvement in the Bracero Program. I complemented our conversation with research on the working conditions and the exploited cheap labor. That was a part of my family history I did not know about.

But even after the program, I got some of it, but I didn't really get it. Like I would get all happy when white people would tell me, "Congratulations, you got in without affirmative action. See, it's not needed." And I was like, yeah, that's right! I started seeing a lot of my Chicana friends from the summer program getting involved in student organizations though, and it was through conversations with them that I finally began to understand the Chicana and Chicano perspective. It just all started coming together, my growing-up experiences, my conversations with my uncle, the way I had treated my family, especially my dad for being born in Mexico. I finally got it. I realized I had been privileged by the educational system and that's why I wasn't willing to see things differently: to see them differently would mean to bring myself down from my false pedestal and recognize that others struggled more than me.

By the end of my first year I started calling myself Chicana. At that point it meant having a lot of pride in who I am and having an awareness of the issues that affect us and a commitment to do something about them. I was angry because I was made to believe I was better than all my people. I realize I had kind of been taught to make fun of my own self by making fun of my own people. Now I also understand that Chicana and Chicano is not exclusive to Mexican Americans; it's more than that. It's about constantly struggling to be more aware, a process of self-education and learning from other people, other raza. I go back home now and seriously try to understand and appreciate my parents and family a lot more because I realize I have a lot to learn from them. It's sad, but there was a point when they couldn't help me with schoolwork anymore, and I kind of felt like they were ignorant, like they couldn't teach me anything else. Those were the messages I was getting at school. I missed out on those years I could have appreciated my parents more.

I think if you're gonna call yourself a Chicana that implies you're gonna be actively involved. It's a politicized statement. It means you're trying to understand what's going on in your community and you care enough to do something about it. It can be something as simple as talking, challenging, questioning, or getting other people to open their minds by raising consciousness, it's about speaking out and representing. For me it's also about working with youth, community organizations, garment workers, and laborers. As the MEChA gender and sexuality coordinator, I work a lot with youth; it's my passion, and it brings me hope for a better future.

In terms of activism, people have this perception of activists as protestors, or crazy people, but protesting is just one branch of activism. I have been involved in protests, but there's so many other ways. I guess my definition of activism is doing something that tries to eliminate certain problems in struggling to make life better. Not necessarily your life, but the lives of your people, whoever you identify with or those you care about. So I consider myself an activist, especially when dealing with issues of gender and my work with Chicanas.

Teachers

Henry. I got into the university I always wanted to attend, and my first two years there I still had the same type of mentality. I remember working part-time at the police department, and sometimes a couple of African American cops would come and tell me about how messed up our society was. I used to sit there and listen, and it made sense for the most part. But after that half-hour conversation, I'd think, oh, that was cool, and that's it. So it just didn't take hold. After my second year I transferred to another university because I needed to get away from here. When I got there I took a job as a peer counselor for transfer students of color and poor whites.

The peer-counseling program, sponsored by the university affirmative action program originally started during the late 60s, had a two-week intensive training session we had to attend. During those two weeks, we talked about issues of gender, race, homosexuality, and that made my eyes go, wow! It's almost like you're living in the dark and somebody shines a flashlight, boom! All of a sudden you wake up and realize everything you believed and thought isn't true. From that point on my whole life just changed. First my thinking changed as I reanalyzed my life, and then my actions in terms of what I wanted to do. I always wanted to be a cop or a FBI agent, but then I started thinking about serving the community through teaching.

I got involved with student organizations that helped youth of color. We'd bring them to campus and give them tours and stuff, run summer leadership programs, and help them transfer from community college. I also started taking classes to help me learn even more. I took a class on Malcolm X, I read his autobiography, and I listened to some of his tapes. I just felt good! It's almost parallel to when people find God! All of a sudden they feel like they're woken up and have a rebirth. That is what it felt like, like I was born again as a Chicano. I also developed this urgency to make change because it's like an obligation to raise consciousness to help others understand what I didn't understand until I was much older.

So, if you're really gonna create societal change, you just can't change your mind and say, wow, things are really screwed up, but realizing things are screwed up, you gotta go out there and be much more proactive. I still see it that way: that's why I'm a teacher. I think you can raise consciousness and really have some kind of impact on the future. Now, how great that impact is sometimes I really question, but you still have to give it a shot even if you get pessimistic sometimes. When I graduated, though, I wasn't really prepared to go right into teaching, so I became a substitute teacher.

Then I realized that at the university a lot of times we live in bubbles, and when you get out to the work force, that bubble bursts because all of a sudden you don't have people around you that think like you do. It's not that you stop believing what you do, but you're much more reluctant to act in ways that you're used to or to express your opinions because of people's attacks. Sometimes those attacks have real-life consequences like losing your job. So as a substitute teacher and now as a full-time teacher, I don't hang out with anybody at work because I don't feel like getting into arguments. I've had more conversations with people where I feel like I get more out of this wall [taps wall]. I tell my wife sometimes it's just not worth engaging somebody in a conversation if you know it's not gonna change their mind.

After three years of subbing, I realized I wasn't as effective as I wanted to be because substitute teaching is more like babysitting. So I got into the PhD program at the University of California. It was the best decision I ever made because I got so much more theory than I would have ever gotten in a credential program. I learned about issues in education and what teachers go through, I did research, and I read Freire's *Pedagogy of the Oppressed* and that totally changed my outlook on teaching. I learned that what's fair for one student may not necessarily be fair for another. I eventually got back into teaching through coaching. I was the JV baseball coach at a local high school, and then some of the parents requested I interview for a position that opened up, and I dropped out of the PhD program and took the job. I was ready to teach full-time by then.

Juanita. In college is where I slowly got my formal education in being Chicana, Mexicana. I didn't go through a miraculous transformation. I don't know what it is, but in college you seem to be attracted to your own kind. So I went to a MEChA meeting once, and it just seemed too wild for me. The guy facilitating the meeting was practically calling for a war, and to me, coming from such a sheltered environment, that just seemed crazy. Today I could be that guy because I've changed so much I could easily be the MEChA president, but back then I was just another person.

I found out I could get a minor in Chicano studies with my history major and it would only take a few more classes. So I started taking Chicano studies courses. I remember my first class was on *corridos* (Mexican ballads). I didn't know the value or the long history of corridos; I just knew it was the kind of *tan tan* music my dad listened to that I didn't like. The professor was Chicano and he was great. We did a research paper on a corrido, then he took us on a university vanpool to a cantina in Tijuana and hired a *conjunto* (band) to play all the corridos we studied. I was amazed. I just started learning so much and really began to understand issues and be critical of the system, and to appreciate my culture and family. I would come home sometimes and share the information with my parents and sisters.

Growing up, my dad told me some of the same information, but I would just dismiss him back then by saying, "Ay apa (oh dad), you're just so down on American [white] people! Ay apa, what you say can't be true, you only went to third grade! ¡Qué me vas a enseñar a mi?! (What can you possibly teach me!)" So now my father would say *ves* (see), I told you! And he said, "Well, if this is what I'm paying for for you to finally believe a PhD instead of me that's fine as long as you learn something!" [Juanita begins to cry.] I'm sorry. [sobbing] It's just that he told me that and that made me remember how bad I used to treat him and think he had nothing of value, or just nothing important to teach me [crying intensifies and interview is ended].[12]

I grew up so sheltered and other Chicano students had all these experiences, and it was just so interesting to listen to them and hear the same things my dad would tell me. That was all good for me and being around Pedro, my husband. Seeing how he couldn't go visit his family in Mexico was hard. He couldn't really go visit his mom for many years until after we got married and he got legal residency. Hearing about the *coyotes* (human smugglers), how they charge so much money to get people across the border and about how they rape women, it all taught me so much. So at the university and through my husband I got my formal Chicanismo and Mexicanismo, but more my Chicanismo because now that we're married I realize being born and raised here is a totally different experience.

When I was getting ready to graduate, I decided to become a teacher, a bilingual teacher, and work in the same community where I came from, but before I set foot in a classroom I made sure I got my teaching credential. I always felt it was unfair and racist that the teachers that could get emergency teaching permits were the ones who were to teach bilingual classes. Why would such unprepared new teachers be the ones to teach the kids that needed the most experienced teachers? I thought it was racist of the institution to allow and even encourage that, and if you wanted to teach English Only students, you could not set foot in a classroom without a teaching certificate. So I ended up staying another year and got my bilingual, cross-cultural teaching permit and participated in the raza graduation ceremony because by then I was more comfortable with myself.

Graduate Students

Miguel. The university I attended was about 97–98 percent white. I was the only Chicano, Latino, Mexican, in a five-floor dormitory. I think there was like one black student too. I was very isolated and alone, and it was there that a great sense of pride and liberation in who I was emerged. I was admitted as an engineering major, so I was taking all the hard sciences and barely passing, and I wanted to double major in Spanish literature. I took a class just for fun that dealt with Spanish-speaking people's experiences in the United States and included the Chicano Movement and events of the 60s and 70s. The professor was involved in a lawsuit against the Spanish Department because she had been denied tenure and the department had a history of denying tenure to non-Iberian and non-white professors; she was a first-generation Chicana. She won, by the way! I quickly became involved in issues and struggles pertaining to Chicanos/as, but especially those of the first generation. By the fourth year, I dropped out of the engineering program and decided I wanted to become a teacher.

There was an instrumental professor there, a Chicana who focused on issues of race and self, especially of Chicanos of the first generation. It was in these classes that my culture was valued in a university setting and it was a very empowering experience. It was an eye-opener that sparked my activist perception. I realized I could speak for who I am and can speak for others like me. I decided to teach because all of this helped me realize I had something to offer. I realized what I had experienced was beneficial to others. I really did have a strong sense of giving back to the community by raising consciousness. I decided to work where I felt I was most needed and became an activist teacher. To me, an activist is a person who looks beyond their own situation and is able to place themselves in wider community goals rather than just their own.

Therese. I knew early on that I was going to college, and sure enough I ended up at the University of California, and it was in college that my identity was solidly strengthened. Actually, Latino organizations put me through college because I got scholarships from them. So it was very real for me who paid for my education and who kept me in school. I knew I was going to get involved with those organizations in order to give back. I was so homesick though that I tried to transfer to another university, but through getting involved I got more adjusted. First I joined a Chicana women's group on campus, and I found them to be strong, intelligent women, but a little too risqué for me because their strength and experimentation with sexuality conflicted with my morals. So I became a Mechista [MEChA member] instead.

Through MEChA I got really involved in campus and community issues. When my brother started attending that university as well, we were both arrested on a march and takeover we did on one of the local bridges, and my dad was so upset because he saw us on the news. That and similar experiences empowered me as a Chicana. I remember coming home all fired up and talking to my grandparents about being Chicana, and they were so offended. My grandpa was like, "Don't you ever call yourself that! We worked hard to get rid of those stereotypes, and I served this country because I am an American! And here you are saying, no, I'm different, I'm a Chicana!" He explained to me that the term Chicano was used derogatorily during the time of the Zoot Suit Riots; he was in the Navy and my grandma was a Pachuca,[13] so these are sensitive issues for them, but for me it was empowering.

I took as many Chicano studies classes as I could fit into my schedule, but I didn't major in Chicano studies because I thought it might hurt me careerwise. I majored in U.S. history and communication to keep my options open because I wanted to be a lawyer, and I wrote my honors thesis on protest movements. My intentions to become a lawyer changed when I took the LSAT and during the test a woman had a seizure and no one got up to help her. After a couple of minutes, a woman and I got up and called an ambulance. I couldn't believe after what happened people were more concerned about how this would affect their scores instead of the woman's well-being. So I walked out and decided that's not where I wanted to be. It was inspiring to take classes with professors of color; it was almost like, yeah, one of us made it, but more than anything it was inspiring to see through their example how they wove their activism and passion with their professional lives.

I got involved in a lot of things as an undergraduate. A group of us started this Chicano/Latino pipeline project to get mujeres to go on to graduate school right after undergraduate school. I also got an internship with a local Latino organization and was able to do research on immigration, education, access to higher education, and I just had access to all this data on issues that were important to me. I also wrote for our student newsletter and different magazines. All of that helped me get into a master's program in education at an Ivy League university. There, we did a lot of organizing around issues too, especially those affecting Latinos in

California after Proposition 209, with fellow students that today are very involved and have high visibility within the community.

Academically my Ivy League experience was not all that challenging and my doctoral experience is the same. The curriculum is so conservative and there is so little room for change. But, I've learned to play by the rules. I've learned how to be good at getting A's, and I figure I need this degree to go out there and better serve my community, so I'm better off with it than without it. My views as a Chicana activist have also changed. They've evolved from like everything's racist and the system is corrupt, to how can I make the system work for me. How can I do my part to change the system enough to impact people?

Professors

Phillip. I got a good deal through a soccer, football, and leadership scholarship to attend a private, overwhelmingly white university in the western United States. There, I experienced some of the worst isolation in my life. I was truly an outsider in terms of race, class, culture, politics, and especially religion. The university was over 96 percent white and had a tiny student of color population, some African Americans, Polynesians, and a few Latinos. I mean, I had to change my political science major because I could not deal with the right-wing Republican professors and their curriculum. Coming from a John F. Kennedy family tradition, I couldn't handle the culture. But it was also there that I really started to reflect on who I was in many ways, but especially ethnically and class wise.

I missed Mexicano culture. I missed it especially being in that white environment where you're almost forced to seek out people like yourself to survive, to handle it there. There were a few international, very wealthy students from Mexico, probably more than there were Chicanos, and they would all hang out in the basement of the library and use the TVs there to watch *novelas*. I didn't speak great Spanish, and we didn't have much in common, but just to be near them was enough for me. Until one day a Chicana from Texas came up to me and asked if I was Mexican American. She invited me to a group meeting other Chicanos on campus were going to have. Finally, I had access to the few other Mexican Americans, Chicanos at my university.

There were like six to eight of us and it was great to be around people of similar backgrounds, so we formed a club and did a lot of activities together. It was our little network, our little *familia*. We assigned readings to each other because we didn't have Chicano studies classes. We covered topics like the UFW [United Farm Workers], César Chávez, the Mexican Revolution, immigration, and did presentations for the group. We basically taught ourselves about ourselves and this forced me to search for who I was. We also did *balet folklórico* (folkloric dance), mini-conferences, and outreach to increase the number of Latinos on campus. We had a weekly festival of cultures and tried to represent the Latino culture through Mexicano traditions, dances, food, and educational sessions.

At the university I also started to recognize some of my privileges, and I asked myself, how could I be at this kind of university and not do something to help Mexicanos? I soon came to the realization that I could not be doing this just for my own benefit and whatever I did was going to also benefit other Mexicanos. I was in preparation to devote my life to helping Mexicanos in some way. When I was younger, I always wanted to be a doctor or lawyer, but I decided I wanted to be like a director of multicultural affairs and just recruit Chicanos and students of color to the university. I would help design programs to help them graduate and send them off to graduate school. That's what I was going to contribute to the community.

I definitely identified as an activist on campus and not just by the leadership positions I held but also by what I wanted to do in those positions. I define activism as trying to make change, to enact change, to accomplish some kind of change in society. We had an agenda to increase the representation of Latinos on campus, and we did it by designing our own recruitment program and by using some back-door techniques to get students in. By then, I was already working on my master's, and when I finished, I took a job in student affairs in a liberal arts college in the Midwest. There, I worked with student of color organizations, and one of the things we did was start a people of color conference focused on issues of race, gender, class, and sexual orientation. It went really well, but I decided to return to the West and became an academic and MEChA advisor at a state university. It was a strategic move because of my activist kind of agenda and desire to effect institutional change.

Then I realized that the people with the power to call the shots are the deans, vice presidents, and presidents, and if I wanted to call some shots, I needed a doctorate. So my motivation for a doctorate was basically my activist agenda for institutional change. I applied to doctoral programs and did my PhD at a university with a sizeable Chicano/Latino student and faculty population, and it was a great experience. I was finally being nurtured in a very Chicano, Mexicano environment. I did struggle with the typical graduate student dilemmas such as does publishing really make a difference, but my activist agenda pretty much remained the same.

Anabel. After struggling with my dad to sign the financial aid forms, I went away to a local public university. I lived in the dorms and I loved it! I started off in the hard sciences, but felt very isolated because there were literally no women in any of my classes. So I changed majors and decided to minor in education and started learning more about Chicano issues. It was more like taking these random classes because there weren't any ethnic studies departments at that university during that time, but I definitely took classes. Later, as a student teacher, I was placed in a very elite white school and I didn't like it, so when I finished, I looked for a job working with Latino and African American students. Those were the kids I wanted to work with, the kids that didn't have access. It was a very humbling experience because I really was exposed to all of the inequities in education.

A lot of programs were started in the spirit of affirmative action at that time, and I was recruited by a local university to teach "English for Chicano Students." I saw how much potential there was in these students and began to feel this strong sense of commitment. My commitment just grew and became larger during each part of the career. While I was there, I also got my master's. I really loved that job, but ended up moving out of state with my fiancé and took a job at another university as a coordinator for UMAS [United Mexican American Students]. Now they had some real hyped-up Chicano activism there!

I mean, students carried guns; they took over buildings and demanded that the Chicano faculty and administrators they considered sellouts resign. It was really turbulent. Being the youngest member there, I negotiated with the students and ended up being the co-director for this program along with a student activist. Boy, did they educate me in activism; I mean, this was real hardcore and I survived. I became involved with boycotts, women's issues, and Marxism. There was a Marxism study group, and we got involved in study sessions and support work from migrant farm workers to national liberation fronts. That's when I started to see the value in coalition building rather than the strictly Chicano nationalist agenda UMAS had.

Through connections I became the academic coordinator of all the minority programs at the university and worked with very sexist men of color. I grew politically and began to realize there were serious roadblocks to doing transformative work, credentials being one of them. There was definitely more clout over people with PhDs, so I decided to get mine. My decision was solidified after one of the departments on campus decredited some of our ethnic studies classes and a group of us organized a major student takeover of a building. By then I had established a vast network of scholars of color nationwide, and everyone knew it was a blatantly racist action on the department's part. They eventually gave in and recredited our courses, but it was obvious you had to be part of certain clubs to raise issues. So I needed the degree to have the authority to speak or nobody would listen.

I was very clear in how I was going to use my PhD. It was going to be about creating transforming spaces to raise consciousness and to destroy myths about my community. If you could transform these spaces in the university, then you could do a whole lot, so that was my commitment. That's why I'm in education because I didn't see as great a transformative potential in other departments. I think in education you can make systemic change—have a better shot of having access to students who already have an inclination to do something to help. I can prepare people to start thinking about things differently because these are the same people that are going to come back and teach our kids and who were screwing them up in the first place. It is very clear that some kids get labeled in negative ways over and over and the problem is systemic, not the kids. So teaching is important to me, but research is also because I love debunking myth after myth about our community.

I struggled through my doctoral program because I had to do my course work twice because I had a baby. There is also a lot of sexism and sexual harassment in the academy. I mean, as a graduate student you are so vulnerable and some people take advantage of that, especially when you have everything riding on just one person. I think it's criminal to use your power in any way against graduate students. But I finished and through national Chicano connections was able to get a postdoctoral fellowship here at the University of California and was later hired as tenure-track faculty. So my trajectory at times seems amazing to me, like how did I get here?

Identity Shift

Although each experience was unique, all of the participants experienced both a conceptual and procedural identity shift consistent with the worldview and practices of Chicana and Chicano activist identity. This shift to a Chicana and Chicano activist identity led participants to an awareness of their activist agency. Activist agency, for the participants, stressed that activism was embedded in daily, conscious, critical practices and demanded that participants actively seek out opportunities for change. "That's the way it is," or that the system functions the way it does, was not the end of the conversation for Chicana and Chicano activist educators, but a hopeful beginning to think about making change. One of the ways participants sought to make change was by raising consciousness.

Raising Consciousness *Pero Con Ganas*!

Raising consciousness was often used synonymously by Chicana and Chicano activist participants with teaching for social justice *pero con ganas.*[14] Commitment to raising consciousness, to the participants, meant educating others from a Chicana and Chicano perspective and also engaging in teaching informally whenever possible in moment-to-moment opportunities as a form of day-to-day activism (Urrieta, 2003a). This commitment to raising consciousness also coincided with participants' formal decisions to pursue careers in education, especially in urban contexts.

Informally, raising consciousness involved sharing their new or perhaps renewed knowledge and views with peers, as well as with family members. For example, Andrea, who was darker skinned and came from a family oppressed by fellow family members who privileged lighter skin, discussed how she taught her younger sister to be proud of their indigenous heritage.

> I started to tell my sister, especially about color . . . My family is darker than any of my cousins, and for that reason . . . we're not the favorite family . . . we feel discriminated even by our grandparents, aunts and uncles. So I called my sister and told her . . . we have to be proud of our color. My sister's the darkest one and she's always felt unattractive, even as a young girl, because of it. I told her to be proud 'cause that's our . . . indigenous heritage. So little by little, I had to make change first in my family and have them understand where . . . these negative views came from.

Andrea believed she helped to deconstruct negative conceptions with her family by raising consciousness. Andrea said she especially helped her sister better deal with whitestream models of body image and beauty, often used to oppress all women, but especially women of color, and encouraged her sister to see herself as a beautiful woman.

In some cases, raising consciousness with family members helped participants conceptually corroborate family knowledge with their new perspectives, and at other times, it caused conflict with more traditional and conservative perspectives, such as religious perspectives. In Juanita's case, what she learned in her college Chicana and Chicano history courses corroborated well with the version of history her father shared with her years earlier. Juanita, like several other participants, suffered and expressed painful regret for having devalued her parents' and relatives' perspectives and knowledge.

In Johnny's case, his new progressive political inclinations as an undergraduate came into conflict with his father's conservative ideas about meritocracy and welfare. Ruth, as a Chicana lesbian activist, found that she could no longer participate in the strict religious life her family practiced. Regardless, all participants expressed a strong desire to "raise consciousness" about the issues they felt were important for self and community empowerment, even if those issues caused conflicts.

Participants reported that the shift to Chicana and Chicano activist identity motivated them to formally enter careers in education to raise consciousness and to "give back to the community." Henry said: "From that point on [becoming a Chicano activist], my whole life just changed. First my thinking changed as I reanalyzed my life and then my actions in terms of what I wanted to do. I had always wanted to be a cop or a FBI agent, but then I started thinking about serving the community through teaching." Most participants became educators and returned to their home communities, to the barrios. Some returned as teachers, others as counselors, school administrators, or researchers.

Working in urban K–12 schools in some capacity or another was significant for all participants. For example, Miguel, a graduate student, was previously a bilingual teacher, and four of the six professor participants had served as teachers and/or counselors and administrators in K–12 urban schools. About teaching at the university level, Pedro stated: "My goal as an educator is to make people think critically about the reality they live in. I am convinced if they do that, they will want a different world than the one we are in. . . . I see that practice in a classroom as activism. It is the space in which I am politically working toward . . . a better world, it is a more humane world and that's where I do it." Pedro, like the other Chicana and Chicano activist educators, continued to fuse his activism within his work in education.

Other participants who continued on to graduate school to raise consciousness in the academy through research and teaching also focused on minority, especially Latina and Latino, urban education issues. Working in teacher education programs was especially attractive for Chicana and Chicano activist educators in higher education. In 2002, Raquel left her middle school classroom in the inner city to join a doctoral cohort of graduate students in education. Approximately 45.8 percent of the participants in this study worked or had worked in urban inner city K–12 schools, while all of the undergraduates intended to work in urban K–12 schools as teachers. The remaining participants had not formally worked in K–12 urban schools as educators, but had extensive opportunities and experience, including doing research in inner city schools, especially with minority students. Participants like David, Anabel, and Phillip, for example, who did not have extensive teaching experience in K–12 schools, focused their research agendas on Latina and Latino students' linguistic and cognitive needs, as well as issues of access to higher education.

Many of the participants, like Mariana, reported being inspired by the critical and progressive professors who taught them, as well as by the materials that they read, such as Luis Moll's work on funds of knowledge, to enter the field of education. While some participants recalled with happiness the teachers who had made an impact in their lives in school and wanted to return and emulate them, other participants remembered with anger and pain the teachers and counselors whom they did not want to be like and purposefully returned to the barrios to "undo the harm." Rodrigo, an undergraduate already working as a paraprofessional in an elementary school, commented that he wanted to become an elementary school teacher, like I did years ago, "if anything to give the kids back their real names" *en español.*[15]

Chicana Activist Perspectives

To the majority of Chicana activist participants, social justice included a struggle on a variety of "isms." Isms referred to different forms of oppression, including gender, racialization, class, and sexual orientation, but was certainly not limited to these. Chicanas had a better appreciation of the isms because of their H-I-Ps, especially their experiences with multiple forms of oppression. Chicana activists were by far more willing to discuss issues of sexuality and sexual orientation than their male counterparts.

Andrea most eloquently expressed what most Chicanas articulated as their Chicana activist perspective. "Unless we have social justice that is based on race, class, gender, sexuality, all of these things at the same time, then we're not really creating social justice. If we're not understanding immigration, we're not understanding capitalism, and [if] we're not understanding racism, homophobia, all of these things, then we're not really understanding justice. I think that's what a lot of Chicanos and Chicanas tend to do: when they become racially conscious, they forget about the others."

For Andrea, raising consciousness as a Chicana activist was based on pursuing social justice that highlights multiple forms of oppression, not just racial oppression. About Chicana and Chicano scholars focusing strictly on access issues in education, Andrea said: "I've heard too many Chicano or Chicana activists say: 'We wanna get our people into good positions. We wanna get them into college. We wanna get them into the middle class.' That's a really poor goal if you're not challenging the class structure."

Andrea raised crucial points with regard to focusing activist attention on particular goals, such as educational mobility, without incorporating broader conceptions of activism for social justice, rather than just activism to gain access. The focus on getting into "good positions" reflects uncritical aims that translate into "poor goals" in Andrea's and other Chicanas' perspectives of activism.

Sexuality and sexual orientation were also essential to Chicanas' perspective of activism. Andrea and other Chicanas believed these to be non-issues or afterthoughts for most Chicano and some Chicana activists.

> In terms of sexuality, I think that's the last thing people are encouraged to explore in terms of their identity. I think a lot of times we don't even know how to talk about it as Chicano and Chicana activists and intellectuals. We think it's something only gay and lesbian and bisexual people have to deal with. Even in Chicano studies classes, it's still such an afterthought unless you're gay, lesbian, or bisexual. I think that's a real atrocity that people aren't pushing themselves to look at yet another really important aspect of oppression that continues to plague, not only our community, but society as a whole. Women's issues . . . they're always second nature. They're always . . . put in the back burner and need to be at the forefront.

Andrea and other Chicanas considered sexuality oppression "a really important aspect of oppression." They contended that all people working for social justice needed to be more aware about sexuality as well as women's issues. Andrea observed these essential issues are "second nature" or "put in the back burner," when they "need to be at the forefront."

Chicanas envisioned a perspective on activism focused on social justice that included challenging a variety of isms, not just racialized oppression. Because of their complex and multilayered experiences, Chicanas' perspectives on activism for social justice put gender issues at the forefront, while not ignoring the importance and relevance of sexuality and sexual orientation as an area of struggle.

Complex Processes

Conceptual and procedural self-authorship are important because identity production is not just about performing a new understanding of oneself but also about believing one is who one thinks one is. When both a procedural and conceptual shift occur, a more complex (not necessarily more complete) process of identity production occurs. There is no rigid or sequential pattern to this process.

People (in this case Mexican Americans) with particular life experiences are more easily recruited or drawn into particular figured worlds, while exposure in figured worlds may not necessarily lead to identity production. Some participants shared that they were at first dissuaded from identifying as Chicanas and Chicanos because of the militant ethos (I. García, 1998) they were exposed to. Chicana and Chicano self-making in these cases became a long process, while others experienced conversion-like experiences (Diawara, 1994) like Henry.

Younger participants like Julián, Rodrigo, Isadora, and Daniel encountered the Chicana and Chicano identity during their K–12 schooling experiences, but did not understand it. Other participants like Therese, a graduate student, were actively involved in Chicana and Chicano activist practices in their communities through older Chicana and Chicano mentors and family members, but did not conceptually understand the history or herstory and worldview of Chicana and Chicano activism until their undergraduate experiences. Miguel, for example, reported that while he embraced conceptually the politics of the Chicana and Chicano worldview as an undergraduate and later engaged in procedural activism as a former middle school teacher, he did not begin to completely author himself (both conceptually and procedurally) as a Chicano activist educator until graduate school.

Identity production is thus not linear, developmental, or a staged arrangement. Identity production may or may not follow a pattern even within the cultural means of a figured world (Holland et al., 1998). The conceptual and procedural aspects of a more complex identity production can be interconnected and may seem indistinguishable, or may be experienced as separate and partial depending on the place/space and time. Identity production also varies from individual to individual, even within a highly pre/scripted figured world. For example, while the 1960s and 1970s aspects of the Chicana and Chicano activist macro figured world may seem stagnant (or outdated), it is not quite the same figured world or identity as it was back then. Identities, like figured worlds, are always in a process of change and transition despite the durability of their cultural means.

Chicana and Chicano activist identity production in local Chicana and Chicano activist micro figured worlds is important in understanding how some Mexican Americans and other people can *become* Chicana and Chicano activist educators and/or embrace a strong desire and urgency to raise consciousness pero con ganas. Chicana and Chicano activist educators' struggle and commitment to work and change whitestream schools was consistently a part of being a Chicana and Chicano activist. This commitment was fundamentally important to their decisions to pursue careers in education and work in barrio school settings.

Chicana and Chicano activist identity production in figured worlds illustrates the fluidity, flexibility, and contextual significance of this process, while simultaneously highlighting the consistency of people's desire to produce more complex identities. For Chicana and Chicano activist educators, coming to realize they could help raise consciousness as educators, formally or informally, was due primarily to their immersion in Chicana and Chicano activist figured worlds. Chicana and Chicano identity functioned as a semiotic mediator, a constant and consistent reminder of their struggle for social justice and their activist agency.

Implications for Urban Education

Two broad implications for urban education can be drawn. The first implication relates to the ever-increasing demand for Latina and Latino teachers to serve the growing Latina and Latino student population. While local Chicana and Chicano activist figured worlds in colleges and universities encourage in Chicana and Chicano activists an "incredible desire to raise consciousness" (teach for social justice), few schools and colleges of education make active and formal attempts to recruit and support Chicana and Chicano students to enter teacher education programs. Chicana and Chicano students often lack information about how to pursue teaching as a career, and while colleges of education are only minutes walking distance away from ethnic/Chicana and Chicano studies departments in most universities, they are seas apart culturally and in terms of access. In addition, classes and majors in ethnic studies (Chicana and Chicano, African American, Native American, Asian American) are often devalued by education programs, and students find it difficult to take on additional course work (especially for financial reasons), or to double major, to pursue a career as an educator. Colleges of education can create outreach programs to actively recruit future teachers of color from ethnic studies departments.

A second implication complements most colleges of education's mission statements with social justice goals. In general, social justice translates into requiring education students to take one or two required courses with some kind of "diversity" focus. My suggestion: why not require that preservice teachers who will be working for the most part with urban students of color also take courses in ethnic studies departments to complement their teacher education course work? Specific ethnic studies courses that deal with historical oppression in terms of race, class, gender, and sexual orientation of people of color would complement the required "diversity-focused" course work with a more challenging perspective. All students, but especially sheltered students with low levels of critical, social, cultural, and political awareness of historically oppressed groups in the United States, have a lot to learn from ethnic studies courses, especially if they seek to be effective, supportive allies, and authentically caring educators. Through these courses, future educators of urban students can too learn not only to teach but also to raise consciousness, not only by teaching for social justice but also by teaching for social justice pero con ganas. The following chapter explores Chicana and Chicano activist educators sense-making and negotiation between their activist commitments and institutional expectations in whitestream schools.

5
Chicana and Chicano Educational Activism

The Chicana and Chicano activist educators in this book used the metaphor "playing the game" to make sense of their struggle to change whitestream schools from within.[1] The metaphor was generated directly from participant interviews. Twenty out of twenty-four participants used this metaphor (independently) to make sense of their struggle to work change into whitestream schools. I use it to specifically explore participants' expressed understanding of Chicana and Chicano educational activist agency. I also acknowledge that Chicana and Chicano activist educators simultaneously reproduce and resist power inequalities (Foley, 1990) by playing the game (Urrieta, 2005a).[2]

In Chicana and Chicano activist communities, as in other activist communities, the *vendido/a* (sellout or traitor) is someone who betrays his/her loyalties to a group or cause.[3] According to Smitherman (2000), playing the game and selling out allude to a way of expressing an awareness of consciously participating in the system of white institutions and power in U.S. society. Although Smitherman does not offer a definition of playing the game, she defines a sellout as "an African American who isn't DOWN WITH the black cause, one who betrays the race and compromises the COMMUNITY'S principles, usually for personal gain. . . . By extension, anyone who GOES FOR SELF and abandons his or her group's collective mission" (200; emphasis in original). Smitherman's definition of sellout is similar to the Chicana and Chicano vendido/a (A. Rendón, 1971), while playing the game is defined as participation in the system, but with alternative activist motives.

Chicanas and Chicanos' highly political and social justice agenda helped the participants understand the notion of playing the game at a conscious level, but in very complex and, at times, contradictory ways. The "tipping point"—of when a person plays the game or is in danger of selling out—because of its subversive yet compromising, even complicit, role in the process of whitestream indoctrination, was arbitrary.[4] Negotiating identity and activist commitments raised important questions because different interpretations reveal that there is more of a gray area than the two extremes allow.

Activist Educators

Participants described themselves as active agents, as activists in whitestream schools. To see themselves as activists in schools, participants reinterpreted activism from how it is traditionally understood to how they practiced it in their daily lives, on a moment-to-moment basis. Although some participants continued engaging in more traditional forms of activism, such as marching, boycotting, protesting, and walking out (especially the undergraduates), all of the participants valued highly their daily practices as activists because of the consistency of these practices over time. The alienating nature of whitestream schools led participants to talk about their daily interactions (proactions and reactions) as "strategic" and "calculating." For several, situations for "strategizing" arose from opportunities available to them in new roles or positions of power. Teachers, for example, had relative control over their classrooms, while professors often had academic freedom to dictate their curriculum. Participants' day-to-day practices were embedded with the hope that their practices would lead to what some referred to as a "domino effect" or a "ripple effect" to bring about larger societal change. Institutional degrees, to the participants, were often a complement to their activist identity, a means to enable, rather than disable, their activist agency, especially since the motivation to acquire these university degrees was to gain power to make greater changes to benefit marginalized communities. New forms of Chicana and Chicano activism were enabled in ways to be further explained, while activism was redirected from its traditional, romanticized focus. Participants felt like they were doing "something" and defined activism broadly as working for social justice and cultural change. Urgency for social change for all participants was more of a "hope" for long-term and "small," but meaningful, effects, rather than immediate or large "revolutionary" outcomes.

A rigid definition of activism does not encompass the range and degree to which the participants' activism was interpreted and reinterpreted. Participants always pushed for reinterpretation and change. How much reinterpretation was allowed was based on ambiguous notions of when a Chicana and Chicano activist educator was still playing the game, versus when a Chicana and Chicano had sold out. The tipping point between playing the game versus selling out varied from individual to individual, but the general understanding of a sellout as someone who betrays the collective cause for personal, mostly economic, gain or prestige did not. Participants believed that by playing strategically, the game could be changed, and playing was seen as a means to a greater end.[5]

"Don't Hate the Player, Hate the Game!"

Chicana and Chicano activist educators defined the game in the following ways. Henry, for example, stated: "Yeah, you know. I've realized there's a game out there, and then when you get into the workforce, you realize that not everybody agrees with you. You can't say what you want, and I think that's a big part of the game is knowing what to say, when to say it, and who to say it to."

Part of the activist agency invested in the daily practice of playing the game is the awareness of what the game is and how to play it critically. Henry's view of the game is learning how to do what is considered culturally or socially appropriate in whitestream society. Raquel also understood the game, but disagreed with its practices: "I know how to play the fuckin' game, but the game is fucked up! You know, it's fucked up? I'm not about playing power against other people, you know? Or all these like fucked-up ways that institutions would have you relate to people, or see people." Raquel too knows that the game is about power and learning how to navigate the power structures of whitestream society without compromising one's sense of self (J. Gutiérrez, 2003).

Playing the game was also understood as a means to acquire rank, power, or prestige to work change into the game from within for the betterment of marginalized people and communities. Alicia brought up the concept of playing the game during an interview and talked about it in the following way:

> ALICIA: I feel like I don't fit in the establishment sometimes. I do in a sense that I can play the game. I'm really good at that. But yet, it's some of the things I do and the way I conduct myself I think sometimes that ends up . . .
>
> LUIS: What do you mean by playing the game and how do you play it?
>
> ALICIA: [Speaking with a stronger tone of voice] *I play it very well.* The game is being able to talk to the white folks and be . . . And talk

> to them on their level and the way they're used to talking and learning how to keep certain things about my background, or the way I've grown up, or my being Mexican . . . leaving that to the side and kind of fitting in to what they're used to, their middle class, white values. Hypocritical! Sure, sure, um, does it bother me? Yes! Sometimes I go to sleep thinking, fuckin' hypocrite! I get really down on myself. Does it get me where I wanna go? *You're damn right it does!*

Although Alicia is not comfortable with playing the game and feels like a "hypocrite," she plays to continue her activist social justice agendas in teaching in a primarily Mexican American continuation high school. As a former single parent and continuation high school student, Alicia's mission and goals are clear.

> I went to continuation school and I was always seen as trash, 'cause of my kids. So, what I bring to the classroom is my experiences and the fact that I'm somebody who was not supposed to make it. I was somebody who was looked down like I was trash, like I was a nothing, like I was stupid, like I had messed up my life. Like I had dug a hole I could never get out of 'cause I had kids, because of where I was from, because of what I could and couldn't do. I'm one of the people who was never supposed to make it, but I did! And it's not to say, oh, pat myself on the back and say, oh, I'm wonderful! It's to say if the kids could see this, you know how much hope I could give to some of 'em that think they're lost already too and they can't be found anymore. My God, they're just babies!

Alicia later reflected on balancing out her multiple worlds and wondered if activist educators like herself can survive working in whitestream schools without compromise. She stated:

> I'm a teacher and am here in an educational setting and teaching kids and working with white people. Yet, their ideas are so different than mine, and I fully identify with being working class. And it causes conflict because again, it doesn't fit. It doesn't fit unless I play the game. And I don't always like playing the game because then I feel bad at night sometimes. I feel like a hypocrite. I feel like I've almost . . . not kissed ass, but . . . it's just like, why don't I just quit playing the game? I don't know. But then, I don't know, if you stop playing the game I don't know that you could actually survive.

"Survival" and continuity are important for Alicia because playing the game allows her the space to author herself as an activist educator and to continue working as a teacher doing the kind of work she wants to do and "going where she wants to go." Going where she wants to go does not involve personal and economic self-gain, but grants her the access that she needs to impact the lives of students in similar situations to the one she was in when she was their age.

Interestingly, Alicia equated white racial identity with being middle class, as did several other participants. Not only was Alicia "racializing" class (Hatt-Echeverría and Urrieta, 2003), but she was also indirectly defining her understanding of the game. For Alicia the game was not only about race, gender, biological reproduction, and educational success issues in whitestream schools but also about social class. Alicia, despite her new social position and income as a teacher, still claimed to "fully identify with being working class." Alicia's understanding of multiple oppressions was reflected in her herstory-in-person (H-I-P), by society's negative positioning of her single-mother status and living in poverty as low-class "trash," and other experiences she tried to conceal from her colleagues such as, for example, having to feed her children candy bars for breakfast during those difficult times.

Other phrases and words participants used to describe or allude to playing the game included Samuel's "being strategic," Mariana's "bending rules," Henry's "doing what you have to do even if you don't agree," Jaime's "infiltrating the system," and Rodrigo's "jumping through hoops to get to where you want to go." Bourdieu's concept of rules highlights that the rule (like the game) does not (completely) determine practice "when there is more to be gained by obeying it than by disobeying it" (22). The gain for the participants was not in social or economic gain, but in the spirit of giving back to the community. Playing the game involved a conscious awareness and understanding of activist agency (with its potential and limits) in working within whitestream schools with the motivation to ultimately change these schools (even if minimally).

None of the participants embraced the game, but all played it and were conscious of that even if they did not like it. Samuel stated:

> I think we all play it [the game] in a limited sense, some to a higher degree than others. I play it just as much as I want to. But, I'm maladjusted to these types of games, and I don't like these types of games these people play. I wear my heart on my sleeve. So, I'm not good at

being strategic. I'm not good at swallowing pain, and I don't play the game well at times. And that's fine with me. I think for me when the point comes when I ever start to adjust and start liking these games will be an indication I've lost something along the way, you know? Now the game is fucked up in a lot of ways, man, but we all play it to a certain extent 'cause we all show up here [the university] every day.

Samuel recognized the danger in playing the game and "losing" (negotiating) parts of himself as well as "swallowing pain" along the way. Samuel did not like the game because it was often experienced in painful ways, and he admitted that he was not good at playing it. Even with these considerations, Samuel was also conscious of his participation in it. This awareness of participation in the game is precisely where the activist agency to improvise change in whitestream schools lies.

Playing as Activist Agency

Critical innovation and improvisation are the starting points for change when people in practice (as we all are) are conscious and aware of their agency, especially activist agency. There are always moments that elicit our response in social/cultural and professional interactions. The fulfillment or lack of fulfillment of those expected responses depends on the agency people have to respond accordingly or not. Participants were aware of their activist agency in playing the game. The "playing" in playing the game is important because performance in the game was seen as strategic and activist and always had the potential to work change into the imperfections of the system.

Part of the energy invested in playing the game was precisely because the participants saw or knew of the "imperfections" or incomplete totality of the game or system. Most of the participants were well versed in social theory and knew that the totality of the system like hegemony cannot be perfect (Gramsci, Hoare, and Nowell-Smith, 1971). If it were a total system, a revolt would surely occur. When talking about her work in the classroom as a form of activist agency, Raquel shared: "I think what we're trying to do (as activist educators) is find those cracks in the system, *no*? . . . Because like hegemony, their control isn't perfect. It's not perfect. It's not total, even when we get to a place where we feel it is." The "cracks" Raquel refers to are the imperfections of the game (system) and the very sites to exert activist agency at the right time and in the right spaces. Like the interstices in Foucault's (1990) analysis of power, the cracks in Raquel's interpretation are the sites of opportunity to exert activist agency. When the willingness to seek out the cracks in the game is surrendered, activist agency is also "sold out" with this loss of will, and the rules/system/game become(s) normalized.

David's example (to follow) illustrates how playing the game allows for the exercise of agency through improvisation, especially when encountering new positions of power. According to Holland and colleagues (1998), improvisation can be mediated with artifacts and discourses in self-directed symbolization. Self-directed symbolization means that people plan and strategize for change and use symbols, discourses, artifacts, and other cultural means to help mediate the desired outcome. David, who reflected on his accomplishments, illustrates this type of improvisation well.

> Because I've been in the right place at the right time, I've been able to do some things. Whether it's in government, whether it's on a school board, whether it's as an administrator, just being involved in a set of policy conversations which utilize research to make better decisions about educational equity and access to resources, particularly for minority kids, and more specifically for Latino kids and Latino adults, not just kids. But, I think I have contributed to that agenda. Again, not just myself, but a whole bunch of folks like me. I think we've all . . . with our research and our activism made a difference.
>
> In government, putting in that every school receiving federal funds had to have a program to serve limited English-proficient students. [Speaking emphatically] *That was not there before; it is there now.* And it will probably always be there. I'd say again not just because of me, but I happened to be in a position where I could write that into the bill. I could argue for it, and I could be sure politically it got adopted thanks to some Latinos in Congress. It wasn't all my doing but I was there. And I can say maybe if I wasn't there it might not have happened, or someone else would have to do it. And so I would think those are some very specific policy and practice, and I hate to say this, and scientific contributions I may have made, or helped others make, that . . . made a difference.

Issues important to highlight in David's case in terms of playing the game and activist agency include the importance of time and space (context) and of being in the "right place" at the "right time" to "do some things." This positioning is not a random occurrence of "luck" because players in the game have/or make space for activist agency (although at times heavily constrained) to author themselves and their practices in the game. David's credentials, research, rank, and prestige enabled his recruitment into a position of power: the figured world of government and politics. Space and time (context) cannot be underestimated; neither can being aware (by strategically playing) of when a "crack" in the system emerges, or can emerge, and how activist agency can be self directed and exercised within the cracks in the system. So, while activist agency is strategic and may involve some degree of self-direction (planning), it is also practiced and actualized in spontaneous, moment-to-moment interaction in which a player seizes available opportunities to change the game.

Activist agency is also invested in creating and using networks and coalitions, the "bunch of folks like me" that David mentioned. Through associations of like-minded people (activists) in similar positions who are willing to take risks in exercising activist agency by playing together, David considered his work in government and in public policy to have "made a difference." David recognized that his critical decisions and crucial actions in power positions brought about legislative change to benefit the Latina and Latino community at a national level.

David understood the agency invested in his social, cultural, and professional positioning. This example of access to power forms the "secondary benefits" Bourdieu (1977) refers to when alluding to the "prestige and respect which almost invariably reward an action apparently motivated by nothing other than *pure, disinterested* respect for the rule" (22). In David's case, he used the respect and prestige acquired through his academic credentials and work as a scholar to "write" and to "argue" his activist agenda to make "better decisions" for "educational equity and access" for minorities, but especially the Latina and Latino community. His voiced emphasis on "that was not there before, it is there now" and the statement, "Maybe if I wasn't there, it might not have happened" is recognition and self-authorship of his activist identity and agency in playing the game.

Readers considering themselves to be more grassroots activists might wonder if what I'm proposing is really activism. The temptation to judge or to create a Richter scale of activism and authenticity limits on who are or are not real activists is what makes studying daily moment-to-moment activism a complicated issue. Appreciating the activist agency embedded within my participants' practices is critical for network and coalition building. Collective networks have far more potential for change than intergroup conflicts over who the real activists are and what real activist practices should look like. When different interest groups, even within the same ethnic/racial group, focus their attention on fighting with each other, this internal conflict distracts them from the larger goal of challenging the whitestream structure in U.S. society.

Moving activism a step further metaphorically, although without the professional experience David had, Jaime, an undergraduate, provided the most active description of the activist agency in playing the game. He referred to playing the game as a form of "infiltration" of the system: "You do have to play within the system, but you infiltrate the system. . . . If not, you're just . . . outside the system. You're not accomplishing much. You're wearing yourself out. . . . That's what you have to do. That's what I'm going to have to do. . . . You should have a goal. Goals. If you stray too far away, then you just fell into the system you're trying to infiltrate and change."

For Jaime, playing the game was necessary, but he framed it within an activist agenda for change. By focusing on goals and not "straying" too far from accomplishing them, Jaime said participating in the system is a form of "infiltration" with the potential for institutional change.[6]

Normalizing the Game

According to Alim (2004), the response, "that's the way it is," with "it" referring to the system, usually marks the end of a conversation about questioning white supremacy and the whitestream inculcation process, when it should be the beginning of a theoretical and practical dialogue for social/cultural change. "Why are things the way they are?" is an essential question and critical point of departure for activists. The statement "that's the way it is" is usually a self-defeatist response that normalizes the game by taking the agency out of the dialogic interaction process, the space between reproduction and resistance, structure and agency.

The uncritical, almost mechanical performance of the expected prescriptions of the system is theoretically when "selling out" occurs (either consciously or unconsciously). According to Rafael, people who "surrender" to "that's the way it is" do not live in the "real world," but in a destructive "artificial world." "I don't think they're [people] in touch with their world. They're very much an active part of . . . the artificial world around us. And some of them may understand how it [the system/game] works, but they've surrendered themselves to the 'Oh, well, that's the way it is.' 'Cause the world really is not concrete and asphalt and all that, the world is really trees, forests, dirt, sand. That's the real world. That's reality. The natural world is the real world. This is not natural."

Rafael argued that participation in the system should be a compromise and never a complete surrender. He warned: "It's pretty hard not to [invest in the system] because it's so much a part of us, but there's little things we can do. There's little things we should be doing. 'Cause the system is not just ultimately destroying us, it's destroying the world, the natural world. Once the natural world goes, that's it. This artificial illusion called city and city-state is gonna just collapse."

Rafael proposed the following solution for playing the game: "Keep on trucking. Keep doing it [activism]. Don't ever sell out to the system . . . completely, though. To a certain degree we all do. I have. Anyone in the system has to have sold out to a certain degree. Teachers, to be a real teacher, a true teacher, don't sell out completely. Make it a 60/40 proposition. Not even a 50/50. Sell out 40 percent, live simply, and keep the 60 percent of yourself."

Rafael's statements and "formula" for playing the game without selling out (completely) support the perspective that Chicana and Chicano activist educators simultaneously reproduce and resist power inequalities by playing the game. The ways that participation in the system serves to legitimize it was greatly debated in the 1960s. Consciously playing the game and being aware of their activist agency was a constant struggle (or point of contention) for most participants. Participants always had alternative motives, activist motives, other than being "pure, disinterested" "rule" followers.

Since there are no clear definitions of where the line is drawn between playing the game and selling out, this dilemma leads to multiple tipping points and complex issues. Accusations and judgment over selling out abound in general, as do competition-like bouts of who is more "down" (committed) with the cause, but it is in daily practice and through a cultural production lens that activist agency can be assessed in its current, post–civil rights, institutional, professional activist practice. Indeed, all participants refused to conform to the justification "that's just the way it is." Chicana and Chicano activist educators continued to look for the "cracks" in the system to exert their activist agency, whether through a conscious and formulated compromise such as Rafael's, or through other interpretations of the potential of playing the game.

For Raquel, to stop working for change and trans/formation in whitestream schools would be to simply "give up on the world," and she refused. She said: "I hope if I ever get to this place where I'm saying you can't possibly resist in these institutions [whitestream schools] and you can't possibly find space in which to develop transformative . . . sh!!!" Raquel made a sharp sound and raised her hands in disgust and continued, "I've given up on the world!!!" Consistent with the Mexican folk saying, *la esperanza muere al último* (hope dies last), for Raquel to give up on the world implied a surrender of her activist motivations and hope, which she refused to do.

People of color who stop working for change in the system, for Henry, are no longer people of color. Henry equated the refusal of some "Hispanics" to change the game to being white and middle class: in essence, to selling out. Henry equated Hispanics' support of the power structure of privilege that ultimately disproportionately benefits whites to ideological whiteness. Participants generally refused to "surrender" and accept the justification that the system cannot change or that they did not have sufficient agency to act upon the world.

The dilemmas behind playing the game and selling out were often unresolved. Some expressed guilt, while others affirmed that they were not sellouts. Anabel, for example, stated: "I definitely don't see myself as a sellout, well maybe because I still have a working-class existence. I don't have a big home. I mean, I certainly have a good life, but I certainly haven't . . . I'm not among the elite so?" Anabel justified that she had not sold out by identifying with being working class, again "racializing" class. She also reconfirmed her community commitment by stating that, as opposed to a white professor, to be an activist scholar for her was not a choice, but a responsibility. Anabel added, "I don't see it [to be an activist educator] as a choice when your community is in crisis. For me, this is where white academics . . . don't understand the white privilege. . . . They don't have a community they see a felt need for at all. They don't see it, so they don't feel a pull, they don't understand it . . . at all." Community commitment and community crises placed an immense burden of responsibility on Chicana and Chicano activist educators to struggle to change whitestream schools. Participants like Anabel expressed that they did not see their activist commitments as a choice, but as a necessary community responsibility. When responding to the issue of "guilt" amongst some Chicana and Chicano activist educators over "not doing enough" or about the fear of being called a sellout, Elena simply concluded by saying, "If someone feels guilty about that [selling out], then they're probably somewhat of a sellout."

Generally, participating in the game uncritically, not seeking the opportunities to exert activist agency, or not seeking the allies and networks to create change in whitestream schools all contributed to the normalization of the game. The justification "that's the way it (the system/game) is" (to the participants) represented a call to surrender, when hope (*la esperanza*) for change was lost and agency was subverted. Participants said that when hope is lost (*cuando la esperanza muere*) is when people become pessimistic, cynical, and sometimes direct their energies to capitalist self-gain. Recall Smitherman's (2000) sellout, a person who is "abandoning his or her group's collective mission." "That's the way it is" to Chicana and Chicano activist educators is not an "acceptable" answer and, most important, not the end of the conversation, but only the beginning.

With particular attention to the concept of cultural production, the "playing" in playing the game is the conscious awareness and exertion (whenever possible) of activist agency. Activist agency is resisting structural oppression in reactive and reductive ways, as well as through productive, proactive, conscious, and creative activities at all moments of practice. Chicana and Chicano activist educators were aware that a game (whitestream/malestream system) is in force and that the critical performance of playing in *that* game can lead to gains toward social justice and change. The normalization of that game and the subsequent full surrender to that system is what constituted selling out. This normalization, or complete surrender and uncritical participation in the system, occurred when Chicanas and Chicanos lost la esperanza in the Chicana and Chicano vision of a better world.

None of the participants embraced the game, and all realized that it is an unavoidable reality, but the system is not total and complete. Like hegemony and power, the system has "cracks" in it, allowing for the exercise of agency, especially activist agency, at the "right time" and in the "right place." Participating (playing) in the game and the activist agency involved in playing were important to the participants, as well as recognizing the dangers of being content with "limited," and/or "short-term" gains, particularly their actions that could normalize the game. For Chicana and Chicano activist educators in whitestream schools, there was an ongoing struggle to not just play the game but also to change it. Playing, in this sense, became more of a strategic exercise of activist agency, an agency more likely to seek out and seize opportunities for change.

Community Commitments

The community commitment of Chicana and Chicano activist educators took on three levels of responsibility: (1) a responsibility to the larger Chicana and Chicano, Latina and Latino imagined community in the United States, (2) a commitment to forming alliances with other historically oppressed groups with similar ideologies, as well as white allies, both in the United States and abroad, and (3) a responsibility to local community issues. Chicana and Chicano activist educators' commitment to local community issues or those issues closest to their everyday lives and current career trajectories made whitestream schools their most immediate targets for change.

Participants generally defined activists as people with a critical literacy of the world who understood the issues that affected not only raza but also all oppressed people. Having this critical conceptual literacy was only a step toward activism. To be an activist educator meant also doing something in the physical world to challenge oppression in whitestream schools. Doing something is where variety in interpretation occurred. Doing something meant different things to different participants. These activities ranged from formal protests to teaching a unit on the genocide of Native Americans to fourth-grade students. Consistent across participants' narratives about activism was a sense of urgency to act upon the world in support of and for the educational rights of the communities that they felt most committed to.

Negotiating Change in Four Contexts

Negotiation was the process by which Chicana and Chicano activist educators *understood* the expectations whitestream schools had of them and *made sense* of their activist agency to maneuver themselves (play) within and around those expectations. Maneuvering, especially around those expectations considered to be oppressive, was interpreted as an activist strategy for change. Strategizing for change involved a dialogic process by Chicana and Chicano activist educators to evaluate which activist practices they could, or could not, fuse into their practices as educators.

Participants believed in the possibility that playing the game could be a means to a greater end. Time and context were important to what were considered "appropriate negotiations" of activism in particular whitestream schools. In spaces like the university environment, certain forms of activism like protests and marches were practiced more often than in K–12 whitestream schools, while more direct person-to-person contact and personal decisions were often seen as more strategic forms of daily, moment-to-moment activism. Despite the differences in practices, participants expressed a commitment to change whitestream schools and viewed themselves as negotiators for change. Participants' final narratives of the four contexts researched will now be presented.

Undergraduates

Julián. I'm really involved in several projects I consider important. The first is MEChA's [Movimiento Estudiantil Chicano de Aztlán] annual Raza Youth Conference. We target the Chicana and Chicano, Latina and Latino community and bring over 1,100 high school students to campus. We bring community spokespeople like Antonia Darder, Sal Castro, and Michelle Cerros to motivate students to consider higher education. We have Danza [Aztec dance groups], out of respect for our indigenous ancestors, and in general, the conference provides students with information about college and financial aid they might not get otherwise. Different community groups come and give workshops or presentations and focus on gender and sexuality, on organizing *mujeres* (women), on sweatshops, on Zapatismo, and on identity issues: topics students don't typically talk about in school. During lunch we have a college fair, and local Spanish radio station DJs play music and give out prizes. There is a parent component to the conference held in Spanish because we realize parents don't get a lot of information on college, especially in Spanish. We end with a speaker, usually a Chicana or Chicano professor. This event is very rewarding, and I look forward to it even though it's so much work.

My second involvement is with a university committee that addresses outreach and student recruitment issues by funding outreach projects. The project we run works with two local high schools. We do peer counseling, mentoring, and tutoring to get Latino students to this university. The university component of this project works on creating a university policy to raise the minority presence on campus. Since Proposition 209, the percentage of Chicano/Latino students at this campus has dropped by almost 50 percent. There's twelve people on this committee, only three people of color. Two of us are students and one Latina professor, who may as well be white; the rest are all white. For being an admissions/recruitment committee, they have no community or student input, except for us, but it's hard because there's only so much we can say and do when facing people like the vice chancellor who's also on the committee.

I will give back to the community by becoming a high school teacher when I graduate, an activist teacher. Education is just so important because it leads you to understand yourself, your struggles, and your identity. Educational justice can help create social justice, and social justice can help create other types of justice needed. For me, I went through a lot in bilingual programs and so that will be my focus, even if it's now illegal, that, and access to higher education. Before, I used to think a lot of the kids in my high school didn't come to higher education because they didn't work hard enough; now I know they were never given a chance.

Isadora. Through MEChA we offer Chicana Leadership Retreats, and it's amazing what Chicanas go through, especially older Chicanas in abusive relationships and stuff. It's like, first you're told not to feel proud of who you are culturally, then you're told that you're ugly, and some are sexually abused. There's just so much pain, there's a lot of violence, a lot of disrespect towards women and girls. That is where my commitment and activism is centered now. Later I plan to teach. I don't want to be a policymaker. That's too behind the scene. I want to be directly involved.

Ever since I worked with my uncle I wanted to teach, but now even more so. I want to be more actively involved in my community, and I realize our raza youth are brilliant! They're just put down a lot. There are low expectations of them, but there is so much potential there. Before, it was just like I want to get Chicanas and Chicanos into college and just stop there. Now I want to get Chicanas and Chicanos into college, and I want to see them bring along another fifty with them. I want to facilitate in my future students a sense of self-empowerment and community commitment.

I realize in institutional settings you have to make compromises, like with testing, right? I know as a teacher I have to administer standardized tests, but I can also have a critical discussion with students on why these tests suck. I guess it's about playing the game, like doing certain things that don't go with my personal ideology but are enforced by the institution. If you're not taking enough risks, you're compromising too much, but it's hard though because selling out can be an unconscious process too. I mean, it's hard to keep struggling, to keep being critical of everything, and people just get tired, especially when you're the only one. But again, I think when you start worrying about your own personal gain and you stop looking at the bigger picture, that's when you've sold out. I want to always be an activist, especially as a teacher. I don't want to sell out!

Teachers

Henry. At first, my whole focus in teaching was on students of color, but slowly I realized if you don't teach white students about privilege and oppression to change their mindset, how are things ever going to change? If you don't bring whites into the fold and say, hey, this is what's going on and this is the role you play in it, you are missing a huge part of the population that needs to be educated and informed. So every semester I focus on themes that get my students to think critically about issues and what they can do to make change. I see it like a trickle-down thing where I send the message, and hopefully they become active and send the message to other people as well.

Activism is sometimes seen as you gotta pick up a picket sign, or you have to do a boycott. I think activism is any time you make a concerted effort and go out there and change things. Where you don't just realize how messed up things are and are not doing anything about it. If you know things need to be altered, then you find an avenue you feel fits your strengths and go out there and try to make change. For some people that could be writing a book, like Kozol who wrote *Savage Inequalities*. That's his way of trying to say things are messed up and we need to change them. I'm an activist. I think my strength is working with young people and passing on the information I'm trying to give them, but also drawing from them the information they don't always realize they have.

There's a major game to play out there. Like when you join the workforce you realize not everyone is going to agree with you. You can't say what you want and that's a big part of playing that game, knowing what to say, when to say it, and who to say it to. The same is true for me as a teacher, like what I talk about or the way I talk about things with my students is not necessarily the same around my colleagues. Sometimes I don't want to get into it; I don't want to hear their mouth. Getting your teaching credential is part of playing the game. You have to pass these tests, regardless of how irrelevant they are to your profession. There are so many facets of playing the game. It's not simplistic at all. I mean, it goes anywhere from how you play the game in your classroom, how you play it school wide, out in the baseball field, how you deal with testing, how you deal with administrators that treat students like shit and you don't agree with them. How do you approach that situation? It's tough. You've gotta have multiple personalities essentially in order to survive.

My views about making change have also changed. I tend to get more pessimistic now, even about me teaching because I realize I may not really see the changes I'd like to see in this country, not in my lifetime. But that doesn't mean I'm going to stop being involved; even if one day I do stop teaching, I'll find some organization to get involved with or something. But when you see propositions like 187, the anti-immigrant, 209, the anti-affirmative action, and 227, the English only, passed as laws, then you do get a little down. It's like, instead of making progress we are going in reverse. And even through my teaching, yeah, maybe some kids do acquire a more critical perspective and begin to see the importance of race in this country, but I'm only one lonely voice compared to everything else, including other teachers giving them the exact opposite message.

Regardless, when you come to the realization I did as a Chicano and you don't find it critical to somehow make change, then you're not a person of color! You're just not! You're white 'cause you don't give a shit! That's the way I see it. So if you really have a heart and you realize how fucked up things are, then you need to get out there and do something about it. So what if you're middle class and you're living pretty good! The poor in this country are expanding day by day; how can you sleep comfortably at night with your hundred-thousand-dollar job and nice house, knowing so many people are suffering?! I mean, you benefited as a Chicano and became middle class out of the backs and dead bodies of other Chicanos who suffered. That's ridiculous! So that's why my mindset, that's why I do what I have to do, and that's what mainstream people don't have to do if they don't want to because they're already sitting pretty.

I realize institutions enforce conformity, but in some ways the level of that conformity is up to the individual. Some people feel pressure to conform to the point they give up their activism. They usually say it's taking too much of their time. So, without a doubt, institutions enforce conformity, but there's a spectrum, and some people conform a lot more than others, while others are able to hold on more to who they are. But, how many people who do not get involved in institutions are actually able to say they made a major impact? Like who do we have right now, like a Malcolm X or Martin Luther King, that's an activist, that's not part of an institution and is really trying to make change? I can't think of anyone.

So I don't think it's so much about an either/or, black or white thing anymore when it comes to selling out: it's more about the gray areas. If you are a Chicano activist, and you enter different institutional arenas with the intention of changing them, then it's gotta involve negotiations and compromises. It's like watching a movie. You don't always just love or hate it, there are always elements of movies you appreciate and others you don't. It's the same with people, and the same can be said for the situation in this country: for some, it's so messed up nothing can be done about it so why even try? For others, this is the greatest country in the world, and it's better than most places so just stop complaining and enjoy your piece of the pie. But I don't want to live in Disneyland, and I hate to think nothing can be done either. Do I feel guilty about not doing enough sometimes? Yeah, I do, but that's part of my whole motivation to continue.

Juanita. With my credential in hand I was able to be a bit more . . . pushy, I guess you can say when it came to getting a job. I remember I asked for specific things from the principal in order to accept the job, and my dad and husband thought I should just be grateful I was getting a position. I took the job and I began to get really involved; I got the teachers on the move when I got here. The principal who hired me, *aunque era Latino* (even though he was Latino), had parents from Mexico and everything, *no hablaba* (didn't speak) a word of Spanish, but *hay veces pienso que se hacía pendejo* (sometimes I think he would just play stupid). He would hire people as bilingual teachers, and he wouldn't even know if they spoke Spanish! Hello! So I pushed him on that, and from then on, I became part of the hiring committee and would interview candidates *in* Spanish. So he started hiring more bilingual teachers; we made sure they were speaking Spanish and were proud of it.

I just became very active. Like, we didn't have any books in Spanish in our school library, so I gave him a hard time about it until we finally got some. We had notes and letters going home to parents incorrectly written in Spanish—what an insult to the parents! At first I translated, and now another teacher who is better in Spanish corrects them, but we also have a new secretary that is fully bilingual. I also translate at parent meetings and am involved with the school and district bilingual advisory committee. I started to also put pressure on our local high school to increase their college attendance rates. I went over there and asked one day what the college attendance rate was, and the counselor looked so proud when he said they were now up to 21 percent! I looked at him in disbelief and said, "Oh my God, you should be embarrassed!" So I started this program with the local community college to increase their college attendance rate.

I'm also committed to taking my students on a yearly field trip to a local prestigious university. It's amazing, but I think something so simple can make a big difference, even if it is a hassle to get buses, emergency permits, lunches, and all that bureaucratic stuff. It's all extra work, and most teachers are not willing to do it. But I think the little things matter, even the way we teach a lesson. For example, my kids have to write journals with their parents almost every day, just to make sure their communication with their parents is ongoing. I allow them to write them in English and Spanish, even though it's against the law. I try to incorporate a lot of what I learned in my credential program, especially what I read in Paulo Freire's work on critical pedagogy and Luis Moll's work on funds of knowledge.

Most of the time I feel like I can get away with a lot here, or like I'm in a safety zone, especially after Proposition 227, but I think I'm partly responsible too for creating it. When I first started, few people were critical here and almost no one took risks. Now we have eleven fully bilingual teachers here, barely enough for our school, but all very, very proud of their roots and pro-bilingual. We have Adriana who goes all out for national Hispanic Awareness Month, which she calls Chicano History Month. We have Johnny, who is so proud of his Mexican roots he had a *banda* (Mexican folk music band) at his wedding and not a single song in English. Ana, and some Salvadoreños, and the younger Chicanas and Chicanos especially like to rub it off on just how proud they are, but it's great! I think all the white teachers are used to us, and our pride, and they just kind of go along with it. They really don't have a problem with it, unless they aren't saying anything. So it's really quite nice here.

For the Cinco de Mayo program you might have noticed how most of us, the Chicanos, did very critical performances. We see it as an opportunity to raise consciousness with the parents too. There was the farmworker protest music, Johnny's students' critical historical rendition of the Battle of Puebla and the French invasion of Mexico, and my kids did "Una Mañanita Alegre" [song] by Los Lobos, and I chose it because it has the same verses in English and Spanish. That's because I have twenty students this year, ten of which are English Only because their parents wouldn't sign the permits for bilingual instruction. Through that song, I was able to make them all sing half of the song in English and half in Spanish. I don't know if you noticed but I had this little *gringa* (white girl) go out there and shout ¡*Viva México!* (Long live Mexico!). I did that on purpose because it's so sad that a lot of my Latino students don't want to speak Spanish anymore. I wanted them to see what they see as the status symbol was yelling in Spanish too and there's nothing wrong with it, they have nothing to be ashamed of.

I'm working on funding to start an after-school language academy next year. I think we'll be teaching three languages, including Spanish, Italian, and French. I'm doing this so there isn't such a negative stigma attached to the Spanish and also to create a safe place for those kids who do want to continue learning, reading, writing, and speaking Spanish. How ironic we have to create a safety zone to speak our own language, right? Maybe this will help the other kids to feel proud of their language and who they are. So the shame doesn't, well, if it's gonna happen, at least it doesn't start so early.

I have become a silent activist, even though I like to talk a lot. I'm a silent activist in taking what's near me, finding the injustice, getting angry at it, and trying to do something about it here at our school. I mean, I am interested in what happens everywhere else, but now that I'm over thirty I realize I can't do it all. I have to stay here; whatever happens here I have control over, not what's out there. I would love to see a lot more Latinos go to universities, and not just community colleges. Not that there's anything wrong with community colleges, but for students to be inspired to go on to major universities and not just stop at a BA, get a master's! You know, get a doctorate, go on and do wonderful things and still be Latino, still be Chicano. And be proud you're that. You know, be a doctor and help out your community! But, on a more realistic level, right now and right here at this school is what matters most to me.

Graduate Students

Miguel. I taught third grade in a small, primarily agricultural community in the San Joaquin Valley for six years. The student population was 99 percent Latino, 70 percent of which were migrant farm workers. While I taught, I got my bilingual cross-cultural teaching credential and later a master's in curriculum and instruction at the local state university. But, I had idealized and romanticized notions of giving back, especially since the wider community was also overwhelmingly predominantly Latino, with the exception of a few older Japanese Americans. I quickly became very involved with, and committed to, the students and their families. I wanted to be a voice for the voiceless and those were the Spanish speaking students in the community. But my idealism was shattered by the reality that people are people and politics are politics regardless of race. All of the politicians and community leaders in this town were all second- and third-generation Mexicans and they played dirty and were against any kind of change, especially change to benefit the first-generation immigrant.

I was very conflicted as I tried to give my service in a war zone where basically my own people like me were screwing my very own people like me. Immigrant and language status created a situation in the school and wider community where recent immigrants were treated like second-class citizens. I tried to counter this through my teaching, but I also became actively involved with the city council, the local board of education, and the teachers' union. Through larger involvement I began to see the importance of policy issues that eventually brought me to graduate school. I see the relevance of second-language-learning research being produced, but I feel it ignores the larger policy issues.

I felt I had good ideas that were not being listened to and were not going to be listened to unless I had the proper credential, the PhD. As a proactive teacher you are inundated and fully immersed in your classroom and never have time to think about how you fit into the larger structure, and I felt the most effective changes were in the larger arena, for example, where issues of school finance are handled. As a teacher I was able to implement some change, but I realized those changes I could make were going to be limited. I also realized the issues of the classroom cannot be divorced from the issues of the larger community, and micro-level issues were interrelated with macro-level issues, and thus the importance of policy.

As a graduate student in educational policy, I still consider myself an activist not only in my academic work but also through the activities I decide to engage in. For example, I sit on numerous committees, one of which is the affordable student housing committee. Through this committee we stopped the university from taking affordable housing away from graduate students, especially in this area where the housing cost is outrageous. But, most important, I think through my work and conscious decisions as a researcher and future scholar.

For example, at first I was uncomfortable with my role as researcher, especially when entering primarily Latino communities. I think what my white colleagues saw as "interesting" and novel, for me was not. I saw the Latino school sites we studied as yet other manifestations of experience, very private experiences we had no right to go into and write about. I think my role as researcher and my university affiliation also made me suspect in the Latino community. Was I going to sell them out? With time, I have begun to reconcile these issues and to see the value of research.

My biggest struggle was entering the classroom as a researcher because as a teacher the classroom was sacred to me, and I felt like an outsider invading the space in my new role. I also felt a strong commitment to give back. If I was given access to the site, then it was with the condition I give something back. I think I've negotiated between myself as a Chicano and the research process because I realize I can't carry the burden all the time. So, for example, when teachers ask for feedback, I usually alternate and give them feedback only on the days I don't take fieldnotes, so the days I do take fieldnotes I can distance myself from the data a bit more.

I still see myself as an activist, a researcher, and an academic. But this is an evolving or perhaps supplementary academic activism according to what I have been trained to do, and it reaches an audience often too comfortable with who they are and their own intellectualized definitions of the way things work. I think it's a different strategy. When I was younger I was trained in grassroots activism, and this activism is for a different audience. The middle class, to me, is a more important, schooled audience because it has the most pull, and when you provide alternative perspectives to this audience, you can have greater change. But my role in the university does not undo my responsibility to community. I often speak to community groups and provide information in Spanish to Spanish-speaking parents on how to better play the game and navigate the educational system. So, my role in the community is just as important as my role in the institution, and it's not community service. It's part of who I am.

To reach the middle-class audience, though, I now have to take on the role of assistant professor. This is a new academic culture that sometimes is quite challenging, from the social niceties of cocktail parties to the very elitist culture of the academic conference, especially in policy studies. I will play that culture when I have to, but not at the expense of my primary culture because I realize I can't become like everyone else [whites] because I'm not like everyone else. I can't and don't want to change who I am as a Chicano academic, and that comes with other dilemmas and burdens.

One of those burdens of people of color is we are always in a position where we have to educate whites about social justice issues because they won't do it on their own—not out of their own motivation. That's the whole burden thing: how far are you gonna carry this burden? Because you're gonna have to stop everywhere on this journey to help whites understand different perspectives, and the bad thing is you're gonna have to do double time after to catch up. Another is the issue of having to prove you're smart. It's not enough to have earned a degree because there is always the doubt maybe you didn't really deserve it. Yet another is the issue of having to represent and be the spokesperson for your racial group and at times for all minorities. And I refuse! I'm not going to be a spectacle. I'm not going to play the game of educating every white person I meet and much less of having to prove I'm smart and worthy of a top-ten university job.

In policy circles I'm often one of two or three minorities; usually, the other minorities are black. Most often I'm the only Chicano/Latino, and not only is my physical presence important but also the alternative perspective I bring to the table. My goal is to shed more light on ignored issues. Issues of race and how minorities might be affected seem to be secondary. In general, policy makers and analysts feel if they address general issues they will automatically address race issues. I think those sort of assumptions are the ones that I can begin to provide a little more information on. I represent something different. I've lived something different, and I have a strong sense of duty and responsibility to express that in my work. Now I have the ability to express my differences and different perspectives, and it would be a shame if I didn't.

Therese. I see my activism now as being more professional. It's like a professional type of activism. How can I use the tools and the skills that I've acquired through my educational experience to raise money for community education groups, for example? I want to make a larger-scale impact, to make sure models that don't exist exist, especially in this post-209 no–affirmative action era. As a researcher, I want to be on admissions committees with big policy people who are just pushing paper. I want to actually present and confront them with informed research on access to higher education issues for the Chicano/Latino community. I think I'm just starting to evolve, and I don't know to what degree it's good, or it's just changing.

I mean we still do, the Chicano organization I'm affiliated with, we still support all these grassroots groups. Almost everyone in there is a leader of different organizations, but I think there comes a point where you realize your strengths, and you're like, okay, what can I do with those strengths and how can I be most effective with my time? Regardless, education to me is key, especially higher education because it's the doorway to opportunity. Education really enables you to see the world through a whole different lens. I think our community lacks in the number of Chicana mentors in education. I mean, there are a few like Patricia Gándara, Angela Valenzuela, and Kris Gutiérrez, but not many. I want to be one of those Chicana mentors.

Professors

Phillip. The activist agenda to me was to increase the representation of Chicanos and other students of color on university campuses, to increase graduation rates, and to increase our presence in graduate school. Now the agenda's matured into preparing the next generation of Chicanos committed to improving the social conditions of the Chicano community. So I'm not interested in having brown faces with white middle-class dreams, or middle-class "Highspanics." I'm not interested in working with students who just want to get a nice cushy job and make a whole lot of money. I'm interested in working with students who come from communities where they had to overcome a lot of barriers to even get to college. It's about helping Mexicanos who are more working class, poor working families, that have been able to overcome that and help them go to college so they can then return and help their communities.

It's been as a professor that I've gained a sense that it is important to do scholarship, and that's kind of where I'm also at now. I can see a little bit more value, actually the activism involved in being a scholar. I'm now seeing activism has different forms; it's not all about protesting, concrete outcomes, or tangible outcomes. Sometimes activism has more abstract ways, less tangible ways. So I feel a little bit better about what I do as a professor and still see my work as activist kind of work. I think I've been able to produce some knowledge and ideas practitioners can actually use, some activists can use, and say, yes, this is what we want to change. There is power in changing the way a conversation is going, changing the topic of a conversation, or informing the structure of a conversation. I just published an article that got quite a bit of attention, and I was invited to be the keynote speaker at this student retention and recruitment conference. I had the mike to talk to seven hundred people on what they needed to do to increase the Chicano presence on the predominantly white campus: to me that's activism.

I think education is a place of liberation when you think about activism. Education is the most fertile ground to liberate yourself, your mind, economically, socially, spiritually, in every way, through education. And it has been used as a tool to oppress by those that have controlled it, but to me it is a tool of liberation. So I'd rather not walk away from it, but walk right towards it and try to change it through my activist agenda as a scholar. I consider an activist agenda the kind of work that shakes things up. It's not doing safe research; it's doing the research and producing the knowledge that's controversial, that has resistance and a strong critique against it. I think that's one way of determining whether your work is making a difference. If it's causing some resistance, then you must be producing something that's threatening because people don't like change.

As a kid I wanted to be the best I could be, and I cared about others. I was exposed to people in suffering, either myself or others, and that contributed to who I am. Those things kind of combined when I went to college and started focusing on who I was as a Chicano, my class, and then developing an activist agenda. It began when I was little, but it coalesced, came together in college. The activist has always been with me all the way through. I've just shaped it in different ways. It'll always be with me; I don't think I'll lose that. I think everything I want to do is all about that mission. How it's manifested has changed a little, but it'll come back spelled differently as I get older. I mean, I may be sixty years old and run for political office. I'll still be an activist, but a different kind of activist than I am now.

Anabel. It's hard being at this university because no matter what you do you're never really part of their [white professors] club, not that I want to be really, but they just find ways to let you know that you're not one of them. There are always assumptions made about you and your identity, and there is never any recognition for our accomplishments. They [whites] always see our accomplishments as like sneaky strategies rather than accomplishments. The major gatekeepers in this business are white women and white liberals. Maybe they want to hold on to their newly acquired stronghold? But white liberals are making a killing of us in the academy; they really pimp us a lot. I see them taking so much of what we live and talk about, repackage it into this palatable thing that [white] people rave about, but they're the very ideas that we've lived, talked, and written about, and we don't get cited! We don't get acknowledged or identified in their sources, and white women and liberals take it and make it theirs! It's an issue of invisibility.

What keeps me going is that I've created a tiny place where I think we're still trying to do transformative work. And I hate the bureaucracy of it, but it is so gratifying to see students go through significant ideological, intellectual transformations in my classes. That's all part of my activism because I can't separate teaching from research, from my politics, from my work in communities—they are always mutually informing. My work in communities is especially important because it keeps me humble and grounded, especially around teachers, because if you don't get it and are trying to BS [bull shit] them, they'll tell you! I also enjoy mentoring students because I know how important that was for me. To this day I don't make major decisions without consulting with a more senior Chicano scholar for advice.

It's very easy to get caught up in this bureaucracy, but keeping up the work is how you know you're committed because there's a lot of what I call Shake 'n' Bakes out there. Shake 'n' Bakes are people that have no consciousness most of their lives and then instantly become radicals. They become diehard, and later on, it kind of fizzles off when they leave the university space. For me, formal education did not play the biggest role in solidifying my political identity that is also clearly connected to my ethnic identity. It really came from doing grassroots work and then putting a lot of things together to make larger connections between class, race, gender, sexual orientation, colonialism, and globalization and moving into really trying to understand the isms and also the contradictions we all have. That awareness I really didn't get from formal schooling; it came from informal study groups and community work.

It's not enough for me to say: "I'm Chicana. I'm going to be a role model and be visible. I want to open doors." I mean, that's nice, but that doesn't get at the real issues. And a lot of times, we are coerced to think that's all we really need to do here, and that's because as educated, critical people of color anywhere, we are of high risk to status quo society because by our very nature we want to disrupt it. So the system considers us all high risk. The issue of selling out is real because there are people who make conscious decisions not to link their work to the betterment of community, but even to set it up as a dichotomy is problematic because people have different trajectories. Some people never shift and others do, but I don't personally give up on anybody. Anything that's dichotomous oversimplifies things. I mean, I find that the reason lots of us get into this business is because we have felt this need for change, we have a community in crisis, we see it, and we want to do something. If you're really committed, it's not something you wait for tenure for. Being an activist after tenure is a privilege for white liberals; we don't have that luxury.

I also think it's simplistic to say that just because I'm here that's activist. I think that's just too simple. Although being here and being on the right committees can really help spur some transformation, you have to go there knowing that. It just doesn't happen haphazardly. I know when I was division head I could admit so many students of color without worrying. So you can make some very minor difference, but you're just making a difference in the same system. I think our work can help people think in radically different ways, but who reads our research? I feel that way sometimes and tend to get more pessimistic about how much we can actually do.

The best I can do is see what kind of transforming space I can create for my students here and through my research because as the right becomes more and more powerful, the work we do becomes less and less valued. Conservatives are saying those of us who are interested in looking at social practices, in looking at culture, that our work is by definition pseudo-science. That's the move of the country, so it's gonna be harder and harder and harder for the work we do to be used at the national policy level. The curriculum's gonna get more and more into a national identity, one identity, and it's gonna make it much more difficult to raise issues around a radical multiculturalism and diversity. That doesn't mean we'll give up. But it's gonna be very difficult to rely just on our research, and I think we'll have to take more activist stances than we do right now.

Four Contexts of Chicana and Chicano Educational Activism

The variety of perspectives presented is useful in understanding the complexity of the issues and the multitude of experiences. Every participant said, thought, and was doing something to change whitestream schools, although essential dilemmas about activism arose for all of the participants. High expectations of themselves as Chicana and Chicano activist educators pushed them to find ways of adapting to local environments, to understand power dynamics, and to strategize for change while maintaining strong community ties. Each participant found ways to negotiate activism, appearance, behavior, language, identity, and worldview perceptions according to the spaces they occupied, with the hope for "greater ends" change.

Compiled ethnographic data on all twenty-four participants is reported in the following sections. All ethnographic data were collected between 2001–2003; however, communication and follow-up informal conversations with some participants continue to the present. Specifically, each participant was shadowed for one day at their host institution. Participants were also observed at marches, tutoring sessions, teacher workshops, organization support meetings, and their presentations at national conferences, as well as at weddings, *quinceañeras* (fifteenth-birthday celebrations for Latinas), soccer games, and churches throughout the duration of the study. Twelve weeks of participant observations were also conducted with a male and female participant at two local public universities in 2002. In addition, two years (2001–2003) of observations were conducted at a local elementary school's community plays and performances such as the Winter Holiday Show, Cinco de Mayo program, and other school/community events.

Undergraduates

The daily activist practices reported and observed of the undergraduates included a variety of activities. While more traditional forms of activism were present, such as marching and protesting at the undergraduate level, these were not the day-to-day activities reported by participants and observed by me. Taking on a variety of leadership roles in committees regarding university diversity issues and the recruitment and retention of minority students were important to the majority of participants. All six undergraduate participants worked extensively in recruitment efforts through programs that mentor and tutor high school students either individually or collectively. Chicana and Chicano student organizations such as MEChA encouraged undergraduates to establish relationships with local low-income Latina and Latino high school students. Positions in summer orientation programs for incoming minority students were particularly important jobs to pursue for more advanced undergraduates. Summer programs were seen as places to raise the social justice consciousness of incoming students. Organizing and hosting youth conferences for Latina and Latino high school students were also highly valued activities, especially as a forum to provide information about college and financial aid to students and parents in both English and Spanish.

Several undergraduates were involved in promoting cultural awareness in the university community through educational and political forums aimed to raise consciousness (teach) about social, racial, and gender inequalities. Participants also coordinated activities for raising consciousness with local communities about local community issues such as Latina and Latino laborers, especially sweat shop workers, and became involved with school boards in Latina and Latino neighborhoods. Amongst the Chicanas, there was a deep commitment to offer retreats and conferences for women and girls to address issues of sexism, homophobia, abuse, and patriarchy. Half of the participants were already involved in education by volunteering as teacher's assistants or working closely with professors doing research in community-based education and after-school programs that served primarily Latina and Latino students in working-class neighborhoods.

Teachers

Teachers were observed making critical daily decisions about their classroom curriculum, pedagogies, and student evaluation techniques and methods, and about social and political interactions with colleagues, parents, and community members. Curricular material and unit plans were usually prepared using culturally relevant teaching materials and drawing actively from the students' cultural background and languages. The formal, standard curriculum was usually altered (without lowering academic expectations) to meet the needs of the students and the community, often with the understanding that students needed individual assistance. Teachers felt that their expectations for student performance were higher than those of whitestream teachers working with the same students. The primary goal for all of the teachers in the study was to encourage critical thinking skills in the students, to get them to question society and the establishment, as well as develop healthy and proud images of themselves and of their culture.

Chicana and Chicano activist teachers were observed to encourage and welcome parental participation, and most had an "open door" policy, even when whitestream school policies attempted to prevent this. Whitestream policies require parents to make appointments before visiting or to schedule parent conferences during work hours. Chicana and Chicano activist teachers welcomed parents at any time during the school day as well as made arrangements to do home visits or scheduled meetings with parents early in the morning or late in the evening.

Five of the six teacher participants purposefully lived in the community where they taught and participated actively in community social and cultural events such as parties, soccer games, church activities, and grocery shopping. All of the participants were teaching in the same or similar schools to those that they attended as children, including Alicia, who taught at a continuation high school for pregnant teens. At Johnny's wedding, which I attended in 2001, for example, many of the guests were his students' parents, as well as some of his former students. Rafael was also asked to be a *padrino* (godfather) for several of his former middle school students' *quinceañeras*. Community for these participants really meant participating in and forming lasting social and even religious pseudo-familial bonds with community members outside of the classroom environment.

Other teachers, like Juanita, were observed translating at parent meetings to encourage Spanish-speaking parents' participation in school. Using Spanish actively and proudly in the classroom and in the community for several of the teachers was a way to model assertiveness and cultural pride to their students. For all of the teacher participants, making themselves accessible as community members and making the school more open to parental participation and influence was important. Similar to Ladson-Billings's (1994) findings with African American teachers, Juanita, for example, commented that she "dressed up" for her students and parents as a sign of respect. She added: "When parents come to school and see teachers in shorts, T-shirts, and *chanclas* (sandals), that conveys the message to them that teachers don't care about their profession or about the kids and community. In Mexico teachers are highly respected, and they sure dress up!"

Although two of the teachers I observed, Henry and Raquel, expressed feeling very isolated and without much support for their ideas, ideals, and work, other Chicana and Chicano activist teachers helped create safety niches and networks of support within and outside the whitestream schools where they taught. Juanita, for example, became involved in the hiring process that helped create a niche of eleven Chicana and Chicano activist teachers, including Johnny, and a safe space where bilingual and bicultural education, for the students, teachers, and community, was maintained after Proposition 227. Most of the teachers reported that collaborating with each other was important and that such collaboration helped them strengthen their work with students, as well as share their lives and life experiences openly with the community. Chicana and Chicano activist teachers often talked of creating an extended *familia* (family) with the community that helped to positively link formal education with the families that they served.

The teachers observed were also involved in networks of Chicana and Chicano activist or socially conscious educators. These community and professional networks were often used for social, emotional, economic, and academic support and as sources of ideas and pedagogies for their ever-evolving classroom practices. Rafael, for example, was involved in a writing group for teachers that met monthly to share experiences, teaching tips, lesson plans, and materials through Taller de Escritores (Writer's Workshop). Raquel, through networks of community and parent support, was able to secure a large grant for a reading program to enhance the educational experiences of English Language Learners at her school.

Organizations that provided support networks for teacher participants included the California Association for Bilingual Education (CABE), with umbrella subgroups that used poetry and other forms of writing for cathartic self-expression of ideas and frustration. Another organization was the California Consortium for Critical Educators (CCCE), where educators of all levels, but primarily K–12 classroom teachers, met to discuss ideas and projects for liberation using critical pedagogy. The annual meeting of the National Association for Chicana and Chicano Studies (NACCS) was also reported as a place where several participants in all of the four groups in this book enjoyed supportive encouragement for their activist educator work.

Graduate Students

Given the rigorous, highly structured socialization process of graduate school, activism for graduate students was thought of as each individual's academic work and the personal decisions each made in terms of research methodologies, conferences to attend, books and articles to read, mentors to emulate, and ultimately career choices. Questions and decisions arose for participants regarding research and the researchers' long-term commitment to her/his informants (similar to Villenas's 1996 healing process as a Chicana ethnographer). Several graduate students expressed making decisions not to work on certain projects or with specific professors despite the personal and career networks or advantages such projects or connections would bring them. Because of ethical considerations, to accept to work on these projects would compromise their Chicana and Chicano activist identities and political orientations. In these situations, Chicana and Chicano graduate students reported being sought after by white researchers to translate, to transcribe interviews conducted in

Spanish, or to help them gain entry (establish legitimacy) into certain communities. At times, the participants considered the research being conducted as disrespectful to Latina and Latino communities and refused to participate.

Documents like research papers, essays, syllabi, and proposals revealed that activist graduate students made conscious and important decisions on what theories to work with, methodologies to use, and academic sources to reference. These students were also observed being active in class discussions where their efforts to raise consciousness (teach) were often met with "verbal abuse" and dismissal by whitestream peers and professors. Often, such consciousness-raising efforts created the perception of them as "radicals" by their peers.

Career choices also became very complex for graduate students when they debated the career trajectory they wished to follow. All of the graduate students were aware that the choices they made as students would impact their future careers. Some had committed in advance to teaching working-class students at primarily Hispanic Serving Institutions (HSIs), mainly mentoring teachers, or in community colleges. Other participants saw themselves merging researcher/scholar identities with their activist orientations and social justice agendas. Participants pursuing the research university route expressed a commitment to mentoring Chicana and Chicano students at top universities by creating, or helping to maintain, existing Chicana and Chicano, Latina and Latino pipelines of access to these institutions and spaces. Despite all of the differences, participants expressed a will to transform the whitestream academy.

Most participants were observed to be at least peripherally involved with student organizations on campus such as MEChA and other groups that focused on issues of gender, sexuality, or recruitment to graduate school. A few Chicana and Chicano activist graduate students occasionally mentored undergraduates and, in some cases, high school students and often served as sources of support and information for them and their families. Rita, for example, spent quite a bit of her time mentoring and helping male undergraduate students at her institution. This included not only academic mentoring but also helping out monetarily and with rides to visit their families. Two other graduate students were observed to volunteer periodically in local K–12 schools. Participants often reported that they found balance in their lives through their connections to the "world" outside of the university by volunteering and doing community activist work. Andrea, for example, started a community and graduate student partnership organization. In this organization, Latina and Latino graduate students used research and access to resources to help community members take stands against California's anti-bilingual education policies.

Professors

The professors, like the teachers, were also active in altering the curriculum (syllabi) by using more critical educational pedagogies that have traditionally contributed to the conceptual identity production of Chicana and Chicano activist students (undergraduate and graduate alike). Student evaluation, support, and mentorship were actively informed for professors by a Chicana and Chicano activist subjectivity and consciousness. Relationships with undergraduate students were important, but relationships with graduate students where pseudo-familial ties were established seemed longer lasting and more meaningful. Mentorship, where a Chicana and Chicano faculty member functioned as a sponsor, a *madrina* or *padrino* (godparent) to the graduate student, according to David, was important for retention in graduate school.

> Once you're in a position where you can help others, then you ought to do it. That's just the responsibility you have, mainly because there may not be that support for those individuals elsewhere. It's the old padrino, madrina syndrome. When you baptize someone, you have a responsibility. The devil is not supposed to take that person. [laughs] Should anything happen to the parents, you're supposed to do it. When you marry someone, you're the padrino: you have responsibility to help them, nurture them, support them. It's not just an honorific relationship; it's a responsible relationship.

In both undergraduate and graduate school, it was often through the work of professors and mentoring relationships that Chicana and Chicano activist identity was strengthened for students and alternative epistemologies were explored.

Professors had a strong commitment to teach and do research in areas that supported and presented alternative epistemologies and perspectives. For the professors, this commitment involved doing academic work in areas such as social justice education, addressing equity issues in schools, fighting for equitable resource allocation, providing critical analyses on race/ethnicity, informing school policy, lobbying around language and immigration issues in schools, and supporting affirmative action. All of the activist professors incorporated such issues in their syllabi in courses they were hired to teach, while others taught extra courses they were not getting credit for teaching or paid to teach in order to do this. All of the participants expressed a "political twist" and controversial element to their research agendas. "Debunking myths" in research previously used by whitestream researchers to stereotype and oppress minority communities was a common goal.

Professors were often a resource for Chicana and Chicano students on their respective campuses (undergraduate and graduate) as well as to Chicana and Chicano students nationally who often sought out their assistance. Their commitment to "opening doors" was taken very seriously. Opening doors also meant maintaining Chicana and Chicano networks across different university contexts, locally and nationally, that enabled for the flow of Latina and Latino students through higher education pipelines. These networks were maintained with the goal of increasing Chicana and Chicano student representation at all levels of secondary education. For participants in research universities, Chicana and Chicano networks were not limited to other scholars in elite universities, but included professors at state universities and community colleges as well as graduate students, teachers, and community members at all levels and in different fields or disciplines. Network members included people in government organizations, legal organizations such as Mexican American Legal Defense and Education Fund (MALDEF), the National Council of La Raza (NCLR), and other policy forums created to address Latina and Latino community issues. Networks often provided social, emotional, academic, legal, political, and other forms of support for participants.

Professors' activist commitment also involved the creation of what some called "transformative spaces." Transformative spaces included research fieldsites, classrooms, offices, research centers, after-school programs, migrant student education summer programs, and minority new student orientation programs. Research and teaching were considered important in creating these spaces because funding sources enabled the professors to make these spaces available to students (of all races). Large research grants also allowed professors to fund students through their graduate education programs, while doing community-related research. Professors working in teacher education programs focused on teaching their students how to use critical pedagogy and teaching them about diversity issues and multicultural education to make their future classrooms sites of transformation and learning for Latina and Latino K–12 students. Professors working with master's students, especially the two working at state universities, reported preparing and encouraging several of their students to attend elite universities to do doctoral-level work.

The public "voice" was also of great importance to the professors, not only at academic conferences where observations were conducted but also in speaking to a variety of different audiences. Professors were observed giving talks on public issues even when they did not get official university credit or financial compensation for their service. Many wrote for local newspapers, radio, and television to present a more critical perspective on educational issues affecting the Latina and Latino community. Professor participants felt their connections to K–12 education, and to K–12 teachers and community educators, were important and, in many cases, helped to keep them grounded, honest, and humble in their professional and personal lives. With the hope of influencing the direction of the academic and policy conversation, many engaged audiences as keynote speakers and "experts," even when the expert label made them feel uneasy and critical of their voice and work.

Three professors took on leadership positions locally and nationally. One participant served in the U.S. Department of Education, while the other two worked in policy circles and used evaluation research to address issues of standardized testing, to question the validity of the SAT, and to study minority student access to higher education, as well as K–12 programs affecting the larger Latina and Latino community. Professors' involvement in faculty search committees was also perceived as being instrumental in hiring more Chicana and Chicano, Latina and Latino faculty in their departments. Their participation in graduate school admissions committees also allowed them more opportunities to recruit and, in many cases, admit, or commit to working with, incoming Chicana and Chicano, Latina and Latino graduate students.

Chicanas Impacting Chicanas

Chicanas focused their efforts on raising consciousness by also centering gender issues. For Ruth, this was an important part of her mission as a Chicana activist educator, even though she struggled over the number of Latinas she could reach out to. Ruth stated:

> How can I influence the lives of other Chicanas so they can see other possibilities for themselves besides getting married and having a truckload of kids? You can be a beautiful woman, and you can care about your physical appearance, but you can also care about your intellectual power. I go through Latino neighborhoods, but I can't help but think a lot of young women don't see the options they really could have because they've never discovered their intellectual power. They probably have discovered their sexual power or their domestic power before they even discover they have intellectual power to change themselves and the world around them.

Raising consciousness among other Latinas was an important part of the work Chicanas, regardless of their age, envisioned.

Isadora, like Ruth, had a similar passion for working and raising consciousness with other Latinas.

> I've worked [with] a lot with girls. We put on Chicana retreats. Or leadership retreats. . . . We all go through things as Chicanos and Chicanas, but just to hear the things Chicanas go through . . . in terms of, I mean older ones who have been in abusive relationships, right? A lot of them have self-esteem—I mean, first you're told not to feel proud of your culture, right? Then you're told you're ugly. . . . And a lot of them have been sexually abused. I think there's just so much pain there we haven't talked about or addressed. That's really important to me just 'cause I've become really close to a lot of the students. It's sad they have to go through all that. So, I think . . . there's just a lot of gender issues, there's a lot of violence, a lot of disrespect towards women and girls. And it doesn't have to be that way.

Isadora, like Ruth and most of the other Chicanas, mentioned the focus of her activist work with Chicanas. Isadora also expressed her concerns and pain in working with mujeres and the issues they faced on a daily basis. Isadora was especially sympathetic to older Chicanas' experiences with oppression, especially those who had survived abusive relationships.

Additional Chicana Concerns

Other issues Chicanas expressed concern over included reproduction issues and the difficulty of balancing having children (and families) and careers because of imposed gender limitations. For Alicia and Anabel, that was a particularly difficult issue because they were both single mothers while they completed university degrees. Many of the younger Chicanas were inspired by older Chicana role models, especially prominent Chicana scholars. While most Chicanas found their career trajectories inspiring, others expressed concerns. Therese, for example, admired Chicana faculty mentors, but was concerned about not finding a lifetime male partner and especially about having children. These issues became more important to Therese when she realized that many of her role models were single women who did not have children, but pets instead. This made Therese and other Chicanas who shared her concern wonder if they would have to make choices between having "amazing careers or having amazing families."

A few of the unmarried Chicanas expressed concerns over suitable marriage partners. Most were not willing to compromise their Chicana feminist positions, but were also resentful that "some Chicano men can't deal with educated, intelligent women." A few Chicanas expressed resentment over educated Chicanos marrying white women. Therese said: "I was more concerned about who these Chicano professors were marrying and I was like, 'Ahhh, he married a white woman!' I was like 'Man, they're all marrying white!' [laughs] And now all my girlfriends are marrying white . . . and so I'm like, 'Oh my God.' So I'm more concerned about their personal choices because it's important. It's a statement." To Therese, choices in marriage partners, like all other aspects of life, were political statements. To Therese, the personal is political indeed.

Another issue important to Chicanas was physical appearance. While this clearly was not an issue for all of the mujeres, it was critical for a few. For Alicia, worried about playing the game and trying not to stand out in her work environment, this was an important issue: "Even the way I dress. The colors I wear, everything is bright. My makeup is very bright. Like, in your face colors. I don't look like a typical mom. And it makes me feel kind of embarrassed sometimes. And I have to keep trying to tell myself: 'I am me. I am *me*. This is the way I *am*! Don't change for anybody!' But I feel like . . . I feel like I don't fit in the establishment sometimes."

Alicia's struggle over her physical appearance was part of her struggle with the dilemma of "playing the game" and fitting "in the establishment." How much she should compromise in terms of dress in whitestream schools was at times a difficult issue for her. Therese expressed similar concerns, but seemed to be more comfortable with her compromise. One thing Therese asserted was that she would not give up her bright red lipstick. Anabel also expressed issues over physical appearance, but this was in response to white students commenting that she dressed inappropriately for a professor. Anabel said: "I just, I love clothes, I have fun with them. I think it's very Chicana to have fun with how you look. I mean it's been around me all my life. It's how everybody I know is." For Anabel, as for Therese and Alicia, their style of clothing and colors of choice mediate their Chicana identity. The unspoken prescription of what is "appropriate" in terms of physical appearance is also a reflection of whitestream/ malestream (gendered) norms.

Making Worlds by Playing the Game

The third context for the production of identities, according to Holland and colleagues (1998), is in world making. From Vygotsky's studies of play and analyses of the historical emergence of several figured worlds, Holland and colleagues conclude that through "serious play" new figured worlds may come about. Social play, or the "arts and rituals created on the margins in newly imagined communities" (272), can help people develop new competencies to participate in or further develop these new, sometimes marginal, figured worlds. In these new (novel) figured worlds lies the possibility for making/creating new ways, artifacts, discourses, and acts, perhaps even more liberatory worlds. When fully concretized, Holland and colleagues say that world making brings us back to the first context—figured worlds.

Chicana and Chicano activist educators were involved in making worlds by exercising their activist agency in whitestream schools. Although they often existed and worked from the margins and under heavy constraints, they created spaces for possibility in their own work and through the networks of support they established and nurtured. In their niches of safety, for example, in their support groups or even in their own classrooms, Chicana and Chicano activist educators imagined and worked toward their vision of a better world by "playing" strategically, although negotiation and compromise are not easy.

In their marginal positions as activist educators, participants reported that their Chicana and Chicano activist identity was sometimes more prominent in some spaces and contexts than others, or around certain issues or incidents versus others. In some spaces/contexts, Chicana and Chicano activist identity was highlighted by the participants, while in others, different labels such as Latino or even Hispanic were used strategically. For example, David was nationally identified as a Hispanic representative when he worked for the U.S. government even though Hispanic is a term not particularly embraced by Chicana and Chicano activists. The Hispanic identification did not diffuse his commitment as a Chicano activist or his Chicano worldview. David considered it strategic to be able to accept this high-rank positioning given his political orientation and Chicano vision for change. Another participant called such identity negotiation a strategic form of "situational ethnicity," alluding to Spivak's (1993) notion of strategic essentialism.

The "playing" in playing the game highlights the conscious awareness and exertion (whenever possible) of activist agency, or the possibility to make worlds not just in the abstract but also in practice through day-to-day, moment-to-moment activism. Activist agency in this theoretical framework was not just about resisting structural oppression in reactive and reductive ways but also about productively and proactively attempting to make change in line with the Chicana and Chicano activist figured world vision at all moments of practice. Making worlds occurs in the margins and often begins as play. Play expands the possibilities, and daily activism exercises the agency to make the play a reality. Hope, *esperanza*, is essential to bring about changes in the game and to continue working toward replacing the old game with a new one. Participants were aware that a game (system) is in force and that the activist performance of playing in that game can lead to making worlds of change that expand the cracks in the system to make new possibilities viable in the struggle for social justice.

Implications for World Making

The greatest possibility for change has always been in making worlds, working to expand possibilities for social justice, and in imagining possibilities that seem unimaginable. All revolutionary ideas begin somewhere, even if at first in the imagination. Educators committed to social justice can learn, network, and cooperate with Chicana and Chicano activist educators working toward making worlds of possibility exist. As Latinas and Latinos increasingly become the majority population in the nation, and especially in schools, whitestream practices must change. The white population is an aging population, and it's in their best interest to share power and in schools to educate, not just school, the younger population. Education should not promote erasure, myths of meritocracy, and whitestream and malestream norms as mainstream. The democratic proposal that this country was founded on must adapt to the diversity of this nation. Mexican America, like African America, Native America, and Asian America, is part of the United States. It's time the United States also becomes a part of these, its people. The day-to-day and moment-to-moment activism of Chicana and Chicano activist educators is a step in the struggle for change.

6
Transas, Movidas, y Jugadas and the Struggle to Change Whitestream Schools

Significant events occurred when I was completing this book. Most notable were the mass demonstrations by Latinas and Latinos, especially youth, against proposed anti-immigrant legislation HR 4437 in various cities across the United States. Working in Chicana and Chicano studies at the University of California made my decision to work on my book manuscript instead of joining the first march in April 2006 a personal dilemma. I felt guilty for not being out there with the rest of the marchers. I felt especially guilty because I knew a lot of the more active Chicana and Chicano students on campus and because I had followed the communication that went on prior to the event. I walked on campus hoping students or other faculty would not see me there instead of at the march in Sacramento.

I also knew that I had a deadline to meet and my writing time was limited due to family responsibilities. Losing out on a writing day would mean another week less to finish and more time away from my children. The guilt, however, was too strong, especially when I saw on television the number of people who did join the protests. On May 1, 2006, I made a conscious decision to join the march against HR 4437 in Sacramento, and it was an incredible experience. There is power in numbers and in being able to express collective discontent. Some tactics I did not agree with, such as waving the U.S. flag only instead of waving Mexican and other national flags along with it, but perhaps I too was holding on to a romanticized discourse of Chicana and Chicano activism.

Since then, I've wondered what the effect of the May 1 marches and boycott were on those observing. What did whitestream viewers think about Latina and Latino immigrants now? Who would decide if that was the real activism?

In terms of my work, what would some of the protest organizers think about the Chicana and Chicano activist educators in this book? Would they think that the participants' everyday activism is not real activism? I was at the march, and so were some of my study's participants: we marched together. But, I still question if writing this book is an activist stance, or if this book will only benefit me and my career; I have indeed devoted a significant amount of time to this project.

After completing the study that this book is based on, I no longer think there is a prescription for activism, nor is there only one branch of activism. I have come to appreciate people's individual and collective agency in the struggle for change. "Playing the game" is not an either/or situation, as it is usually made out to be. In the 1960s, the goals for change seemed clearer than those of today. Discrimination and exclusion were very real and obvious, and so the targets for change were also clearer. Because racism and discrimination have mutated and evolved, and continue to mutate and evolve into more sophisticated forms and subtle practices, the activism of today is not the same activism of the 1960s. We are not dealing with the same clear and obvious targets, although when it comes to immigration the racism is becoming blatant. Because of color-blindness rhetoric, we now have racism without racists (Baker, 1998; Bonilla-Silva, 2006), and for Latinas and Latinos, language is used as a proxy for race (K. Gutiérrez and Jaramillo, 2006). The mobilization around HR 4437 demonstrates that collective activism is possible when the attack is made clear.

Despite the collective effort in the spring 2006 marches, there was a murmur of judgment placed on people who only showed up to the marches, but were not involved in the organizing efforts. Bouts of who was more involved and who deserved more recognition ensued. Generational differences also played out in how activism was interpreted. For some activists, the marches did not go far enough, for others they were just about right, and yet, for others, they went too far.

Placing judgment on other people's participation in activism is divisive and self-righteous. In activism, some people are willing to risk more, perhaps because they have less to lose. However, it should be emphasized that there are different ways to participate. Delgado Bernal's (1998a) work on rethinking the role of Chicana activists in the 1968 East L.A. school blowouts is an example that leadership is not restricted to our traditional notions of it.[1]

The meaning of activist and activism, especially for those working from within institutions like whitestream schools, still needs to be rethought. Rethinking does not mean a less-grassroots activist stance with a watered-down political agenda is better, and certainly not that activists working in institutions are changing the system to a greater extent than anyone else. If anything, I acknowledge that Chicana and Chicano activist educators both resist and reproduce the system of power in place, but I am not interested in that dichotomy. I am interested in the space of practice (activism) in between the two axes.

Continuity of Movement Struggles

The macro Chicana and Chicano social movement that officially started in the 1960s, but had been building prior to that, is not dead and lives on in micro local figured worlds. Whittier's (1995) study of political cohorts in the women's movement is illustrative of what I am arguing in terms of activism trajectory. Whittier contends that the feminist movement continues through different generational cohorts in the radical women's movement she studied for three decades in Ohio. She called these micro cohorts political generations. Whittier asserted that for these women: (1) collective identity remained consistent over time, (2) even though protest declined, movement veterans carried movement elements into other institutions or other social movements, and (3) new members enter the movement and redefine its collective identity according to their current context. This movement continuity, of course, was not without struggle.

For the Chicana and Chicano activists studied, identity also remained consistent over time, even though it is less fashionable and perhaps more unacceptable today to call oneself Chicana and Chicano than it was thirty years ago. This sample included a wide age range, yet the basic definition of Chicana and Chicano identity remained consistent in its attention to ethnic/cultural pride, self-determination, and decolonization. For older participants, the focus was on Mexican and Mexican American communities, while younger participants had a more inclusive vision that included all people of indigenous heritage and other Latina and Latino communities. Some of the younger participants were also involved with international movements, like the Zapatistas and Mujeres de Juárez. For *mujeres*, Chicana identity centered women's and sexuality issues as well as class and racialization in the fight for social justice. Like Whittier's feminists, the larger cultural means of the Chicana and Chicano identity remained, but not without change.

Although protest activities came in waves, as they did in 1994 against Proposition 187 and in 2006 against HR 4437, participants took the Chicana and Chicano worldview seriously. The desire to raise consciousness *pero con ganas* was especially salient and consistent. Significant narrators, or the most influential voices, took this worldview with them to white-stream schools and exercised their agency when appropriate to share the Chicana and Chicano vision of a better world with others. Whenever and wherever possible, participants sought to raise the consciousness of those around them. Through sustained action and activity within local micro figured worlds, new members entered new micro cohorts and political generations that also contributed to self-authoring and re/defining Chicana and Chicano identity.

The 1960s grassroots social movements challenged intellectual elitist culture and pushed the boundaries and purposes of intellectual work (Muñoz, 1989). The inclusion of marginal, racialized, and gendered voices in Chicana and Chicano micro cohorts slowly fused activism, public intellectualism, and academic scholarship into Chicana and Chicano identities that do all of these—the activist scholar, teacher, educator (Villenas, 1996; Padilla and Martínez, 2005). Discourses about activism and institutional participation have also become prominent. For Chicanas and Chicanos, *educación*[2] has never ceased to be important to the community (Sandoval, 1991; Pérez, 1999; Delgado Bernal, 1998b; Valenzuela, 1999; Acuña, 2000).

The larger macro Chicana and Chicano social movement continues through micro figured worlds in local context. Chicanas and Chicanos shared the view that the *causa* (cause) and *lucha* (struggle) live on, and this was observed in micro cohorts that maintained the continuity of movement struggles. As opposed to the earlier movement that worked from outside institutions, some of these new local micro figured worlds now strive to make change from within institutions.

Working from Within

Chicana and Chicano activism is important at all levels of whitestream schooling. Because whitestream curricula and pedagogy in U.S. schools does not nurture ethnic/racial minority identities, K–12 schooling is in need of more Chicana and Chicano activist teachers and their allies with social justice agendas. Activist educators at any level are more willing to take the necessary risks to enhance the schooling experiences of Latina and Latino and other students of color whose experiences are only minimally addressed in whitestream schools.

There are key roles and sites for change at all levels of whitestream schools (K–graduate school). And although not all Chicana and Chicano activist educators are personally connected with each other through official and extensive networks, everyone who is actively trying to change whitestream schools is involved in this struggle. Given the formidability and bureaucratic nature of whitestream schools, daily practices of activism are important in creating more democratic spaces at all levels. All institutions enforce conformity, but the level of that conformity is determined by individual and collective compromises. Daily actions to enforce inculcation (institutionalization, status quo society, "that's the way it is"), or to disrupt it in key, often unnoticeable, ways, are determined through individual decisions, actions, and choices. Individuals in conscious activist practice constantly seek out the "cracks" in the system.

Understanding their activist agency, even under the burden of whitestream schools' expectations and boundaries, helped Chicana and Chicano activist educators maintain a positive outlook about change. Without a hopeful outlook, Chicana and Chicano activist educators would no longer see the point in their struggles. Instead of developing a cynicism about changing the entire structure of society, Chicana and Chicano activist educators focused on their own situational context (space, time, and place) of struggle as the site of transformation. Collective action cannot be underestimated, but individual daily, moment-to-moment practice is equally important in the struggle for change. Reinterpreting activism and activist practices according to different local sites and contexts was important.

Identity production is important because activist identities produce activist agency, an agency that is more likely to seek out, or to create, opportunities for change. Interpretations of what it means to be an activist, and how those interpretations change over time through individual and social experiences, are also important. The younger participants in the study wanted immediate change through direct action and had a strong sense of urgency. Older participants continued to hope, *mantenían la esperanza*, for change, but interpreted activism in a different manner. In some ways, they were less focused on immediate and large-scale utopian change, but in others they were more hopeful, *con más esperanza*, in terms of what they referred to as the "ripple," "domino," or "trickle-down" effect of everyday activist practices for long-term change.

Activism was generally talked about by all participants as "strategic," "situational," "calculated," and "improvisational" instead of solely organized around romantic physical manifestations, such as marches or protests. Participants made calculated decisions in terms of what issues were worth the battle and which were not. Perhaps because some participants had a better understanding of power, working on certain issues or engaging certain people were seen as a waste of their time and energy. Henry, for example, said:

> I don't hang out with anybody [at work] because I don't feel like getting into arguments. And sometimes I've had so many conversations with other people since college that I feel like I get more out of this wall than I do talking to people. It's like it's no use; it really isn't. Some people you are not gonna convince, you're not gonna change them, so why even pick a fight or even deal with this sort of issue. I tell my wife, you gotta pick your battle because sometimes it's just not worth engaging somebody in a conversation if you know it's not gonna change them.

Although Henry was very committed to social justice and made this a priority in his teaching and involvement with community organizations, he knew he had teacher colleagues whom he chose not to engage in significant conversations with. Henry commented that such conversations were "draining" and sometimes emotionally "disturbing," and he would rather save his energy for working with students and having positive relationships with family members and friends. Overall, participants' changing view of activism and activist agency resulted from their engagement with power and the obstinacy of bureaucracy.

Activist Agency

The lives of Chicana and Chicano activist educators highlight that, although institutionalized and faced with many compromises and negotiations, the participants engaged in active and committed participation. Each of the participants was conscious of his/her activist agency, as well as of its limitations and the expectations of the whitestream schools that they worked in. Participants were also critically aware of the contradictions involved in their work and in their lives as both institutional agents and social justice activists.

Whitestream school expectations ranged from taking irrelevant required classes, to administering standardized tests, to taking comprehensive examinations, to obtaining tenure: all of these expectations devalued Chicana and Chicano activism. Participants constantly said formal schooling was both a means of "enabling and disenabling" agency. In some ways, participants acquired power through institutional credentials and positions of prestige, but at the same time felt more pressure to perform to the institutional expectations that came with these accomplishments. In their daily lives as Chicana and Chicano activist educators, they had more access to power, yet were also under closer surveillance by the power structure. Participants were both the products of whitestream schools and in a constant struggle to change them.

Despite the contradictions, there was not one participant who did not see herself/himself as an activist agent for change, especially change that would benefit the communities that he/she felt most committed to. María said: "I am incredibly grateful, and I feel this very strong sense of responsibility that I need to turn that into opportunities for other people. And because I have a particular connection to the Chicano community, it allows me to do that there." Community commitment was a constant "responsibility," as María expressed it, for participants (Urrieta and Méndez Benavídez, 2007). Although participants' interpretations of what activism meant and how change should be brought about varied, they were committed to "doing their part" to make whitestream schools more democratic places.

Existing in multiplicity and being able to juggle contradictions were parts of Chicana and Chicano activist agency in daily practice. All of the Chicana and Chicano activist educators were able to dignify the contradictions of their daily lives in playing the game, often functioning as the very pillars that sustain whitestream schools, while simultaneously looking for moments, cracks, and spaces to disrupt, weaken, or alter the structures of the system. Pedro, for example, saw the classroom, and teaching, as a space to disrupt the status quo: "My goal as an educator is to make people think critically about the reality that they live in. Because I am convinced that if they do that, they will want a different world than the one we are in. . . . I see that, that practice in a classroom as activism. It is the space in which I am politically working toward . . . a better world. it is a more humane world and that's where I do it." What many participants referred to as "minor yet significant victories" and "teachable moments," such as raising consciousness in a classroom for Pedro, often helped sustain and reinvigorate *la esperanza* (the hope) in their active participation and enduring community commitment as worthwhile. Even when the contradictions seemed daunting to most of the participants, *la esperanza muere al último* (hope dies last).

The "colonizer/colonized" dilemma (Villenas, 1996) was constant for many participants, but was not compromising. Chicana and Chicano activist educators maneuvered, sabotaged, and disrupted the status quo.

Active, daily, moment-to-moment activism was part of their struggle to make whitestream schools more democratic spaces even when the bureaucracies of the system seemed formidable, permanent, and unchangeable. The realization that the system is not perfect, as Raquel aptly put it, was of high importance to the participants. Constant struggle and commitment in *la causa* in an active and proactive way was not a waste of time for participants, but a responsibility. The continuity of activist agency in turn sustained local contentious practices.

Resistance versus Reproduction

Active participation is not just about reactive practice, or resistance practice, nor is it about reproductive practices. The focus should be on what happens in between this dichotomy. This dichotomy has received exhaustive attention since the publication of Paul Willis's (1977) *Learning to Labor* and, in many ways, has become taken for granted by theorists. As in any dichotomy, focusing on only two alternatives is problematic. Where is the "tipping point" of when a person is no longer resisting and is reproducing power inequalities? When is a person no longer playing the game and has sold out?

Anzaldúa (1999:100) raised important issues regarding reactive stances, which she referred to as counterstances, and which can be used as a framework for re/viewing activism. This section of her text is worth quoting extensively:

> But it is not enough to stand on the opposite river bank, shouting questions, challenging patriarchal, white conventions. A counterstance locks one into a duel of oppressor and oppressed; locked in mortal combat, like the cop and the criminal, both are reduced to a common denominator of violence. The counterstance refutes the dominant culture's view and beliefs, and, for this, it is proudly defiant. All reaction is limited by, and dependent on, what it is reacting against. Because the counterstance stems from a problem with authority—outer as well as inner—it's a step towards liberation from cultural domination. But it is not a way of life.

Anzaldúa, while highlighting the importance of counterstance as resistance in the process of liberation, also implies that this "shouting," "challenging," "defiant," "reacting" subject is still in the process of forming (healing) a Chicana and Chicano identity. The Chicana and Chicano activist identity involves ambiguity in being able to "stand on both sides of the shore" and see through multiple, opposing eagle and serpent eyes.

Chicana and Chicano activist identity production is a healing process that involves the agency to respond to whitestream and malestream oppression and be proactive even when not reacting to direct aggression (in daily practice). The reactive stance, according to Anzaldúa, is a cornered stance that "is limited by, and dependent on, what it is reacting against." Chicana and Chicano activist agency is informed in practice not just by transformational resistance (Solórzano and Delgado Bernal, 2001) as a "resistance for liberation" that is "motivated by emancipatory interests" (Delgado Bernal, 2001) but also by assuming the agency of the "cultural worker" (cultural production). The activist agency of the cultural worker draws inspiration and knowledge from community culture, collective experience, community memory, and cultural intuition (Delgado Bernal, 1998b) to transform alienating whitestream schools (in multiple, not just cultural, dimensions) (K. González, 2001).

Chicana and Chicano activist educators, as cultural workers/resistors, do not just use cultural resources when cultural clashes or cultural isolation occurs, but they also utilize them with a social justice "commitment to communities" (Delgado Bernal, 2001) that forms part of the macro Chicana and Chicano activist figured world. Identity obviously involves multiple elements, such as gender, class, and sexual orientation. I present mainly the ethnic/cultural identity that was most highlighted by the participants in the study because U.S. whitestream aggression has historically been mostly directed at Mexican Americans in a racialized way. Although gender, class, and sexual orientation are of utmost importance, ethnic/cultural identification of Mexican Americans seemed to be most salient.

Being able to stand on both sides of the shore and seeing through opposing eyes, as Anzaldúa advocates, is a powerful claim not just to ambiguity but also to the multiplicity of selves. I use Bakhtin's concept of orchestration as a complement to the playing the game metaphor. Orchestration, as in musical orchestration, can also be used as a way to think about Chicana and Chicano activist educators' activist internal and external agency between resistance and reproduction.

Musical orchestration involves multiple settings, as in daily life, where sometimes individuals orchestrate their own practice, while at other times people play with other musicians. In yet other situations (if invited or allowed in), individuals play within the orchestration of alien spaces, different tunes, and highly structured dictated orchestration (such as in whitestream schools). Internally, orchestration happens through thinking, an activity that is also agency-informed. One can learn to self-orchestrate one's subjectivity in multiple ways. In one's internal, imaginary orchestration, other worlds are possible, even if the reality is different. Externally, in the physical world, self-orchestration occurs when people strategically enter spaces foreign to them, work with different people, and coordinate their actions to make changes from within, such as through cross-cultural networks.

Chicana and Chicano activist identity production as orchestrated action is about learning to "develop subjectivities capable of transformation and relocation, movement guided by the learned capacity to read, renovate, and make signs on behalf of the dispossessed" (Sandoval, 1998: 359). Chicana and Chicano identity production is both born out of oppression and is in a conscious struggle against it (Anzaldúa, 1999), cognitively and in the physical world. Villenas (1996) also implicitly engages the resistance versus reproduction dichotomy in a similar way as the "colonizer/colonized Chicana Ethnographer."

Villenas highlights the dilemma in coming to terms with her formal education and institutional affiliation as a Chicana graduate student working with poor immigrant Latinas in rural North Carolina. Villenas located herself within the problematic dichotomy of the colonizer and the colonized, yet ultimately resolved the dilemma by seeing her own agency in-between as a Chicana ethnographer: "My answer to the ethnographer-as-colonizer dilemma is that I will not stop at being the public translator and facilitator for my communities, but that I am my own voice, an activist seeking liberation from my own historical oppression in relation to my communities" (Villenas, 1996:730).

Villenas's dialectic of being simultaneously the colonized and the colonizer is an example of the in-between space. Identity and agency cannot be underestimated in Villenas's realization. Like Anzaldúa, Villenas comes to see from opposing sides of the river bank, simultaneously through eagle and serpent eyes (as in the Mexican national emblem), not just as the colonizer or the colonized but also as an activist scholar, the Chicana ethnographer.

Chicana and Chicano activist identity and agency, in this book, is about Chicana and Chicano activist educators working in whitestream schools that would have them contribute to the schooling colonizing enterprise, but who have the personal and collective counter-intent and motivation to transform these schools into more democratic spaces. Chicana and Chicano activist identity production is about understanding activist agency and being able to exercise this activist agency consciously, not only in reacting to microaggressions (Solórzano, 1998) but also in daily practice in proactive, even if more subtle, but possibly more enduring, ways. Chicana and Chicano activist identity production is formed on the basis of individual experience (history-in-person); cultural, collective, and community memory (history-in-system); and through consciousness raising in transformative spaces. Chicana and Chicano activist educators able to juggle multiple selves become key players in the game, able to exist, even if uneasily, as both colonizer and colonized, eagle and serpent, activist and institutional agent, in between reproduction and resistance.

There remain entire bodies of knowledge(s) to be explored in the dialectic between structure and agency, between resistance and reproduction. Activist agency in daily local contentious practice that is motivated by the commitment to active participation has many more resources and is often effective because of its offensive rather than defensive nature. Activist identities that nurture activist agency in the struggle to change whitestream schools are of great importance in sustaining this form of proactive and daily activism within formal educational institutions.

Agency Embedded in Daily Practice

Agency then is embedded in daily relational practice. Being conscious and aware of agency is especially important when encountering new roles and new positions where individual responses and decisions will be made. The particulars of daily responses, or lack thereof, are sites of possibility for multiple activist incursions against systemic racist, classist, sexist, and heterosexist educational barriers.

Daily practice is embedded with agency, perhaps more so than we think. Daily practice can be highly influenced by innovation and improvisation, rather than merely following prescriptions or protocol. Chicana and Chicano activist educators' awareness of their daily activist agency informed the planned spontaneity of their responses. Planned spontaneity refers to activist educators' actions that appeared to be spontaneous to their colleagues, but were actually planned and premeditated before the actions were taken. In positions of power, Chicana and Chicano activist educators sought out the opportunities to exercise planned spontaneity in order to make changes. David, for example, shared the following: "I've been fortunate. I've been in positions where I can make policies, where I can make decisions, everything from this position, to other positions, to department chair, to even faculty member where I could make decisions about students. . . . I've been fortunate to be in those positions where you can do that. You can make gains, 'cause you can."

By altering the expected protocol while in positions of power, David's daily practices contributed to making the formalities and restrictive nature of whitestream schools into more inclusive and transformative spaces. The innovations arising from planned spontaneous improvisations in practice create the possibility of permanently altering patterns of behavior as well as people's subjectivities.

Focus on particulars and daily practice is timely and relevant for people working for social change through ideologies embedded within identity politics and localized new social movements. The idea that an immediate and organized revolution is needed can work counterproductively because it can kill the drive, aspirations, and hope of those working for social change who get tired of waiting for the revolution. Understanding institutions' formidability can lead to cynicism, but an active commitment and conscious understanding of individual and collective activist agency is key to sustaining enduring struggles working from within.

"Moments of transformation," as some participants referred to them, take on larger significance, with greater value, than do the hopes for mass revolution and aspirations for a utopia. Daily activist practice actively seeks the opportunities to exert activist agency within the structures of whitestream schools, at critical moments when room is allowed for decision making and direct intervention. Teachers, for example, according to Spring (2002), make over two hundred independent decisions in their classroom every hour. The classroom is therefore a critical space that can be used for transformative purposes, teaching is indeed political, and everyone with access to a classroom should fight for their academic freedom.

Daily practice then for the educators in this book was about understanding and negotiating their individual and collective activist agency through daily moment-to-moment interactions. Participants indeed straddled roles as institutional agents and activists, both colonizer and colonized, opening doors and also functioning as gatekeepers. Although being in multiple, often contradictory, roles was always a dilemma that worried and demoralized the participants, assuming these roles also created hybrid spaces for opportunity. Daily practice and the activist agency embedded within these hybrid, or third spaces, was a very important part of Chicana and Chicano activist educators' struggle to change whitestream schools. Chicana and Chicano activist educators' hybrid, contradictory location was neither the serpent's nor the eagle's eyes, but both—a unique hybrid space from which to work change into the system from within it.

Rethinking Activism

The images that the words *activism* or *activist* conjure are often bound by stereotypes that have "domesticated" what were once innovative practices in social movements. The action taken by the African American students who entered a diner, sat in the white section, and demanded to be served in Greensboro, North Carolina, for example, was not expected when it occurred. It was planned by the students as part of a larger social movement; the students had a clear goal in mind, but their actions were not expected by the whites, who deliberately refused to serve them. Activities of this sort I call "planned spontaneity"—for those observing, it appears spontaneous, yet there is often a great deal of planning and strategizing that occurs. A classic example is Rosa Park's refusal to give up her seat during the civil rights movement. Grade-school mythology presents her as a heroine and her activist stance as an isolated, spontaneous, uncritical decision, rather than as a planned and strategic part of a community's struggle for equality (Landorf and Lowenstein, 2004).

Today, when a march, demonstration, or protest is held, there are expectations that are usually fulfilled. Police surveillance is usually involved, as well as marked areas where protestors should stand and walk according to the permits they were granted prior to the march. Activism, in its 1960s forms, is known and is in many ways "ritualized." Today, traditional forms of activism persist with credibility, but function more like spectacles, and protest acquires a carnivalesque nature (Sipple, 1991). In the neoliberal world of today, commercial boycotts would be most effective, given the economic implications, and yet consumerist culture is so pervasive that effective and persistent boycotting is difficult to do.

Why then have notions of activism not changed? Why is there a prototype of what it means to be a "real" activist in the Chicana and Chicano community? This book shows that definitions of activism have shifted for Chicanas and Chicanos over the last forty years and that the manner in which people function as activists is different now than in the past. Affirmative action and other programs from the civil rights movements have allowed for limited but significant entry into positions and institutions that were not accessible to Chicanas and Chicanos prior to the 1960s. By this very change in access and entry, the nature of the activism of those committed to social justice and change also changed. Current local contexts provide opportunities to study and exercise agency, especially activist agency in different and currently unexplored forms.

Local niches and networks of activism and contentious practice should continue to be studied with particular importance to local demands for democracy (Holland et al., 2007). Donato's (1997) study of a local California Mexican American community's struggle for justice and equality before, during, and after the civil rights era is an example of such a localized study. The image of the larger collective social movement of the earlier part of the past century with specific activist engagements is indeed in need of rethinking in the U.S. context. By rethinking activism and focusing on locality, context, and situation, new visions of change, as well as prospective challenges, may be identified.

All of the participants in the study saw themselves as activists in different aspects of their daily lives, even though not all engaged in what are traditionally thought of as activist performances. Their definitions of activism varied, but were broad enough to encompass a variety of activities and stances against injustice and oppression. Activities and stances ranged from engaging someone in a critical conversation to participating in a march or protest. For some participants, working for change from within a whitestream school was necessary. Pedro, for example, said, "It is from the inside that steel doors can be unlocked; not by one or two people banging on it from the outside."

Participants in general had moved away from perceptions of activism as an armed struggle or bloody revolution. This perception shifted to having a sustained commitment and active participation in *la lucha* with the hope for larger societal change that most were sure they would not see in their lifetimes. Further studies on activism and local contentious practice should focus on specific contexts as sites of change and transformation with a broader understanding and interpretation of activism. Universities, K–12 schools, and other spaces of Chicana and Chicano activist educator transformation can be studied using the concept of *micro* figured worlds. I propose as well ethnographic methods that focus on the micro figured world as the target of local study beyond the strict fixation on a physical site, or place. Micro figured worlds can be place bound, but can also exist beyond a specific location and encompass, like the borderlands in borderlands theory, a spiritual as well as an emotional space. The data drawn and interpreted from these micro figured worlds can further inform the struggle to change whitestream schools.

Applying the Framework to Whitestream Schools

The concept of figured worlds is part of Holland and colleagues' larger blueprint for understanding and studying identity and agency, which also includes negotiations of positionality, space of authoring, and world making, and few scholars have taken on the full task of using the framework more comprehensively. This concept is useful as a tool for studying identity production in education, particularly sociocultural constructs in education and local educational contexts. Figured worlds can also be used as practical tools for crafting figured worlds of possibility as well as culturally appropriate figured worlds of learning.

Figured worlds can make alternative, marginal worlds a possibility. Two examples will be discussed. Blackburn's (2003) work highlights the experiences of Kira, a lesbian African American urban youth, at The Loft, a youth-run center for LGBT [lesbian, gay, bisexual, and transgender] students, and her activist work on awareness of LGBT issues as worlds of possibility. In these worlds, Kira sought out and used the resources at hand to make room for the perspectives created in marginalized worlds. Jurow (2005) also makes an important contribution by showing how a project-based curriculum (the Antarctica Project) provided the students in her study with a meaningful context for learning mathematics. Jurow asserts that the figured (and imaginary) world proposed by the Antarctica Project shaped students' approaches to mathematical tasks and helped them learn how to apply mathematical concepts to problem solving. Jurow's research highlights the importance of play and imagination for creating and crafting learning possibilities.

These two examples show that figured worlds can be controlled and engineered by students and/or educators to meet the needs of children in specific communities of learners. Chicana and Chicano activist educators, especially teachers and professors, did the same in their daily work. By centering Chicana and Chicano, Latina and Latino perspectives via curricula and pedagogy, they made alternative marginal worlds a possibility. They helped create new figured worlds where Latinas and Latinos were actively positioned positively and where they could create spaces for students to author themselves in different, generally positive, ways.

Positioning is important because, as this book shows, the way teachers position students matters. Positive positioning generally leads to positive academic identities. Although most teachers claim to have neutral stances toward students and teaching, especially white teachers who have not examined their own racial identities and in rhetoric wish for all of their students to perform to their best potential, people are not free of biases, especially biases heavily embedded within our national racial conscience.

In order to disrupt the negative positions offered to students of color, especially African American and Latina and Latino students, educators need to actively position students of color in positive ways, including giving them access to gifted and talented classes and other special programs with culturally appropriate academic, social, and emotional support. Creating figured worlds where students of color are positioned as smart students and are given access to all of the resources and attention given to students in privileged "smart space" will make a difference in their self-figuration. Positioning Chicana and Chicano curricula and pedagogy in prominence for Mexican American students is also important and, coupled with positive student positioning, creates optimal learning environments and culturally relevant, anti-racist figured worlds of learning.

For marginalized students, these specially designed learning environments create a space of authoring where they can construct senses of themselves as intelligent Chicana and Chicano students. In these spaces, students can learn that they do not have to take on oppositional identities and that intellectualism and academic accomplishment are not only associated with white students but also are expected of students of color. Curricula that center the accomplishments and contributions of people of color and analyze the foundational inequality of U.S. society can provide spaces for students of color to author themselves as important people and full members of society with all of the privileges and responsibilities full citizenship brings.

Making worlds, or working toward creating new and alternative figured worlds, goes beyond the self-defeating statement, "that's the way it (the system) is." Making worlds gives marginality and the possibility of opportunity a chance to exist as a legitimate and recognized figured world. Play is important, even if in imagination, because it enables people to make imaginary worlds, revolutionary worlds, into real local micro figured worlds, spaces of practice where people are repositioned and new ways of doing things can emerge. I encourage activist scholars to conduct further studies of native epistemologies as a way to understand how agency is known and exercised by people not of the whitestream, malestream, or heterostream. Centering these marginal ways of knowing and being is a step toward making worlds, reconfiguring the system, especially in education.

El Que No Transa No Avanza

To further theorize activist agency outside of the dichotomy of reproduction versus resistance, I offer an autochthonous theoretical perspective. Folk notions like playing the game, despite the critique, helped the participants in my study maintain their dignity and authenticity while engaging in the struggle to change whitestream schools. Similarly, concepts such as *transas* (transactions), *movidas* (moves), *jugadas* (plays), and *traversuras* (playful mishaps) can and are also used by Mexicanas and Mexicanos, Chicanas and Chicanos to collectively make sense of the power system and their relation to it. These concepts, which need to be developed further, are an attempt to center practical and ideological folk knowledge in relating to the power structure.

Little scholarly work exists about these folk notions in Mexican and Chicana and Chicano folk knowledge. Work by Buendía and Meacham (1999) found similarities between movidas as Chicana and Chicano sense-making epistemology and trickster tales and the blues idiom in Native American and African American epistemology. Buendía and Meacham define movidas as "movements," and they contend that movidas are part of a coping strategy used by Chicanas and Chicanos to relate to power and to maintain dignity. Movidas, according to Buendía and Meacham, allow Chicanas and Chicanos to recognize the severity of the unjust practices of the white power structure and to unveil unseen relations and motives of power.

Buendía and Meacham's analysis of movidas is important because it reveals that movidas exist in the whitestream system already, but they are normalized and taken for granted, except by people who are subordinated by the system and can perceive the injustice of these practices. The movidas of the whitestream system are the rituals of exclusion to maintain the stronghold of power in the hands of white, wealthy, heterosexual males. From there, power is redistributed to different people with different degrees of access. Generally, but not always, the more people support the whitestream system, the more they are rewarded, in limited ways, by it, depending on who they are. Thus, the most marginalized tend to be those to whom the exclusionary injustices of the system are most apparent.

A shortcoming of Buendía and Meacham's analysis is that movidas, according to their interpretation, are couched in an oppressor versus oppressed standpoint, or positioned as a coping strategy. What I propose is in line with Pérez' (1999:7) argument that one is neither solely the oppressor nor the victim, but rather one who "negotiates within the imaginary to a decolonizing otherness where all identities are at work in one way or another." The transas, movidas, jugadas, and travesuras I theorize from are not just for coping but also for strategizing change in between, in the cracks, in the imaginary with the potential to decolonize. I now revisit the concept of transas as the overarching metaphor for what I am proposing and then discuss the rest of the terms as subsets of transas.

Transas literally means transactions (dealings), which in Mexican folk knowledge are strategic and common, yet usually clandestine, practices used by people with less power to subvert, survive, or get by in the system. There is for the most part a negative perception of transas by mainstream standards in Mexican culture, but from the view of the oppressed *El que no transa, no avanza* [S/he who doesn't conduct such transactions, doesn't advance]. Transas are usually calculated practices that purposefully do not follow mainstream, or in the United States, the whitestream, malestream pre-scriptions, and are conducted to benefit the oppressed against the injustices of the system.

Wealthy whitestream and malestream people most certainly conduct their own transas. In fact, their transas are embedded in the very foundations of wealthy, white, male supremacy, especially in the legal system (Williams, 1991), that the United States is based on. But because the system is normalized to their standard, their transas are perceived as fair, just, and normal. Therefore, the epistemological autochthonous framework I explore here is not surprising because power is never unidirectional, and unjust power dynamics are always contested. The notion of transas should also not be used to condemn Mexicana and Mexicano, Chicana and Chicano cultures either, unless one is willing to condemn white, wealthy, heterosexual, male supremacy first, since transas exist in relation to the existent unequal structure.

The issue of playing the game can thus be analyzed through this lens. Playing the game can be seen as a systematic transa that Chicana and Chicano activist educators engage in to try to subvert the injustices of the whitestream and also the malestream system. Playing the game is a conscious choice that individuals make to participate in (individually or in collectivity) the game, knowing full well that there is the possibility of winning or losing. In order to strategize or play in the game, individuals have to study the game first, decode power, and devise strategies to resist and subvert power. Power is never fully demonstrated. There are spoken and unspoken rules, and the basis to maintain power lies in the fact that rules can, and often do, change to maintain the status quo or to limit access.

The idea of playing the game, however, although commonly understood, remains broad, like a transa, because there are different ways to play the game—countless possibilities to exercise agency. Like in a transa, agency, especially activist agency, remains important for this social practice where strategic performances and responses (or the lack thereof), as well as innovation and improvisation, become key to proaction in the struggle to change whitestream schools. To develop this awareness of activist agency fully, all of the players have to believe in the game (with its pervasiveness and its limits) in order to rationalize their struggle, while recognizing both their individual and collective agency to maneuver within the game. Each individual, as well as collective group, has a place in the game, and for that reason, not just individual but also collective activist agency is important.

Movidas (moves), jugadas (plays), and travesuras (playful mishaps) are forms of transas to help further break down the infinite number of transas that are possible. Movidas are defined here as "moves" rather than movements because moves emphasize the active nature of a movida to carry out a carefully strategized plan. A movida can be conducted individually or in collectivity and consists of multiple transactions that are planned and premeditated with a specific goal in mind. For example, several people working within a specific school might strategize how to propose a specific plan of action, a movida, and get it approved by the school council. A movida is usually a local action that involves planning. Someone at the school might plan how they will present the new plan to the council and who will offer support for it, premeditate what the response will be and how to argue against counterpositions, and eventually try to get their plan approved. If that does not work, what would be alternative strategies? Although to the members not privy to the movida, this process might seem spontaneous and unplanned, as in the civil rights examples offered earlier, to those involved, it is more of a performance of their premeditated strategy in action.

A jugada (play) can be carried out by multiple players on a larger scale by means of networks, extensive communication, and careful internal monitoring. Jugadas consist of several movidas that help players struggle to attain a specific goal. An example of a jugada on a national scale might be strategizing how to hire a specific candidate for a faculty position at a university. This type of jugada can be planned out by having an internal member or members at the university and by carrying on informal communication that makes it appear as though there was not a connection or planning involved in selecting the person desired as a serious candidate for the position. Having people in strategic positions in multiple organizations and levels is required to carry this plan out. This jugada would also require a movida to confront the forces that might oppose this. This type of jugada is carried out all the time in academia by the existing whitestream power structure, but their jugadas are normalized as fair, neutral, and objective. For people with less power, carrying on this type of jugada requires a lot more planning and risk. This is only an example, but many more examples of jugadas are possible.

Finally, a travesura (playful mishap) is also important because it is couched in play. According to Holland and colleagues (1998), play worlds can become real worlds and therefore offer an infinite number of possibilities for change. As playful mishap, a travesura is often used to test the limits of power. Because it is within the realm of misbehavior, there can be serious consequences for stepping outside of the rules to test the boundaries, or the possible permeability of the boundaries. Travesuras, however, can also lead to permanent changes in how things are done. Travesuras are embedded with agency because they form part of the "what if?" of possibility. Because of their playful nature, there may also be less-serious consequences for travesuras, depending on the context. In some contexts, playful mishap can often be excused as ignorance or naïveté. For example, when in a new position of power, someone might decide to playfully change a rule or protocol. If successful, this action could alter the way that things are done from that point forth; if unsuccessful, justification can be made on the premise that the person did not know what the rules were, or how serious the protocol was, or was just kidding.

Together, all of these folk notions offer important Mexicana and Mexicano, Chicana and Chicano ways of understanding agency by the transa of playing the game. They can also be used to further strategize and maneuver in the struggle to change whitestream schools. Often, scholars are driven to study agency from a whitestream and/or from a malestream perspective and miss or misinterpret the agency that autochthonous, Native people know and exercise. The concept of movidas is a minute example of the wealth of knowledge and skills Native communities possess in dealing with power.

Again, because power is not unidirectional, and unjust power structures are usually contested, people in subordinate positions tend to understand and exercise the agency that they have or have made available through their practices of contestation, survival, and resistance. Their autochthonous understanding of their agency is important because it often allows them to maintain their dignity and their humanity in the midst of societies bent on dehumanizing them. Re/thinking the dichotomy of resistance and reproduction is important because it is a reductionist perspective that limits subordinate people's agency to a reactionary counterstance and ignores the creativity of people's ability to survive and sabotage the systems that oppress them.

While critics might argue that the Chicana and Chicano activist educators in this book are contributing more to the problem than to the solution, or others might say that the game (the system) is not changeable, I encourage others to offer other alternatives. What other options for change are available and effective? This book is not about comparison, but about different, mutual understandings in dealing with a common unjust situation. *Si la esperanza muere al último* (If hope dies last), then the struggle of Chicana and Chicano activist educators to change whitestream schools remains a hopeful endeavor.

Implications

For social movements and the study of them, a major implication of this work is that movements do not just die, but change and continue through the work of their members. Sometimes these movements continue in micro cohorts and political generations; in other cases, they become new movements, or their causes influence other struggles. Significant narrators, or what Whittier (1995) called movement veterans, take their perspectives and practices with them and raise the consciousness of other people working on similar causes and struggles. These significant narrators may create new local micro figured worlds that resemble or put the larger movement's causes into practice or may form part of institutions or other organizations where these veterans can continue their activist work.

The participants in this study chose to work in whitestream schools with the goal of changing them to benefit the Latina and Latino students whom they worked with, but the Chicana and Chicano Movement continued through their individual and collective efforts.

Another significant implication for the study of social movements is that academics tend to apply Western models of knowledge to study movements. Some movements, especially those that share non-Western epistemologies, may not follow a Western model. Such movements may appear disjointed, or not coherent, but may actually be following a model that is unfamiliar to Western systems. Indigenous, autochthonous knowledges need to be studied on their own terms, in ways yet to be determined and explored. Sometimes the logic of this logic makes no sense to outsiders, but is logic indeed. Indigenous people and those in subordinate positions have survived and struggled against their subordination in logical ways for centuries. A new way for studying "new" movements is by expanding our theoretical frameworks to include more folk theories. We could better study almost any type of movement in this way, including new technologically driven movements, gender movements, and LGBT movements, to name a few.

An important implication of this study is that identities are not static, sterilized notions of who people are. All human beings share an essence as people. Identity, however, is a manifestation of particular socio-historical, cultural experiences as well as lived experiences that make groups of people different from each other. While all people share in humanity, not all people share the same identities. The notion of *raza* is a good example.

Raza, as mentioned before, does not literally mean race. Race in the whitestream refers to a specific racist context where race has been used to legally oppress some people and elevate others in a white supremacist system. Raza connotes a people with a similar experience with oppression, a history of invasion, and a commitment to struggle for self-dignity and liberation. Raza does not seek racial superiority, but rather equality within the system where raza have been oppressed. To identify as raza, people must have this socio-historical and cultural lived experience because raza come in all colors, shapes, and sizes. This diversity or *mestizaje* (mixture) is not solely what makes raza; raza share a common experience within colonized contexts.

Identities for all people are also not compartmentalized, ordered, or ranked based on theories of psychological and cognitive development. There are no higher or more-developed identities, and there are not culturally pathological identities; each identity makes sense in its own context. Historically oppressed people share identities often full of contradictions because they have had to survive in contexts of contradiction where survival does not always follow a Western, psychological, medicalized, sterilized logic. People of color's survival practices do not always make sense to the whitestream, and they are not meant to make sense to outsiders because this insider folk knowledge is what has ensured our survival. Most important, survival is not always just about resisting; survival sometimes compromises and negotiates with the system/game.

Oppressed people have come to exist in multiplicity as an adaptation for survival purposes that draws on all possible cultural resources, emotions, ancestral wisdom, and ancestral oppression, as well as the struggle for self-determination. This multiplicity is sometimes pathologized as an identity "crisis." As Latinas and Latinos, we are often perceived to have an identity crisis—we allegedly don't really know who we are.

Recently, a young Latina in a summer orientation program at the University of Texas asked me how "we" Latinos can deal with our identity crisis. My reply was that we do not have a crisis—the system has a crisis dealing with us and the diversity we bring. The manufacturing of a Hispanic/Latina and Latino identity crisis is turned around at some point, and Latinas and Latinos are constructed as a problem: we end up having a "crisis." The reality is that whitestream society is having a crisis about us; we simply deal with the confusion we are presented with in schools and in society where we continue to be depicted as enemies and foreigners and are often coerced into disliking our culture, language, and traditions.

In terms of activist agency, it is important to understand that activist agency does not just happen, but rather, it is enabled by an activist identity. Activist identities semiotically mediate a sense of activist agency. This type of agency is much more likely to seek out and/or create possibilities for change. Activist agency also needs to be known: people need to see and understand that they can act purposively in the world. People must study the power structure at both a macro and micro level and weigh the possibilities for change with purpose in the struggle for social justice.

Activist agency is constant, opportunistic, and hopeful. Designated moments and contexts, such as public demonstrations, are important for activist agency, but are not the only moments. Moments to exercise activist agency can occur at any time in daily practice, and activist agents should seize those moments to act purposively in the world. In these moments, activist agency can occur spontaneously or through self-directed symbolization, mediated through artifacts and discourses. Self-direction begins in the mind. Activist agency enables the mind to envision options and allows it to see the possibility of alternatives to society's scripts as steps toward change. Artifacts can help mediate and sustain that struggle, such as the United Farm Workers flag, as its colors and symbols are important in that struggle. Symbols and artifacts' mediational power cannot be underestimated.

Finally, implications from this book can be drawn for different interest groups including Latinas and Latinos, other people of color, and white allies. First, the goals of the Chicana and Chicano Movement for education are really goals to benefit all Latina and Latino students and Mexican American students in particular. Given that the school-age population is rapidly becoming predominantly Latina and Latino, and especially of Mexican descent, these goals should be considered seriously.

The East L.A. school blowouts of March 3, 1968 (Solórzano and Delgado Bernal, 2001) had the following demands: (1) address the high Mexican American student dropout rate, (2) reduce the overcrowded and run-down conditions of predominantly Mexican American schools, (3) dismiss racist teachers with low expectations, (4) end tracking practices that funneled disproportional numbers of Mexican American students into non-academic tracks and into special education, (5) implement curricula that centered the culture and experiences of Mexican Americans, and (6) create quality bilingual education programs.

Similar demands could be made today on behalf of Latina and Latino students. Unfortunately, these issues remain as salient today as they did in 1968. Latinas and Latinos, including recent immigrants, should learn about the Chicana and Chicano struggle for social justice. Mexican Americans and Puerto Ricans have a special political relationship to the United States that should not be ignored and cannot be minimized. Exploring this relationship is key to a more proactive politics of inclusion and educational justice. The struggle for social justice is not just a struggle that benefits some and not others; the struggle for social justice benefits all. Like Chicana and Chicano activist educators, others similarly moved and inspired to work for social justice should think of their daily work as educators as activist political work. Indeed, teaching remains a powerful political act. Like Chicana and Chicano activist educators, let us hold this country accountable to its professed creed, "with liberty and justice for all": all, with no exceptions.

Appendix 1
Profile of Study Participants

Pseudonym	Age	Institution	Position	Region in California
Undergraduates				
Elena	19	University of California	Student	Northern
Isadora	22	University of California	Student	Southern
Jaime	20	University of California	Student	Southern
Julián	21	University of California	Student	Southern
Mariana	22	California State University	Student	Southern
Rodrigo	19	University of California	Student	Southern
Teachers				
Alicia	32	Continuation high school	History	Northern
Henry	32	High school	History and geography	Northern
Johnny	28	Elementary school	Self-contained	Southern
Juanita	30	Elementary school	Self-contained	Southern
Rafael	51	Middle school	Language arts/social studies	Southern
Raquel	32	Middle school	Social studies	Southern
Graduate students				
Andrea	30	University of California	Student	Southern
Daniel	30	University of California	Student	Southern
Miguel	34	University of California	Student	Northern
Rita	30	University of California	Student	Northern
Samuel	31	University of California	Student	Southern
Therese	29	Private university	Student	Northern
Professors				
Anabel	45	University of California	Professor	Southern
David	57	University of California	Professor	Northern
María	46	University of California	Associate professor	Northern
Pedro	38	California State University	Assistant professor	Southern
Phillip	33	Private university	Assistant professor	Southern
Ruth	54	California State University	Assistant professor	Northern

Appendix 2
Selected Participants

Anabel

Anabel is in her forties and a full professor. Anabel is of unknown multiple Mexican American generations in the United States. I first met Anabel in 2000 at a national organization meeting. I have since observed Anabel in various contexts from presenting at national conferences to a twelve-week period of ethnographic observations of her at her university. I mainly observed her teaching and at the many social/cultural interactions that took place in her office, which was a gathering place for students and supportive colleagues. Anabel's students, almost all Chicanos/Latinos with a high number of women, were always very comfortable in the "safety" of her office and research center. Anabel's modest apartment home, like her office, was also accessible to her students and was decorated with traditional Latin American folk art, such as colorful rugs, mats, and paintings. Anabel is a scholar and activist in high demand and always had a full schedule, yet always made time for formal and informal conversations.

Henry

Henry was thirty-two years old when we met for the first time at a coffee shop in 2001. He wore baggy blue jeans, a plaid shirt, and glasses and had short hair. He is a high school geography teacher and baseball coach in a predominantly lower-middle-class to middle-class neighborhood that is racially mixed, but has a predominantly white student population. I was referred to Henry by some of his former graduate school friends. Henry almost completed an education PhD program, but decided that high school teaching was what he really wanted to do. Henry was very articulate and passionate about his beliefs and convictions, and that was evident in our conversations and his physical expressions. I later met his family and was honored by subsequent invitations.

Isadora

Isadora was twenty-two years old when we met at one of the campuses of the University of California in 2002. She was tall and of somewhat dark complexion. Isadora was shy when we first met. She told me she was a fifth-year student and didn't quite feel ready to graduate, but was very excited about becoming a teacher. I first interviewed Isadora at the campus MEChA (Movimiento Estudiantil Chicano de Aztlán) office. It was a small office with two desks, an old couch, and walls covered with posters of the Chicana and Chicano poster art movement. Some of the posters included "Four Hundred and Fifty Years of Chicano History," "Who's the Illegal Alien Pilgrim?" "Chicano anti-Viet Nam War," and "United Farm Workers," amongst others. The posters covered the walls like wallpaper from ceiling to floor. Isadora became very outspoken about gender issues that affect women and girls.

Juanita

I was referred to Juanita by several of the teachers that worked with her as "the activist." I met her in her fifth-grade classroom, where there were several Latina and Latino students engaged in a variety of activities. Juanita spoke to them in both English and Spanish, and they seemed to really enjoy her motherly *regaños* (scolding). She is a first-generation Chicana, a bilingual teacher going on nine years, and thirty years old at the time we first met in 2001. Juanita continues to live and work in the same primarily Chicana and Chicano, Latina and Latino, working-class to upper-working-class community she grew up in. Juanita is deeply committed to the public schools, even though she attended Catholic schools K–12. Juanita seemed very eager to talk and a little nervous when we first met. She dressed in formal attire, wore glasses, and was constantly laughing and trying to make jokes. She made sure she invited me to see the school's Cinco de Mayo community show to partly witness for myself what she helped create in the school and community. This school's community performances eventually became one of my ethnographic research sites for the next two years.

Julián

Julián was twenty-one when we first met and a third-year student at the University of California in 2002. I was doing observation hours in an introductory education class taught by a Chicana professor when we met. Julián, along with an Asian American student, presented a research project on bilingualism and English Language Learners at a local after-school club. Julián was very articulate and had a definite message to convey. He seemed very comfortable, partly because the professor created a safe space for him to talk about this issue, and partly because he is a good speaker.

Miguel

Miguel was about to turn thirty-four years old at the time we met in 2001. He was writing his dissertation and completing his last year of graduate school at the University of California. His doctoral program in education was in public policy. Miguel had already been hired and was ready to move and work at an East Coast University. Several interview sessions were conducted as well as observation hours at his work/school environment in a policy studies center housed in the university and under the direction of his graduate mentor. At the time, Miguel already had extensive research experience and had authored and co-authored important work in his field of study. Miguel seemed to be under a lot of stress and limited for time. His personal appearance and attire (shorts, sandals, T-shirts, glasses, and a beard) during each of our interviews was casual and laid-back. Miguel was very articulate, bilingual, and generous with the time he did have and also with his work.

Phillip

Phillip was in his early thirties and an assistant professor of education when we met in 2002. He was tall, of dark complexion, thin, and dressed in semi-formal attire. His office was in a new building, with new office furniture, and decorated with traditional Mexican folk art such as a wooden mask, colorful painted scenes, and embroidered textiles. Phillip was a very busy person and yet made time to meet with me despite his very tight schedule. Although Phillip was not an academic for too long, he was already extensively published. I have subsequently seen and worked with Phillip on a variety of both academic and service projects over the years. Phillip has since received tenure and is now an associate professor.

Therese

Therese was twenty-nine years old when we first met at a restaurant in 2001. Therese had long, straight, black hair, wore make-up, and dressed in professional attire. Therese was then a PhD candidate in education, but also ran her own consulting business. We continued to meet over a period of months at various places, including a café and her home for carne asada. Along with other colleagues, we subsequently worked on conference proposals, and I continue to see her occasionally at national conferences.

Notes

Chapter 1. Introduction

1. Educators in this book are defined broadly as people who engaged in the practice of raising consciousness about social justice issues. Educators did not necessarily only teach formally in classrooms but also taught informally in multiple ways. The educators in this book consisted of four groups studied: undergraduates planning to pursue careers in education, K–12 teachers, graduate students in education programs, and education professors.

2. Sandy Grande (2000) refers to the whitestream as the cultural capital of whites in almost every facet of U.S. society. Grande uses the term whitestream as opposed to mainstream in an effort to decenter whiteness as dominant. Whitestream, according to Claude Denis (1997), is a term that plays on the feminist notion of malestream. Denis defines whitestream as the idea that while (Canadian) society is not completely white in socio-demographic terms, it remains principally and fundamentally structured on the basis of the Anglo-European white experience. The phrase "whitestream schools" in this book refers to all schools from kindergarten through graduate school and to the official and unofficial texts used in U.S. schools that are founded on the practices, principles, morals, and values of white supremacy and that highlight the history of white Anglo-American culture. Whitestream indoctrination or the teaching (either formally or informally) that white supremacy is normal in whitestream schools is not exclusively the work of whites. Any person, including people of color, actively promoting or upholding white models as the goal or standard is also involved in whitestreaming.

3. *Indígena* literally means indigenous or those of strong indigenous descent who claim that as part of their identity.

4. Aztlán is the mythical land of origin of the Aztecs or Mexica people. In the Chicano ideology, Aztlán is designated to mean the Southwest as the Chicano homeland or the land invaded by Euroamericans.

5. Since I had always worn a Catholic school uniform, a marker of status in a different context, I was unaware of the differences in clothing and clothing styles amongst public school students. Everything seemed to matter, from the shoes to the hairstyle. This, of course, was also an issue in the Catholic school setting, but nowhere near to the same degree, especially when it concerned the

number of outfits required to "fit in," along with the contradiction of not being able to afford them.

6. Obviously these are only a few examples of the new perspectives in revisionist historical interpretations I encountered while at UCLA, but coming to see events in history from different perspectives opened my eyes to the social injustices around me.

7. *Patrón* refers to boss. In local family folklore, usually a patrón is a wealthy landowner, having at his service many workers or *peones*. Stealing the patron's tools is a different take on Audre Lorde's "stealing the master's tools" (1984).

8. "Development" in the study was not used in the same sense as in traditional progressive and prescriptive models in psychology. Development was used as a "proxy" for time, and not a linear Western sense of time but time in relation to the knowledge one gains through human experience, drawing from specific cultural references, or "cultural intuition" (Delgado Bernal, 1998b). Delgado Bernal (1998b:565) refers to cultural intuition as "ancestral wisdom and community memory." Chicana and Chicano identity and consciousness development in this book refer specifically to the knowledge and wisdom one gains through life experiences, or history-in-person.

9. Some participants used Spanish and others did not because they were primarily English speakers or did not feel comfortable talking about academic matters in Spanish.

10. Urrieta and Reidel (2006) define white supremacy as the official and unofficial practices (including racism), principles, morals, norms, values, history, and overall culture that privileges whites in U.S. society. White supremacy of this sort is normalized and often appears as fair and objective practice even to people of color. The white supremacy I refer to in this book is not about individual acts of hate, although these too are byproducts of the white supremacist system.

11. Examples of *raza* considered undesirables by the whitestream, and by other Latinas/os and Hispanics, may include pregnant teenagers, dropouts, or gang members.

12. A term like *raza* alludes to the solidarity existing between people who are the products of local and enduring struggles, and thus respond with intensity to those intense struggles (Brayboy, 2005).

Chapter 2. How the Story Goes . . .

1. The subordination of people of color through colonial enterprises was often especially targeted at the emasculation of men and even more degrading physical violence against women (R. Gutiérrez, 2001). In Mexican America, the use of organizations and police forces like the Ku Klux Klan, the California Vigilantes, the Texas Rangers, and the Border Patrol and other forms of surveillance were specifically used to subdue Mexicans and other people of color (Martínez, 1990).

2. Malestream is the feminist notion to make explicit that what is often considered the mainstream is in reality a product of a patriarchal social order (Warren, 1989). Castells (2006) asserts that in fact patriarchalism is a founding structure of all contemporary societies. Castells (2006) further states that patriarchalism is "characterized by the institutionally enforced authority of males over females and their children in the family unit" (134).

3. The explicit focus on gender and disregard for class and race issues of the white feminist movement did not address the unique experience of Chicanas and other women of color (Pesquera and Segura, 1997). Aida Hurtado (1989) asserts that white women's privileged relationship to white men impeded white women from truly embracing a sisterhood with all women, including poor women and women of color. To do so would mean to jeopardize the relative position of power and close association white women have to white men (as wives, mothers, daughters, sisters, lovers, etc.).

4. Part of the Chicana feminist struggle has been to vindicate Malinche, a slave woman given to Hernán Cortés as his mistress, from being a traitor to a heroine and symbol of cultural and personal survival and resiliency. Malinchista, in Mexican culture, usually denotes a traitor, or sellout.

5. To assert politically the existence of Chicana experiences, it was/is important to include the word Chicana in an effort to disrupt the gendered dictates of the Spanish language and most importantly the gendered norms of Mexicano/Chicano patriarchy.

6. Chicana lesbians played an important role in challenging and deconstructing the sexism and heteronormativity of the Chicano movements (Trujillo, 1991). *This Bridge Called My Back* (Moraga and Azaldúa, 1984) and *Borderlands/La Frontera: The New Mestiza* (Anzaldúa, 1987), now both central to the Chicana and Chicano literary cannon, figured prominently in disrupting the heteronormative scripts of Chicana and Chicano patriarchy.

7. The concept of the new mestiza was first presented by Anzaldúa (1987) in her important book, *Borderlands/La Frontera: The New Mestiza*. Theorist Cherríe Moraga (1983) also contributed to the concept in her emancipatory attempt to link the work of women of color throughout the Americas with the concept of third world feminism.

8. Saldívar-Hull (1999), using Sandra Cisnero's (1991) ideas of *feminismo popular*, also theorizes on mestizaje using the concept of *transfronteriza* (transborder) feminism, all ideas which have been influential in providing alternative epistemological foundations for Chicana and Chicano, Latina and Latino liberatory agendas.

9. This invasion of Mexican territory by U.S. troops was finalized in 1836 in Texas, in 1848 with the Treaty of Guadalupe Hidalgo in parts of Colorado, Arizona, New Mexico, California, Nevada, and Utah, and in 1853 with the Gadsden Purchase in parts of Arizona and New Mexico. Because of this unique history and

long presence in the United States, Chicana and Chicano identity merits attention. This book attempts to refocus attention on this identity as a practice other groups working toward social change within the confines of institutional expectations in the United States and abroad can identify with and learn from.

10. The overall analytical framework of this book is based on social movements and social movement theory (Melucci, 1988, 1989; Epstein, 1990; Beuchler, 1995; Taylor, 1999; Einwohner, Hollander, and Olson, 2000; Pulido, 2006). Infused into the analysis are also anthropological theories of culture, practice, and cultural production, which I use to question the dichotomy of reproduction and resistance when studying identity and agency and the metaphor of playing the game. I especially rely on Holland and colleagues' (1998) theory of identity and agency as well as Mexicanismo, Chicanismo, and Chicana Feminist Theory.

11. deMarrais (2000:161) defines gender as "a more inclusive term (than sex) that refers not only to physiological characteristics but to learned cultural behaviors and understandings."

12. Seemingly neutral concepts like social movement(s), activism, and leadership are very much the products of gendered, patriarchal ideologies. Like concepts such as civic engagement and citizenship in the U.S. context, for example, are racialized to a whitestream standard (and are also gendered), so too are concepts like activist and leader gendered to a malestream standard.

13. Cultural production was most notably influenced by ethnographic studies in anthropology and the field of cultural studies after the 1960s and focuses on how human agency is maneuvered under the structures of the system (Levinson, Foley, and Holland, 1996). According to Levinson, Foley, and Holland (1996), cultural production "indexes" a dialectic between structure and agency: "For while the educated person is culturally *produced* in definite sites, the educated person also culturally *produces* cultural forms" (14). In this study self-awareness or conscious understanding of one's agency is culturally *produced* in educational institutions and in a constant struggle to change them.

Chapter 3. Positioning Mexican American Students in Whitestream Schools

1. A portion of this chapter was previously published as Urrieta, 2004b.

2. Several of the participants' experiences with being positioned as smart in schools, often without fully realizing how this happened, seem similar to members of ethnic communities often referred to as scholarship boys or scholarship girls (L. Rendón, 1992; Lin and Cranton, 2005).

3. Hatt-Echeverría and Urrieta (2003) define racializing class as when people tend to associate "low-class" status to groups considered to be inferior to their own, and "high-class" status to groups considered to be superior. In racialized terms, whites are stereotypically perceived as wealthy by racial minorities and

racial minorities are perceived of as poor by whites, regardless of whether they are or not.

4. *Chúntaro* is a derogatory term used to describe what Latina and Latino, especially Mexican, popular language and understanding would consider a "low-class person" or an "undocumented Mexican." Usually, passing judgment by personal appearance such as clothing preferences, haircut style, etc., would determine who is or is not a chúntaro. It can also be used synonymously with the word wetback, or *paisa*.

5. *Pocho* and *pocha* are derogatory terms used, usually by Mexican nationals, to refer to Mexican Americans or Chicanas and Chicanos whom they perceive to be Americanized, especially those who do not speak Spanish fluently.

6. In this and other sections throughout the book, I will address the findings specifically about *mujeres* (women) in my data. Like Delgado Bernal (1998a), I will not compare the men to the mujeres. Undeniably, we live in a patriarchal system where we men are systematically and consistently privileged. To compare men to mujeres would help to sustain the false image that both men and mujeres are treated equally by society. In a sense, when people or groups are compared (and that goes for race as well), the assumption is made that both have achieved equality not just in rhetoric but also in practice. To compare the two can also lead to already commonly held perceptions of victimization, and that is not an image that I want to sustain.

7. This finding supports Bragaw's (2000) and Ross's (2000) assertions that the social studies curriculum has been fairly unchanged since 1916. With the exception of one student in a well-structured bilingual program, participants revealed that the rigidity of whitestream curricula and pedagogy did not nurture or address Mexican or Chicana and Chicano history or culture.

8. Teaching is generally perceived as a "neutral" activity that, according to Freire (1978), is a highly political act. Warnock (1975) argued that it is a teacher's duty to point out to students what direction evidence points to and that teachers must model how people draw conclusions from evidence. Agostinone-Wilson (2005) further adds that teachers taking a "neutral" stance create an aura of legitimacy of the status quo, subsequently helping to create a passive, spectator-oriented citizenry.

9. Assimilation was one of the strongest, most coercive tools in the colonizing process. Skutnabb-Kangas (2000) argues that assimilation was rationalized to benefit the dominated by promoting the culture, language, institutions, and traditions of the colonizer as superior. Skutnabb-Kangas (2000) states this process follows three steps: glorification, stigmatization, and rationalization. Colonization was rationalized as a good thing meant to benefit the Natives. It was suggested that the Natives should be thankful, for without European uplift, uncivilized savagery would persist.

10. U.S. Census Bureau Demographic Projections, 2008.

11. California Department of Education, 2006.

12. Native elite were coerced to assimilate to the culture of the colonizers in the colonizers' schools (Willinsky, 1998; Coe, 2002). In colonial schools, a few students of Native origin were selected to become cultural brokers between the colonizers and the colonized, while the majority of Natives were excluded from these elite spaces (Coe, 2002). Particularly barred from spaces reserved for men were Native women.

Chapter 4. How Some Mexican Americans Become Chicana and Chicano Activist Educators

1. A portion of this chapter was previously published as Urrieta, 2007a.

2. Eriksonian (1964, 1968) perspectives on identity, often premised on psychological stages of development and based on research conducted with children and adolescents, are purposefully avoided. Studies based on Erikson's work focus on ego identity development and effective psychological functioning rather than on cultural influences in identity production and self-making (Marcia, 1966; Phinney, 1989, 1993; Bernal et al., 1993). Such models suggest a linear, often causal, relationship based on cognitive ability stages and ethnic or racial identity development (Pizarro and Vera, 2001). Phinney's (1989, 1990, 1993) three-stage model of ethnic minority identity development, often cited as the basis for understanding Latina and Latino identity development, is also based on restrictive psychological premises that conflate ethnic identity development with racial identity (Pizarro and Vera, 2001). Most of these perspectives emphasize a strong connection with psychology, are based on survey data and on studies mostly of men, and ignore the dynamic, fluid, and flexible nature of cultural production and individual self-making. A strictly racial analysis of identity development, such as Tatum's (1997), is also not appropriate because Latina and Latino racial identity is more ambiguous and complex. In the past, Mexican Americans, unlike African Americans, have legally been considered Caucasian, but socially did not enjoy equal treatment as whites. Understanding Chicana and Chicano activist identity production therefore demands a cultural analysis that encompasses issues beyond a strictly racial analysis because Chicanas and Chicanos, Latinas and Latinos share a racialized experience, but come from different racial backgrounds, phenotypes, and experiences with race.

3. *Raza*, contrary to most whitestream analyses of the term, does not mean "race" in the literal sense of what race means in the U.S. white supremacist context. Raza connotes a people with a similar social, cultural, and historical experience with oppression. A term like raza alludes to the solidarity that exists between people who are the products of local and enduring struggles, and thus they respond with intensity to those intense struggles (Brayboy, 2005).

4. Vera and de los Santos (2005) point to certain types of university courses as sites of what they refer to as Chicana identity construction.

5. Significant narrators, or "the owners of the most influential voices" (Sfard and Prusak, 2005:18) of this identity discourse, functioned as key carriers of the cultural messages about being Chicana and Chicano activists and were also those with the greatest impact for action.

6. Reyes (2006) also provides an example of how Mexican American students struggle, not only with negative concepts about their own people but also with negative and deficit perspectives about their own intellectual abilities.

7. Displaying the Mexican flag did not mean that the participants rejected their U.S. citizenship, but rather that they were actively proud of their cultural heritage, which to some of them has been conveyed as something negative in whitestream schools (Urrieta, 2004b).

8. K. González (2002) specifically identifies the alienating and marginalizing contexts of the predominantly white university as social, physical, and epistemological spaces.

9. Studies (S. Hurtado, 1994; Schneider and Ward, 2003) have found that Chicana and Chicano, Latina and Latino student organizations on college campuses are important to Chicana and Chicano, Latina and Latino student recruitment and retention at predominantly white universities.

10. Chicana and Chicano identity arose conceptually in the 1960s as a process of self-determination in an attempt to challenge U.S. domination and the invasion of Mexican and indigenous territory. Therefore, part of the process of Chicana and Chicano self-making had to do with conceptually understanding this reversion of history/herstory and coming to identify, with dignity, as a member of the colonized group.

11. Multiplicity has become central to Chicana and Chicano activist discourse through the work of Gloria Anzaldúa (1999:85). About existing in contradiction, Anzaldúa wrote, "Hay veces que no soy nada ni nadie, pero hasto cuando no lo soy, lo soy" (Sometimes I am no one and nothing, but even when I am not, I am). Self-making as Chicana and Chicano activists and the orchestration of multiple selves continue over time and are enhanced with experience.

12. The rest of Juanita's narrative was compiled from data from subsequent interviews and conversations.

13. Pachucas and Pachucos are Mexican American youths who developed their own subculture during the 1930s and 1940s in the southwestern United States, including their own clothing style and speech.

14. The Spanish term *con ganas* does not have a literal translation that will do it justice. It is a colloquial saying that implies not doing things for doing things' sake, but doing things with a purpose, doing things with passion, doing things with everything you've got. A similar saying in English, although not quite with the same sense of purpose, nor conveying the same emotion of struggle embedded in language (N. González, 2005), would be "giving it your all."

15. One of the first things that students from Spanish-speaking households experience in whitestream school environments is that their names are changed by their teachers and/or peers (i.e., María del Socorro becomes Mary, Alejandro becomes Alex, Enrique becomes Henry, etc.)

Chapter 5. Chicana and Chicano Educational Activism

1. A portion of this chapter was previously published as Urrieta, 2005a.

2. Playing the game versus selling out is an extension of the reproduction versus resistance debate and the dialectic between structure and agency in social movements. Few empirical studies have focused on the "gray areas" in between either of these dichotomies' extremes. This chapter uses this concept to theorize Chicana and Chicano activist educators' positions on activist agency and the dialogic relationship between reproduction and resistance, structure and agency.

3. People sell out for different reasons varying from the need for self-preservation when persecuted to individualistic greed for economic gain (Urrieta, 2007b). In white working-class culture, a version of the sellout is one who "puts on airs" (Hatt-Echeverría and Urrieta, 2003), while among certain genres of music, musicians going mainstream may be considered sellouts.

4. The arbitrary nature of the playing the game versus selling out issue complements Scott's (1990) analysis of the complexity of public performances between dominant and subordinate groups through hidden transcripts or, in this case, in formal educational spaces.

5. Bourdieu (1977) articulates a means to a greater end well: "Thus, quite apart from the direct profit derived from doing what the rule prescribes, perfect conformity to the rule can bring secondary benefits such as prestige and respect which almost invariably reward an action apparently motivated by nothing other than *pure, disinterested* respect for the rule" (22). "Pure, disinterested respect for rules" (following rules) was for Chicanas and Chicanos the mask hiding a conscious Chicana and Chicano activist educator's intentions for change.

6. Infiltration has traditionally been a tool used by neoconservatives and government agencies to dismantle and integrate violence in grassroots organizations and identity-politics social movements. FBI agents and undercover police officers frequently infiltrated Chicana and Chicano organizations and often instigated violent actions and tactics (Vigil, 1999).

Chapter 6. *Transas, Movidas, y Jugadas* and the Struggle to Change Whitestream Schools

1. Delgado Bernal (1998a) proposes an eye-opening cooperative leadership paradigm to understand the participation of women in grassroots activism. This paradigm consists of five dimensions of activity that include more malestream

activities like holding office and acting as spokesperson, but also include networking, organizing, and developing consciousness (124). Holding office and acting as spokesperson are also expanded to include a variety of different types of office positions and acting as unofficial spokesperson in networking, organizing, and consciousness-raising efforts. Through this more inclusive perspective of what constitutes leadership, Delgado Bernal sheds light on the activist participation of Chicanas in the 1968 school blowouts, while challenging us to reconsider our malestream ideas and conceptions of what constitutes leadership. Most important, Delgado Bernal does not compare Chicana activists to Chicano activists, but centers the experiences of eight Chicanas as the focus of her groundbreaking work.

2. About the concept of educación in Mexican American culture, Valenzuela (1999:23) writes: "Educación is a broader term than its English-language cognate. It refers to the family's role in inculcating in children a sense of moral, social, and personal responsibility and serves as a foundation for all other learning. Though inclusive of formal academic training, educación additionally refers to competence in the social world, wherein one respects the dignity and individuality of others."

Bibliography

Acuña, R. 2000. *Occupied America: A history of Chicanos.* 4th ed. New York: Longman.

Agostinone-Wilson, F. 2005. Fair and balanced to death: Confronting the cult of neutrality in the teacher education classroom. *Journal for Critical Education Policy* 3 (1). <http://www.jceps.com/index.php?pageID=article&articleID=37> (accessed August 27, 2008).

Alarcón, N. 1990. Chicana feminism: In the tracks of "the" native woman. *Cultural Studies* 4 (3): 248–256.

Alexander, B. K., G. L. Anderson, and B. Gallegos. 2005. *Performance theories in education: Power, pedagogy, and the politics of identity.* Mahwah, NJ: Lawrence Erlbaum Associates.

Alim, H. S. 2004. *You know my steez: An ethnographic and sociolinguistic study of styleshifting in a Black American speech community.* Durham, NC: Duke University Press.

Alvarez, R. R., Jr. 1995. The Mexican-US border: The making of an anthropology of borderlands. *Annual Review of Anthropology* 24: 447–470.

Anderson, B. 1983. *Imagined communities: Reflections on the origin and spread of nationalism.* London: Verso.

Anzaldúa, G. 1987. *Borderlands/la frontera: The new mestiza.* San Francisco: Aunt Lute Books.

———. 1990. *Making face, making soul/haciendo caras: Creative and critical perspectives by feminists of color.* San Francisco: Aunt Lute Books.

———. 1999. *Borderlands/la frontera: The new mestiza.* 2nd ed. San Francisco: Aunt Lute Books.

Baker, L. D. 1998. *From savage to Negro: Anthropology and the construction of race, 1896–1954.* Berkeley: University of California Press.

Bakhtin, M. 1981. *The dialogic imagination: Four essays by M.M. Bakhtin.* Ed. M. E. Holquist, trans. Caryl Emerson and Michael Holquist. Austin: University of Texas Press.

Banks, J. 2003. Multicultural education: Historical development, dimensions, and practice. In J. Banks (ed.), *Handbook of Research in Multicultural Education,* 3–29. 2nd ed. San Francisco: Jossey-Bass.

Bernal, M. E., G. P. Knight, K. A. Ocampo, C. A. Garza, and M. K. Cota. 1993. Development of Mexican American identity. In M. E. Bernal and G. P. Knight (eds.), *Ethnic identity: Formation and transmission among Hispanics and other minorities*, 61–79. Albany: State University of New York Press.

Beuchler, S. M. 1995. New social movement theories. *Sociological Quarterly* 36 (3): 441–464.

Beverly, J. 2000. Testimonio, subalternity, and narrative authority. In Denzin and Lincoln (eds.), *Handbook of Qualitative Research*, 555–565. Thousand Oaks, CA: Sage Publications.

Blackburn, M. V. 2003. Losing, finding, and making space for activism through literacy performances and identity work. *Penn GSE Perspectives on Urban Education* 2 (1): 1–23.

Blackwell, M. 2003. Contested histories: Las hijas de Cuauhtémoc, Chicana feminisms, and print culture in the Chicano Movement, 1968–1973. In G. F. Arredondo, A. Hurtado, N. Klahn, O. Nájera-Ramírez, and P. Zavella (eds.), *Chicana feminisms: A critical reader*, 59–89. Durham, NC: Duke University Press.

Bonilla-Silva, E. 2006. *Racism without racists: Color-blind racism and the persistence of racial inequality in the United States*. Lanham, MD: Rowman and Littlefield.

Bourdieu, P. 1977. *Outline of a theory of practice*. Cambridge: Cambridge University Press.

Bragaw, D. 2000. The social studies: The civic process. In *Teaching the social sciences and history in secondary schools: A methods book*, 10–36. Prospect Heights, IL: Waveland Press.

Brayboy, M. J. B. 2005. Climbing up and over the ivy: Examining the experiences of American Indian ivy league graduates. In M. Martinez, P. A. Pasque, N. Bowman, and T. Chambers (eds.), *Multidisciplinary perspectives on higher education for the public good*, 9–26. Ann Arbor: Center for the Study of Higher and Postsecondary Education for the Public Good, University of Michigan.

Buendía, E., and S. Meacham. 1999. *Working the fields with movidas and the blues idiom: Conceptualizing and representing the social in interpretive inquiry*. Paper presented at Reclaiming Voice Conference, Riverside, California, June.

Calhoun, C. 1994. *Social theory and the politics of identity*. Oxford: Blackwell.

California Department of Education. 2006. Public School Summary Statistics, 2005–06: Enrollment and Percent of Enrollment by Ethnic Group for 2005–2006, <http://www.cde.ca.gov/ds/sd/cb/sums05.asp> (accessed August 26, 2008).

Cary, L. 2001. The refusals of citizenship: Normalizing practices in social educational discourses. *Theory and Research in Social Education* 29 (3): 405–430.

Castells, M. 2006. *The power of identity*. 2nd ed. Vol. 2. Malden, MA: Blackwell Publishing.

Castillo, A. 1994. *Massacre of the dreamers: Essays on Xicanisma.* Albuquerque: University of New Mexico Press.

———. 1997. Massacre of the dreamers: Essays in Xicanisma. In Alma M. García (ed.), *Chicana feminist thought: The basic historical writings*, 310–312. London: Routledge.

Castro, T. 1974. *Chicano power: The emergence of Mexican America.* New York: Saturday Review Press.

Chávez, E. 2002. *"¡Mi raza primero!" (My people first!): Nationalism, identity, and insurgency in the Chicano Movement in Los Angeles, 1966–1978.* Berkeley: University of California Press.

Cisneros, S. 1991. *Woman hollering creek and other stories.* New York: Random House.

Coe, C. 2002. Educating an African leadership: Achimota and the teaching of African culture in the Gold Coast. *Africa Today* 49 (3): 23–44.

Creswell, J. 1998. *Qualitative inquiry and research design: Choosing among five traditions.* Thousands Oaks, CA: Sage Publications.

Davies, C. A. 2001. *Reflexive ethnography: A guide to researching selves and others.* London: Routledge.

Delgado Bernal, D. 1998a. Grassroots leadership reconceptualized; Chicana oral histories and the 1968 East Los Angeles school blowouts. *Frontiers: A Journal of Women's Studies* 19 (2): 113–142.

———. 1998b. Using a Chicana feminist epistemology in educational research. *Harvard Educational Review* 68 (4): 555–579.

———. 2001. Learning and living pedagogies of the home: The mestiza consciousness of Chicana students. *Qualitative Studies in Education* 14 (5): 623–639.

Della Porta, D., and M. Diani. 2006. *Social movements: An introduction.* Malden, MA: Blackwell Publishing.

deMarrais, K. 2000. Gender. In D. Gabbard (ed.), *Knowledge and power in the global economy*, 161–169. Mahwah NJ: Lawrence Erlbaum Associates.

Denis, J. C. 1997. *We are not you: First nations and Canadian modernity.* Peterborough, Ontario, Canada: Broadview Press, Collection Terra Incognita.

Derrida, J. 1996. Passions: An oblique offering. In D. Wood (ed. and trans.), *Derrida: A critical reader*, 5–35. Oxford: Blackwell.

Diawara, M. 1994. Malcolm X and black public sphere: Conversionists v. culturalists. In C. Calhoun (ed.), *Social theory and the politics of identity*, 216–230. Oxford: Blackwell.

Donato, R. 1997. *The other struggle for equal schools: Mexican Americans during the civil rights era.* Albany: State University of New York Press.

———. 2007. *Mexicans and Hispanos in Colorado schools and communities, 1920–1960.* Albany: State University of New York Press.

Donato, R., M. Menchaca, and R. Valencia. 1991. Segregation, desegregation, and integration of Chicano students: Problems and prospects. In R. Valencia (ed.),

Chicano school failure and success: Research and policy agendas for the 1990s, 27–63. Philadelphia, PA: Falmer Press.

Einwohner, R., J. A. Hollander, and T. Olson. 2000. Engendering social movements: Cultural images and movement dynamics. *Gender and Society* 14 (5): 679–699.

Elenes, C. A. 1997. Reclaiming the borderlands: Chicana/o identity, difference, and critical pedagogy. *Educational Theory* 47 (3): 459–475.

Epstein, B. 1990. Rethinking social movement theory. *Socialist Review* 20: 35–65.

Erikson, E. 1964. *Insight and responsibility*. New York: W. W. Norton.

———. 1968. *Identity, youth and crisis*. New York: W. W. Norton.

Fanon, F. 1967. *Black skin, white masks*. New York: Grove Press.

Foley, D. 1990. *Learning capitalist culture: Deep in the heart of Tejas*. Philadelphia: University of Pennsylvania Press.

Forbes, J. 1973. *Aztecas del Norte: The Chicanos of Aztlán*. Greenwich, CT: Fawcett Publications, Inc.

Foucault, M. 1990. *The history of sexuality*. Vol. I, *An introduction*. New York: Vintage Books.

Freire, P. 1978. *Pedagogy in process: The letters to Guinea-Bissau*. New York: Seabury Press.

Fry, R. 2004. *Latino youth finishing college: The role of selective pathways*. Washington, D.C.: Pew Hispanic Center Report.

Gallegos, B. 2000. Postcolonialism. In David Gobbard (ed.), *Knowledge and power in the global economy: Politics and the rhetoric of school reform*, 355–362. Mahwah, NJ: Lawrence Earlbaum Associates.

Gándara, P. C. 1995. *Over the ivy walls: The educational mobility of low-income Chicanos*. Albany: State University of New York Press.

García, E. E. 1999. Chicanos/Chicanas in the United States: Language, bilingual education, and achievement. In J. F. Moreno (ed.), *The elusive quest for equality: 150 years of Chicano/Chicana Education*, xxi, 217. Cambridge, MA: Harvard Educational Review.

———. 2001. *Hispanic education in the United States: Raíces y alas*. Lanham, MD: Rowman and Littlefield.

García, I. M. 1998. *Chicanismo: The forging of a militant ethos among Mexican Americans*. Tucson: University of Arizona Press.

García, J. 1996. The Chicano Movement: Its legacy for politics and policy. In D. Maciel and I. D. Ortiz (eds.), *Chicanas/Chicanos at the crossroads: Social, economic, and political change*, xvi, 258. Tucson: University of Arizona Press.

García, M. T. 1991. *Mexican Americans: Leadership, ideology, and identity 1930–1960*. New Haven, CT: Yale University Press.

González, G. G. 1990. *Chicano education in the era of segregation*. Philadelphia, PA: Balch Institute Press.

González, K. P. 2001. Inquiry as a process of learning about the other and the self. *International Journal of Qualitative Studies in Education* 14 (4): 543–562.

———. 2002. Campus culture and the experiences of Chicano students in a predominantly white university. *Urban Education* 37 (2): 193–218.

González, N. 2005. *I am my language: Discourses of women and children in the Borderlands*. Tucson: University of Arizona Press.

González Baker, S. 1996. Demographic trends in the Chicana/o population: Policy implications for the twenty-first century. In D. O. Maciel and Ortiz (ed.), *Chicanas/Chicanos at the crossroads: Social, economic, and political change*, 5–24. Tucson: University of Arizona Press.

Gramsci, A., Q. Hoare, and G. Nowell-Smith. 1971. *Selections from the prison notebooks of Antonio Gramsci*. 1st ed. New York: International Publishers.

Grande, S. 2000. American Indian geographies of identity and power: At the crossroads of *indígena* and *mestizaje*. *Harvard Educational Review* 70 (4): 467–498.

Gurin, P., E. L. Dey, S. Hurtado, and G. Gruin. 2002. Diversity and higher education: Theory and impact on educational outcomes. *Harvard Educational Review* 72 (3): 330–366.

Gutiérrez, J. A. 2003. *A Chicano manual for how to handle gringos*. Houston, TX: Arte Público Press.

Gutiérrez, K. D., and N. Jaramillo. 2006. Looking for educational equity: The consequences of relying on brown. In *Yearbook of the National Society for the Study of Education* 105 (2): 173–189.

Gutiérrez, R. 2001. Historical and social science research on Mexican Americans. In Banks and Banks (eds.), *Handbook of research on multicultural education*, 203–222. San Francisco: Jossey-Bass.

———. 2004. Historical and social science research on Mexican Americans. In J. Banks and C. Banks (eds.) *Handbook of Research on Multicultural Education* 2d edition, 261–287. San Francisco: Jossey-Bass.

Gutman, A. 2004. Unity and diversity in democratic multicultural education: Creative and destructive tensions. In J. Banks (ed.), *Diversity and citizenship education*, 71–96. San Francisco: Jossey-Bass.

Haro, R. 2004. Programs and strategies to increase Latinos students' educational attainment. *Education and Urban Society* 36 (2): 205–222.

Harvey, D. 1990. *The condition of postmodernity*. Cambridge and Oxford: Blackwell.

Hatt-Echeverría, B. A., and L. Urrieta Jr. 2003. "Racializing" class. *Educational Foundations* 17 (3): 37–54.

Hendrick, I. 1977. *The education of non-whites in California, 1848-1970*. San Francisco: A & E Associates.

Henríquez, J. et al. 1984. From the individual to the social: A bridge too far. In J. Henríquez, et al. (eds.), *Changing the subject: Psychology, social regulation*

and subjectivity, 11–25. London: Metheun.
Hernández Castillo, R. A. 2001. *Histories and stories from Chiapas: Border identities in Southern Mexico*. Austin: University of Texas Press.
Holland, D., W. Lachicotte Jr., D. Skinner, and C. Cain. 1998. *Identity and agency in cultural worlds*. Cambridge: Harvard University Press.
Holland, D., and J. Lave. 2001. *History in person: Enduring struggles, contentious practice, intimate identities*. Santa Fe, NM: School of American Research Press.
Holland, D., D. Nonini, C. Lutz, L. Bartlett, M. Frederick-McGlathery, T. C. Guldbrandsen, and E. G. Murillo Jr. 2007. *Local democracy under siege: Activism, public interests, and private politics*. New York: New York University Press.
Horseman, Reginald. 1981. *Race and manifest destiny: The origins of American racial Anglo-Saxonism*. Cambridge, MA: Harvard University Press.
Horvat, E. M., and K. S. Lewis. 2003. Reassessing the "burned of acting white": The importance of peer groups in managing academic success. *Sociology of Education* 76: 265–280.
Houser, N., and J. Kuzmic. 2001. Ethical citizenship in a postmodern world: Toward a more connected approach to social education for the twenty-first century. *Theory and Research in Social Education* 29 (3): 431–461.
Hurtado, A. 1989. Relating to privilege: Seduction and rejection in the subordination of white women and women of color. *Signs: Journal of Women in Culture and Society* 14 (4): 833–855.
Hurtado, S. 1994. The institutional climate for talented Latino students. *Research in Higher Education* 35: 21–39.
Inden, R. 1990. *Imagining India*. Oxford: Blackwell.
Jurow, A. S. 2005. Shifting engagements in figured worlds: Middle school mathematics students' participation in an architectural design project. *Journal of the Learning Sciences* 14 (1): 35–67.
Kozol, J. 1991. *Savage inequalities: Children in America's schools*. 1st ed. New York: Crown Pub.
Ladson-Billings, G. 1994. *The dreamkeepers: Successful teachers of African American children*. San Francisco: Jossey-Bass.
———. 2004. Culture versus citizenship: The challenge of racialized citizenship in the United States. In J. Banks (ed.), *Diversity and citizenship education*, 99–126. San Francisco: Jossey-Bass.
Landorf, H., and E. Lowenstein. 2004. The Rosa Parks "myth": A third grade investigation. *Social Studies and the Young Learner* 16 (3): 5–9.
LeCompte, M., and J. Preissle. 1993. *Ethnography and qualitative design in educational research*. San Diego: Academic Press.
LeCompte, M., and J. Schensul. 1999. *Analyzing and interpreting ethnographic data*. Walnut Creek, CA: Altamira Press.
Leont'ev, A. N. 1978. *Activity, consciousness, and personality*. Englewood Cliffs, NJ: Prentice-Hall.

Levinson, B., D. E. Foley, and D. C. Holland (eds.) 1996. *The cultural production of the educated person: Critical ethnographies of schooling and local practice.* Albany: State University of New York Press.

Lin, L., and P. Cranton. 2005. From scholarship student to responsible scholar: A transformative process. *Teaching in Higher Education* 10 (4): 447–459.

Loewen, J. W. 1995. *Lies my teacher told me: Everything your American history textbook got wrong.* New York: W.W. Norton.

Lorde, A. 1984. The master's tools will never dismantle the master's house. In A. Lorde, *Sister outsider: Essays and speeches,* 110–113. Santa Cruz, CA: Crossing Press.

Marcia, J. 1966. Development and validation of ego identity status. *Journal of Personality and Social Psychology* 3: 551–558.

Marciano, J. 1997. *Civic illiteracy and education: The battle for the hearts and minds of America's youth.* New York: Peter Lang.

Martínez, E. 1990. *500 años del pueblo Chicano, 500 years of Chicano history in pictures.* Albuquerque, NM: Southwest Organizing Project.

Melucci, A. 1988. Getting involved: Identity and mobilization in social movements. *International Social Movement Research* 1: 329–348.

———. 1989. New perspectives on social movements: An interview with Alberto Melucci. In J. Keane and P. Mier (eds.), *Nomads of the present: Social movements and individual needs in contemporary society,* 180–232. Philadelphia, PA: Temple University Press.

Menchaca, M. 1999. The treaty of Guadalupe-Hidalgo and the racialization of the Mexican population. In José Moreno (ed.), *The elusive quest for equality, 150 years of Chicana/Chicano education,* 3–29. Cambridge, MA: Harvard Educational Review.

Menchaca, M., and R. Valencia. 1990. Anglo-Saxon ideologies in the 1920s–1930s: Their impact on the segregation of Mexican students in California. *Anthropology and Education Quarterly* 21 (3): 222–249.

Moraga, C. 1983. *Loving in the war years: Lo que nunca pasó por sus labios.* Boston, MA: South End Press.

Moraga, C., and G. Anzaldúa, eds. 1984. *This bridge called my back: Writings by radical women of color.* New York: Kitchen Table, Women of Color Press.

Moreno, J. 1999. *The elusive quest for equality: 150 years of Chicana/Chicano education.* Cambridge, MA: Harvard Educational Review.

Morris, A. 2000. Reflections on social movement theory: Criticisms and proposals. *Contemporary Sociology: A Journal of Reviews* 29 (3): 445–454.

Muñoz, C. 1989. *Youth, identity, power: The Chicano movement.* London and New York: Verso.

Murillo, N. 1996. George I. Sánchez and Mexican American educational Experiences. In James A. Banks (ed.), *Multicultural Education, transformative knowledge, and action: Historical and contemporary perspectives,* 129–140. New York: Teachers College Press.

Nieto Gómez, A. 1997. Chicana feminism. In Alma M. García (ed.), *Chicana feminist thought: The basic historical writings*, 52–57. London: Routledge.

Oakes, J. 1995. Two cities' tracking and within school segregation. *Teacher's College Record* 96 (4): 681–690.

Oboler, S. 1995. *Ethnic labels, Latino lives, identity and the politics of (re)presentation in the United States*. Minneapolis: University of Minnesota Press.

Oropeza, L. 2005. *¡Raza sí! ¡Guerra no! Chicano protest and patriotism during the Viet Nam war era*. Berkeley: University of California Press.

Padilla, R. V. 2003. *The landscape in higher education*. Paper presented at the inaugural meeting of the American Association for Hispanics in Higher Education, Pomona, CA.

Padilla, R. V., and R. C. Chávez. 1995. *The leaning ivory tower: Latino professors in American universities*. Albany: State University of New York Press.

Padilla, R. V., and R. O. Martínez. 2005. Personal stories, voice and presence in academe: A dialogical response to Aguirre. *International Journal of Qualitative Studies in Education* 18 (2): 199–220.

Payne, C. M. 2003. More than a symbol of freedom: Education for liberation and democracy. *Phi Delta Kappan* 85: 22–28.

Pérez, E. 1999. *The decolonial imaginary: Writing Chicanas into history*. Bloomington: Indiana University Press.

Pesquera, B. M., and D. A. Segura. 1997. There is no going back: Chicanas and feminism. In Alma M. García (ed.), *Chicana feminist thought: The basic historical writings*, 310–312. London: Routledge.

Phinney, J. 1989. Stages of ethnic identity development in minority group adolescents. *Journal of Early Adolescence* 9: 34–49.

———. 1990. Ethnic identity in adolescents and adults: Review of the research. *Psychological Bulletin* 108 (3): 499–514.

———. 1993. A three stage model of ethnic identity development in adolescence. In M. E. Bernal and G. P. Knight (eds.), *Ethnic identity: Formation and transmission among Hispanics and other minorities*, 61–79. Albany: State University of New York Press.

Pitt, L. 1966. *The Decline of the Californios*. Los Angeles: University of California Press.

Pizarro, M., and E. M. Vera. 2001. Chicana/o ethnic identity research: Lessons for researchers and counselors. *The Counseling Psychologist* 29 (1): 91–117.

Pulido, L. 2006. *Black, brown, yellow, and left: Radical activism in Los Angeles*. Berkeley: University of California Press.

Rendón, A. 1971. *Chicano Manifesto*. New York: Collier Books.

Rendón, L. I. 1992. From the barrio to the academy: Revelations of a Mexican American "scholarship girl." *New Directions for Community Colleges* 20 (4): 55–64.

Reyes, R., III. 2006. *Cholo* to me: From peripherality to practicing student success for a Chicano former gang member. *The Urban Review* 38 (2): 165–186.

Rodríguez, J. M. 2003. *Queer Latinidad: Identity practices, discursive spaces.* New York: New York University Press.

Rosaldo, R. 1989. *Culture and Truth: The remaking of social analysis.* Boston: Beacon Press.

———. 2003. Introduction: The borders of belonging. In R. Rosaldo (ed.), *Cultural citizenship in island Southeast Asia*, 1–15. Berkeley: University of California Press.

Rosales, A. F. 1997. *Chicano! The history of the Mexican American civil rights movement.* Houston, TX: Arte Público Press.

Ross, E. W. 2000. Social Studies. In D. Gabbard (ed.), *Knowledge and power in the global economy*, 237–246. Mahwah, NJ: Lawrence Erlbaum Associates.

Rueda, R. 1991. An analysis of special education as a response to the diminished academic achievement of Chicano students. In R. Valencia (ed.), *Chicano school failure and success: Research and policy agendas for the 1990s*, 252–270. Philadelphia: Falmer Press.

Ruiz, V. L. 1987. *Cannery women, cannery lives: Mexican women, unionization, and the California food packing industry, 1930–1950.* Albuquerque: University of New Mexico Press.

Rust, V. D. 1991. Postmodernism and its comparative education: 13 implications. *Comparative Education Review* 53 (4): 610–626.

Said, E. W. 1978. *Orientalism.* 1st ed. New York: Pantheon Books.

Saldívar-Hull, S. 1999. Women hollering *transfronteriza* feminisms. *Cultural Studies* 13: 251–262.

Salinas, C. 2000. El colegio altamirano (1897–1958): New histories of Chicano education in the Southwest. *Educational Forum* 65 (1): 80–86.

Sandoval, C. 1991. U.S. third world feminism: The theory and method of oppositional consciousness in the Postmodern world, *Genders* 10: 1–24.

———. 1998. *Mestizaje* as method: Feminists of color challenge the canon. In C. Trujillo (ed.), *Living Chicana theory*, 352–370. Berkeley, CA: Third Woman Press.

San Miguel, G. 1996. Education. In Nicolás Kanellos (ed.), *Reference Library of Hispanic America*, 287–307. Vol. II. Detroit, MI: Gale Research, Inc.

San Miguel, G., and R. R. Valencia. 1998. From the Treaty of Guadalupe Hidalgo to "Hopwood": The educational plight and struggle of Mexican Americans in the Southwest. *Harvard Educational Review* 68 (3): 353–412.

San Miguel, G., Jr. 1999. The Schooling of Mexicanos in the Southwest, 1848–1891. In José Moreno (ed.), *The elusive quest for equality: 150 years of Chicana/Chicano education*, 31–51. Cambridge, MA: Harvard Educational Review.

Sarup, M. 1996. *Identity, culture, and the postmodern world.* Athens: The University of Georgia Press.

Schneider, M. E., and D. J. Ward. 2003. The role of ethnic identification and perceived social support in Latinos' adjustment to college. *Hispanic Journal of Behavioral Sciences* 25 (4): 539–554.

Scott, J. C. 1990. *Domination and the arts of resistance: Hidden transcripts*. New Haven, CT: Yale University Press.

Segura, D., and Pesquera, B. M. 1998. Chicana feminisms: Their political contexts and contemporary expressions. In A. Darder and R. D. Torres (eds.), *Latino studies reader: Culture, economy, and society*, 193–205. Malden, MA: Blackwell Publishing.

Sfard, A., and Prusak, A. 2005. Telling identities: In search for an analytic tool for investigating learning as a culturally shaped activity. *Educational Researcher* 34 (4): 14–22.

Sipple, S. 1991. "Witness [to] the suffering of women": Poverty and sexual transgression in Meridel Le Sueur's *Women on the breadlines*. In D. M. Bauer and S. J. McKinstry (eds.), *Feminism, Bakhtin, and the dialogic*, 135–153. Albany: State University of New York Press.

Skutnabb-Kangas, T. 2000. *Linguistic genocide in education—or worldwide diversity and human rights*. Mahwah, NJ: Lawrence Erlbaum Associates.

Smith, L. T. 2001. *Decolonizing methodologies: Research and indigenous peoples*. London: Zed Books; Dunedin, New Zealand: University of Otago Press.

Smitherman, G. 2000. *Black talk: Words and phrases from the hood to the amen corner*. New York: Houghton Mifflin Company.

Solórzano, D. G. 1998. Critical race theory, race and gender microaggressions, and the experience of Chicana and Chicano scholars. *Qualitative Studies in Education* 11 (1): 121–136.

Solórzano, D. G., and D. Delgado Bernal. 2001. Examining transformational resistance through a critical race and LatCrit Theory framework: Chicana and Chicano students in urban context. *Urban Education* 36 (3): 308–342.

Spivak, G. C. 1993. *Outside in the teaching machine*. London: Routledge.

Spring, J. 2002. *American Education*. 3rd ed. Boston, MA: McGraw Hill.

Stanton-Salazar, R. D. 2001. *Manufacturing hope and despair: The school and kin support networks of U.S.-Mexican youth*. New York: Teachers College Press.

Tatum, B. D. 1997. *Why are all the black kids sitting together in the cafeteria?* New York: Basic Books.

Taylor, V. 1998. Feminist methodology in social movement research. *Qualitative Sociology* 21 (4): 357–379.

———. 1999. Gender and social movements: Gender processes in women's self-help movements. *Gender and Society* 13 (1): 8–33.

Trinidad Galván, R. 2005. Transnational communities *en la lucha*: Campesinas and grassroots organizations "globalizing from below." *Journal of Latinos and Education*, 4 (1): 3–20.

Trujillo, C. 1991. *Chicana lesbians: The girls our mothers warned us about*. Berkeley,

CA: Third Woman Press.

Urrieta, L., Jr. 2003a. *Orchestrating the selves: Chicana and Chicano negotiations of identity, ideology, and activism in education.* Unpublished PhD dissertation. School of Education, The University of North Carolina at Chapel Hill.

———. 2003b. *Las identidades también lloran*/identities also cry: Exploring the human side of indigenous Latina/o identities. *Educational Studies* 34 (2): 147–168.

———. 2004a. Assistencialism and the politics of high-stakes testing. *The Urban Review* 36 (4): 211–226.

———. 2004b. Dis-connections in "American" citizenship and the post/neo-colonial: People of Mexican descent and whitestream pedagogy and curriculum. *Theory and Research in Social Education* 32 (4): 433–458.

———. 2005a. "Playing the game" versus "selling out": Chicanas and Chicanos relationship to whitestream schools. In B. K. Alexander, G. L. Anderson, and B. Gallegos (eds.), *Performance theories in education: Power, pedagogy, and the politics of identity*, 173–196. Mahwah, NJ: Lawrence Erlbaum Associates.

———. 2005b. The social studies of domination: Cultural hegemony and ignorant activism. *The Social Studies* 96 (5): 189–192.

———. 2006. Community identity discourse and the Heritage Academy: Colorblind educational policy and white supremacy. *International Journal of Qualitative Studies in Education* 19 (4): 455–476.

———. 2007a. Identity production in figured worlds: How some Mexican Americans become Chicana/o activist educators. *The Urban Review*, 39 (2): 117–144.

———. 2007b. Orchestrating habitus and figured worlds: Chicanas/os educational mobility and social class. In J. Van Galen and G. Noblit (eds.), *Late to class*, 113–140. Albany: State University of New York Press.

———. 2007c. Sellouts. In W. A. Darity (editor in chief), *International Encyclopedia of the Social Sciences*, 434–435. 2nd ed. Detroit: Macmillian Reference.

Urrieta, L., Jr., and L. Méndez Benavídez. 2007. Community commitment and activist scholarship: Chicana/o professors and the practice of consciousness. *Journal of Hispanic Higher Education* 6 (3): 222–236.

Urrieta, L., Jr., and M. Reidel. 2006. Avoidance, anger, and convenient amnesia: White supremacy and self-reflection in social studies teacher education. In E. Wayne Ross (ed.), *Race, ethnicity, and education: Racism and anti-racism in education*, 279–299. Vol. 4. Westport, CT: Praeger Press.

U.S. Census Bureau. 2008. State population estimates-characteristics. Annual estimates of the population by sex, race, and Hispanic origin for states; April 1, 2000–April 1, 2007 [data table]. Available from U.S. Census Bureau Web site, <http://www.census.gov/popest/states/asrh/SC-EST2007-03.html> (accessed August 27, 2008).

Valencia, R. 1997. *The evolution of deficit thinking: Educational thought and practice*. Washington, D.C.: Falmer Press.

Valencia, R., and S. Aburto. 1991. Research directions and practical strategies in teacher testing and assessment: Implications for improving Latino access to teaching. In G. D. Keller, J. R. Deneen, and R. J. Magallán (eds.), *Assessment and access: Hispanics in higher education*, 195–232. Albany: State University of New York Press.

Valenzuela, A. 1999. *Subtractive schooling: U.S.-Mexican youth and the politics of caring*. Albany: State University of New York Press.

Vera, H., and de los Santos, E. 2005. Chicana identity construction: Pushing the boundaries. *Journal of Hispanic Higher Education* 4 (2): 102–113.

Vigil, E. B. 1999. *The crusade for justice: Chicano militancy and the government's war on dissent*. Madison: University of Wisconsin Press.

Villenas, S. 1996. The colonizer/colonized Chicana ethnographer: Identity, marginalization, and co-optation in the field. *Harvard Educational Review* 66 (4): 711–731.

———. 2001. Latina mothers and small-town racisms: Creating narratives of dignity and moral education in North Carolina. *Anthropology and Education Quarterly* 32 (1): 3–28.

———. 2005. Latina literacies in *convivencia*: Communal spaces of teaching and learning. *Anthropology and Education Quarterly* 36 (3): 273–277.

Villenas, S., and M. Moreno. 2001. To *valerse por si misma* between race, capitalism, and patriarchy: Latina mother-daughter pedagogies in North Carolina. *Qualitative Studies in Education* 14 (5): 671–687.

Voloshinov, V. 1929. *Marxism and the philosophy of language*. Repr., Cambridge, MA: Seminar Press, in liaison with the Harvard University Press and the Academic Press Inc., 1973.

Vygotsky, L. 1978. *Mind in society: The development of higher psychological processes*. Ed. M. Cole et al. Cambridge, MA: Harvard University Press.

Warnock, M. 1975. The neutral teacher. In S. C. Brown (ed.), *Philosophers discuss education*, 159–171. London: The MacMillan Press.

Warren, K. J. 1989. Rewriting the future: The feminist challenge to the malestream curriculum. *Feminist Teacher* 4 (2–3): 46–52.

West, C. 1999. *The Cornel West reader*. 1st ed. New York: Basic Civitas Books.

Whittier, N. 1995. *Feminist generations: The persistence of the radical women's movement*. Philadelphia, PA: Temple University Press.

Williams, P. 1991. *The alchemy of race and rights*. Cambridge, MA: Harvard University Press.

Willinsky, J. 1998. *Learning to divide the world: Education at empire's end*. Minneapolis: University of Minnesota Press.

Willis, P. 1977. *Learning to labor: How working class kids get working class jobs*. New York: Columbia University Press.

Index

About the Author

Luis Urrieta Jr. is Associate Professor of Cultural Studies in Education and Mexican American Studies at the University of Texas at Austin. Dr. Urrieta's research revolves around issues of identity, agency, and social movements in education with a strong focus on Chicana and Chicano and indígena education, identities and activism, and more recently on U.S.–Mexico migration issues. Dr. Urrieta was born and raised in Los Angeles, California, and is the son of Mexican immigrants.